SPITFIRE ACES

TONY HOLMES

Front cover image: On 7 July 1941, an Air Ministry photographer visited Hornchurch and took a series of shots featuring No 611 Sqn aircraft and pilots. This staged image shows Flt Lt Eric Lock, Plt Off Wilfred Duncan Smith, Flg Off Peter Dexter and Sgt William 'Mac' Gilmour striding towards the camera. All four aviators would achieve ace status flying the Spitfire, with Duncan Smith claiming his fifth success the day after this photograph was taken. Dexter, who had actually 'made ace' on 7 July, was killed exactly one week later in a mid-collision with a No 54 Sqn Spitfire over Boulogne-sur-Mer.

Title page image: Wg Cdr 'Johnnie' Johnson, Wing Leader of No 144 Wing, poses with his dog 'Sally' at Bazenville (B2) in the Normandy region of France on 31 July 1944. Spitfire IX MK392 can be seen in the background. Johnson claimed nine aerial victories in this aircraft between 25 April and 5 July 1944.

Contents page image: Spitfire IX EN133 served with No 611 Sqn at Biggin Hill between mid-November 1942 and 14 March 1943, when it was one of three fighters from the Biggin Hill Wing shot down off the French coast by Fw 190s of II./JG 26 during an attack on the latter unit's airfield at Abbeville as part of Rodeo 188. The fighter, seen here fitted with a 30-gallon underbelly slipper tank, was flown by a number of aces serving with No 611 Sqn at this time.

Back cover image: Four Spitfire IXs from No 611 Sqn fly in close formation over Kent on 8 December 1942. The following month Canadian ace Flt Lt Jack Charles joined the unit at Biggin Hill as a flight commander, and he routinely flew BS547 FY-Y. The formation is being led by the then CO of No 611 Sqn, Australian Sqn Ldr Hugo 'Sinker' Armstrong, in BS435 FY-F. He claimed 11 victories in Spitfires, three of them in this aircraft, prior to being shot down into the Channel in BS435 on 5 February 1943. Armstrong's body was never found.

Dedication
This book is dedicated to my late father-in-law, Barry Sawyer, who was born on the day that Spitfire prototype K5054 made its first flight.

Acknowledgements
I would like to thank the following individuals for the provision of photographs and information over the years that forms the foundation of this volume – Peter Arnold, the late Pete Brothers, Norman Franks, Peter Ingman, Phil Jarrett, Wojtek Matusiak, Eddie Nielinger, Donald Nijboer, Andy Saunders, the late Des Sheen, Janusz Światłoń, Andy Thomas, Chris Thomas and the late George Unwin.

Published by Key Books
An imprint of Key Publishing Ltd
PO Box 100
Stamford
Lincs PE9 1XQ

www.keypublishing.com

The right of Tony Holmes to be identified as the author of this book has been asserted in accordance with the Copyright, Designs and Patents Act 1988 Sections 77 and 78.

Copyright © Tony Holmes, 2023

ISBN 978 1 80282 483 4

All rights reserved. Reproduction in whole or in part in any form whatsoever or by any means is strictly prohibited without the prior permission of the Publisher.

Typeset by SJmagic DESIGN SERVICES, India.

CONTENTS

Introduction 4
The Aces 5
  Richard 'Dixie' Alexander 6
  Dick Audet 10
  Douglas Bader 16
  George Beurling 22
  Robert Findlay Boyd 28
  Pete Brothers 34
  Clive Caldwell 40
  Brian Carbury 46
  Jack Charles 51
  Johnny Checketts 56
  Pierre Clostermann 62
  Al Deere 67
  Neville Duke 73
  Wilfred Duncan Smith 78
  Don Finlay 83
  Brendan 'Paddy' Finucane 89
  Bob Foster 94
  Ian Gleed 99
  Colin Gray 104
  Peter Prosser Hanks 109
  Raymond Harries 115
  Svein Heglund 120
  Eugeniusz Horbaczewski 125
  Petrus 'Piet' Hugo 130
  'Johnnie' Johnson 136
  James 'Ginger' Lacey 142
  Don Laubman 148
  Eric Lock 154
  Evan Mackie 159
  Adolf 'Sailor' Malan 164
  Robert 'Buck' McNair 169
  'Dickie' Milne 174
  'Jamie' Rankin 179
  Bill Rolls 184
  Des Sheen 190
  Jackson Sheppard 195
  Stanisław Skalski 200
  Robert Tuck 205
  George Unwin 211
  Lance Wade 217

Bibliography 223

INTRODUCTION

The Spitfire is the best-known British fighter aircraft ever built, thanks to its stunning lines and the exploits of the pilots that flew it, primarily with the Royal Air Force (RAF), during World War Two. Given that more than 20,000 Spitfires were constructed and the aircraft equipped most RAF and Commonwealth fighter squadrons at some point during the conflict, it is unsurprising that four of the RAF's top five aces (pilots who were credited with five or more aerial victories) achieved all of their claims while flying Spitfires. Biographies of those pilots – 'Johnnie' Johnson, 'Sailor' Malan, 'Paddy' Finucane and George Beurling – are contained within this volume, alongside the endeavour and achievements of a further 36 Spitfire aces.

Supermarine's superlative design participated in combat on virtually every front of the war to which the RAF committed fighter aircraft. Although the Spitfire is best remembered for operations with RAF Fighter Command in defence of Britain and on the Channel Front, the aircraft was also widely employed in the Mediterranean Theatre of Operations (where it was used by US Army Air Force (USAAF) fighter groups), with the Far East Air Force (FEAF) over India and Burma, and with the Royal Australian Air Force (RAAF). Aces that saw action in all of these theatres feature in this book.

Aside from British pilots who claimed five or more aerial victories in the Spitfire, aviators from Australia, Canada, France, New Zealand, Norway, Poland, South Africa and the USA are included too. Alongside the more famous names, lesser known aces such as Bill Rolls, Brian Carbury and Don Laubman have earned their place in this book.

To complement each pilot biography, highly talented Polish artist Janusz Światłoń has created 40 profile illustrations featuring an aircraft flown by each of the aces. All the key marks of the Spitfire are included in his gallery of work, ranging from early-production Mk Is flown by Al Deere and 'Sailor' Malan during the summer of 1940, through to high- and low-back Spitfire XIVs assigned to 'Johnnie' Johnson and 'Ginger' Lacey at war's end. In between are myriad Spitfire IIs, Vs, VIIIs, IXs and XIIs in a wide variety of camouflage schemes and markings. Each profile has a caption detailing the aircraft's service history and special markings or insignia applied to the fighter by the ace to which it was assigned.

A brand new Spitfire XIV is put through its paces during an acceptance flight. This variant quickly proved to be a formidable opponent for the Luftwaffe's piston-engined fighters, as Flt Lt Derek Rake of No 41 Sqn noted. 'It was always comforting to know that the increased power of the Griffon would enable me to turn inside and/or out-climb both Me 109s and Fw 190s.'

THE ACES

RICHARD 'DIXIE' ALEXANDER

Richard 'Dixie' Alexander was an RAF 'Eagle squadron' pilot before becoming an ace with the USAAF in the Mediterranean.

Born in Grant Park, Illinois, on 22 July 1914, Richard Lear 'Dixie' Alexander was a keen sportsman, playing baseball and fighting as a professional middleweight boxer prior to working in construction for six years. He joined the Royal Canadian Air Force (RCAF) in October 1940, having had his attempts to enlist in the US Army Air Corps rejected due to his lack of college education. Choosing the RCAF to avoid being drafted into the infantry, Alexander received his wings in Canada on 15 September 1941 and was shipped to Britain the following month. He was assigned as a sergeant pilot to Spitfire IIA-equipped No 133 'Eagle' Sqn at Kirton in Lindsey, North Lincolnshire, in February 1942.

Six months passed before Alexander claimed his first victory, which came during the ill-fated amphibious raid on Dieppe in northern France, codenamed Operation *Jubilee*, on 19 August 1942. While on a patrol with No 133 Sqn soon after midday, Alexander, flying

Flt Sgt 'Dixie' Alexander (standing fifth from left) poses for a group photograph with the rest of the pilot cadre of No 133 'Eagle' Sqn at Biggin Hill on 10 June 1942. Ten of these men had been killed or captured on operations by the end of September 1942.

No 133 Sqn became the USAAF's 336th Fighter Squadron (FS) of the 4th Fighter Group (FG) the following month. After volunteering for operational training instructing duties in the hope of promotion, Alexander, now commissioned as a second lieutenant, was transferred to the 109th Observation Squadron in January 1943. However, he soon received a disciplinary infraction for a flying infringement and duly 'volunteered' for service in North Africa. While ferrying a P-39 Airacobra from England to Algeria in April 1943, Alexander was forced to land in Portugal when his fighter suffered engine problems en route. He finally reached his new unit (the 52nd FG's 2nd FS) four months later after a long spell of internment.

Following almost a year of little action, Alexander engaged the enemy once again from early 1944 after the 52nd FG moved to Corsica to participate in the fighting over Italy with its bomb-equipped Spitfire VB/Cs.

Spitfire VB EN951 was on strength with No 133 Sqn during Flt Sgt Alexander's service with the unit. It is seen here taxiing out at Biggin Hill with future ace Flt Lt Don Blakeslee at the controls – he made five claims in this fighter on 18–19 August 1942, two of which were for aircraft destroyed. Alexander also enjoyed success on the 19th with a victory and a probable as No 133 Sqn attempted to provide air cover for the ill-fated amphibious raid on Dieppe.

as 'Yellow 3', explained in his after-action report that 'just before we reached the target, we were bounced by two 190s, which came down on Yellow Section. I called the break and we turned into them in good time. I was able to follow the second 190 down and fired a couple of short bursts at him.'

Although the Fw 190 escaped, Alexander spotted enemy aircraft attacking the destroyer escort HMS *Berkeley* (which was so badly damaged that it later had to be sunk by other Royal Navy warships) while he was trying to find his squadronmates:

It was then that I saw six Do 217s just as they were dropping their bombs on the convoy. I singled out one 217 and closed to about 300 yards. I fired bursts into him until my cannons were exhausted. I had observed numerous hits, and his port engine was smoking. By this time, we were south of Dieppe and over land, and I continued to fire short bursts of 0.303 as he made a gentle turn, dropped down and crash-landed in a field some two or three miles south of the town.

A pair of Spitfire VBs from the 336th FS/4th FG 'beat up' Debden airfield in the autumn of 1942 prior to splitting up and landing at the end of a patrol. 2Lt Alexander 'brought himself to the attention' of the 4th FG's command cadre for such unauthorised low flying, earning him a transfer out of the fighter group in January 1943.

Finally, on 2 February 1944, he got the chance to add to his solitary aerial success of 18 months earlier when he encountered an enemy aircraft near Malignano airfield, in Italy:

> I was leading an eight-man sweep of the Italian mainland, between Leghorn and Florence, when I observed two aircraft at 'nine o'clock below' on the deck. As I called them in and turned down to attack, I saw several more aircraft on the deck, which I called in as well. I came up on two aircraft, bypassed the first [an Hs 123] and chose to attack an Fi 156 Storch [liaison aircraft]. The Storch pilot did not have a lot of room to turn, but used every bit that he could, and my first two bursts were in the back of him. My third burst was made with all the deflection I thought I could possibly need, and hit him in the tail section. The whole tail section came off, and he made a couple of little spirals into the ground.
>
> I pulled back upstairs to see what was going on, and it was like a great contest of hare and hounds scurrying about. It was a wonder that the entire flight was not wiped out by running into each other, or into the mountains on either side.

When chided by colleagues about his victim, Alexander replied, 'Who knows? He might have grown up to be an Me 109 pilot!' He subsequently downed a Messerschmitt fighter 13 days

One of Alexander's last Spitfire VCs (probably JK777) is seen here after its withdrawal from service with the 2nd FS in March 1944. This machine is believed to be the aircraft in which he made his final Spitfire claims in February 1944. Behind it is Mk VC JG883 from the 309th FS/31st FG, which appears to have had its upper surfaces repainted in dark (possibly olive) green.

2Lt Dixie Alexander poses in front of a Spitfire IX of the 2nd FS/52nd FG at Castel Corsica in February 1944. His unit operated a mixed force of Mk VCs and Mk IXs during this period.

later for his final Spitfire victory. Flying top cover for 24 Spitfires on an offensive sweep over the Viterbo area of central Italy, he had spotted three unengaged Bf 109Gs:

> Two of the enemy aircraft peeled off in a southeasterly direction, and one did a port turn and headed northeast. Apparently, I had not been observed. After making sure that the first two aircraft were indeed leaving the scene, I went to full boost in my Spit IX and went after the Me 109. It was letting down, and still going northeast. This in itself was an advantage because it took me towards the coast, and home. I continued to follow him as he let down at 300mph, not losing or gaining any ground.
>
> The enemy aircraft elected to fly up a valley between two mountain ridges. I closed to about 300 yards and gave him a short burst of both machine guns and cannon. I immediately had a pull to the right on my aircraft and knew that my starboard cannon was not firing. I saw no strikes, and continued to close to about 150 yards, firing another short burst. Again, I saw no strikes. I closed to 100 yards and gave him a long burst of both

RICHARD 'DIXIE' ALEXANDER

This studio photograph of Capt R L 'Dixie' Alexander was taken shortly after he had returned home following a year as a PoW.

cannon and machine guns, while holding hard on the rudder and control column to keep the aircraft from swinging. This time I had good solid bursts in the fuselage and right behind the cockpit. The enemy aircraft immediately nosed violently down and crashed directly into the ground. There was an explosion, but when I pulled up to do a 180-degree turn and fly over the wreck, there was no sign of fire.

I can't imagine how I was able to fire three successive bursts without the pilot of the 109 knowing that he was being attacked. Although the mountain pass was narrow, he still had room to manoeuvre. I can only assume that he was thinking of home, sausage and good German beer. So much for air combat!

Alexander flew his last mission in a Spitfire on 15 May 1944, by which point the 52nd FG was based at Madna, on the Italian mainland. The group switched to the P-51B Mustang shortly thereafter, and Alexander claimed his fourth and fifth victories with the aircraft on 24 and 30 May. The latter kill (a Bf 109) was not credited to him by the US Air Force (USAF) until 1992, however, as he was shot down near Aschbach-Markt, Germany, just minutes after destroying the Messerschmitt. Alexander was captured and spent the rest of the conflict as a prisoner of war (PoW).

Remaining in the USAAF post-war, he served with the P-47 Thunderbolt-equipped 60th FS/33rd FG in Germany until he lost his right arm in a flying accident. Medically retired from the now-independent USAF in February 1948, Richard 'Dixie' Alexander died of a heart attack in Piper City, Illinois, on 19 April 1993.

Spitfire VC JK777/QP-Z of 1Lt Richard 'Dixie' Alexander, 2nd FS/52nd FG, Bocca di Falco, Sicily, August–September 1943

Former 'Eagle' squadron pilot 'Dixie' Alexander joined the 52nd FG in the Mediterranean in July 1943, having made his initial claims with the RAF. Upon his assignment to the 2nd FS, he was frustrated to find that his group was confined to defensive duties, and he first flew this aircraft on one such sortie (a patrol lasting 1 hour 35 minutes) over Palermo harbour on 17 August. He flew JK777 several more times on similar missions in early September. Like other 2nd FS Spitfires, this fighter was marked with the unit's 'American Beagle Squadron' badge on the nose. When he was later allocated his own aircraft, Alexander decorated it with several markings, including a striking shark's mouth. Having eventually become an ace flying P-51Bs, he was shot down in error by a B-24 gunner over the Austrian town of Aschbach-Markt during an escort mission on 30 May 1944. Following its service with the USAAF, JK777 was transferred back to the RAF and flew with No 185 Sqn from Malta.

DICK AUDET

French Canadian Dick Audet achieved the memorable feat of claiming five German fighters destroyed during the course of a single mission.

Born on 13 March 1922 in Lethbridge, Alberta, Richard Joseph 'Dick' Audet was raised on the family ranch in the Milk River valley. Having shown an aptitude for sport, he was offered a position as a PE instructor upon graduation from secondary school, but Audet wanted to fly. At that point he was too young to enlist, so he worked as a stenographer and bookkeeper until he was able to join the RCAF in August 1941. Receiving his pilot's wings and a commission in October 1942, Audet was then posted to Britain.

Following the completion of his advanced operational training in England, Audet was briefly posted to No 421 'Red Indian' Sqn in July 1943. However, his time in the front line was to last just a matter of weeks, as for much of 1943–44 he was assigned to a series of second-line units, including No 691 Sqn at Roborough, Devon. Here, Audet flew a variety of aircraft types on army co-operation duties towing target banners for anti-aircraft batteries. Such flights allowed him to build up a considerable number of flying hours, however, and amass experience in aircraft handling in such disparate types as the Barracuda, Defiant, Oxford and Hurricane.

Finally, on 14 September 1944, following his promotion to flight lieutenant, Audet was posted to Spitfire IX-equipped No 411 'Grizzly Bear' Sqn at Le Culot (B68), Belgium.

Despite his lack of combat flying, Audet was made a flight commander the following month, and he had flown 52 missions by 28 December. Although Audet had successfully attacked ground targets, he was never in the right place at the right time to engage enemy aircraft in the air. That all changed on 29 December.

Leading 'Yellow' Section as it patrolled northeast of Osnabrück, Audet spotted a lone Me 262, followed by a formation of Bf 109s and Fw 190s below and off to the right of it at his 'two o'clock' position. Leading his section of four Spitfires down in the direction of the enemy fighters, he described the remarkable events that followed in his combat report:

No 411 Sqn's full complement of pilots come together for the camera soon after moving to Volkel (B80), in the Netherlands, in October 1944. Future ace Flt Lt Dick Audet is standing directly in front of the Spitfire IX's VHF aerial. He had only been with the unit a matter of weeks when this photograph was taken.

I attacked an Me 109 that was the last aircraft in the formation of about 12, all flying line astern. At approximately 200 yards and 30 degrees to starboard, and at a height of 10,000ft, I opened fire and saw strikes all over the fuselage and wing roots. The Me 109 burst into flames on the starboard side of the fuselage only, trailing intense black smoke. I then broke off my attack.

After the first attack, I went around in a defensive circle at about 8,500ft until I spotted an Fw 190 that I immediately attacked from 250 yards down to 100 yards and from 30 degrees to line astern. I saw strikes over the cockpit and to the rear of the fuselage. It burst into flames from the engine back, and as I passed very close over the top of it, I saw the pilot slumped over in the cockpit, which was also in flames.

My third attack followed immediately after the second. I followed what I believed was an Me 109 in a slight dive. He then climbed sharply and his canopy flew off at about 3,000–4,000ft. I then gave a very short burst from about 300 yards and line astern and his aircraft whipped downwards in a dive. The pilot attempted or did bale

Flt Lt Audet, far left, talks fellow No 411 Sqn pilots through one of his five victories after landing back at Heesch (B88), in the Netherlands, following his 'ace in a day' mission on 29 December 1944.

Audet shot down three Fw 190s and two Bf 109s ten miles west of Osnabrück in a matter of minutes on 29 December, and remarkably, these were his first victories. This official photograph was taken of him shortly after his 'ace-making' feat of arms.

out. I saw a black object on the edge of the cockpit but his 'chute ripped to shreds. I then took cine shots of his aircraft descending to the ground and the bits of parachute floating around. I saw this aircraft hit and smash into many flaming pieces on the ground. I do not remember any strikes on his aircraft. The Browning [machine gun] button only may have been pressed.

I spotted an Fw 190 being pursued at about 5,000ft by a Spitfire that was in turn pursued by an Fw 190. I called this 'Yellow' Section pilot to break and attacked the Fw 190 up his rear. The fight went downwards in a steep dive. When I was about 250 yards and line astern of this Fw 190, I opened fire. There were many strikes on the length of the fuselage, and it immediately burst into flames. I saw this Fw 190 go straight into the ground and burn.

Several minutes later, while attempting to form my section up again, I spotted an Fw 190 from 4,000ft. He was about 2,000ft below me, so I dived down on him and he turned into me from the right. Then he flipped around in a left-hand turn and attempted a head-on attack. I slowed down to wait for the Fw 190 to fly into range. At about 200 yards and 20 degrees I gave him a very short burst but couldn't see any strikes. This aircraft flicked violently and continued to do so until it crashed into the ground. The remainder of my section saw this encounter, and 'Yellow 4' saw it crash in flames.

Dick Audet had achieved 'acedom' in the space of two minutes. This was the only occasion that a Spitfire pilot succeeded in downing five aircraft in a *single* sortie. Audet was credited with the destruction of five more fighters (including an Me 262) in January 1945, and he received the Distinguished Flying Cross (DFC) for his 'ace-making'

A close-up of the new GM2 gyro gunsight fitted to the Spitfire from late 1944. A major step forward in air-to-air gunnery, the GM2 gave the 'average' fighter pilot a much better chance of scoring hits and, therefore, achieving victories. Flt Lt Audet praised the gunsight after he claimed five victories on 29 December.

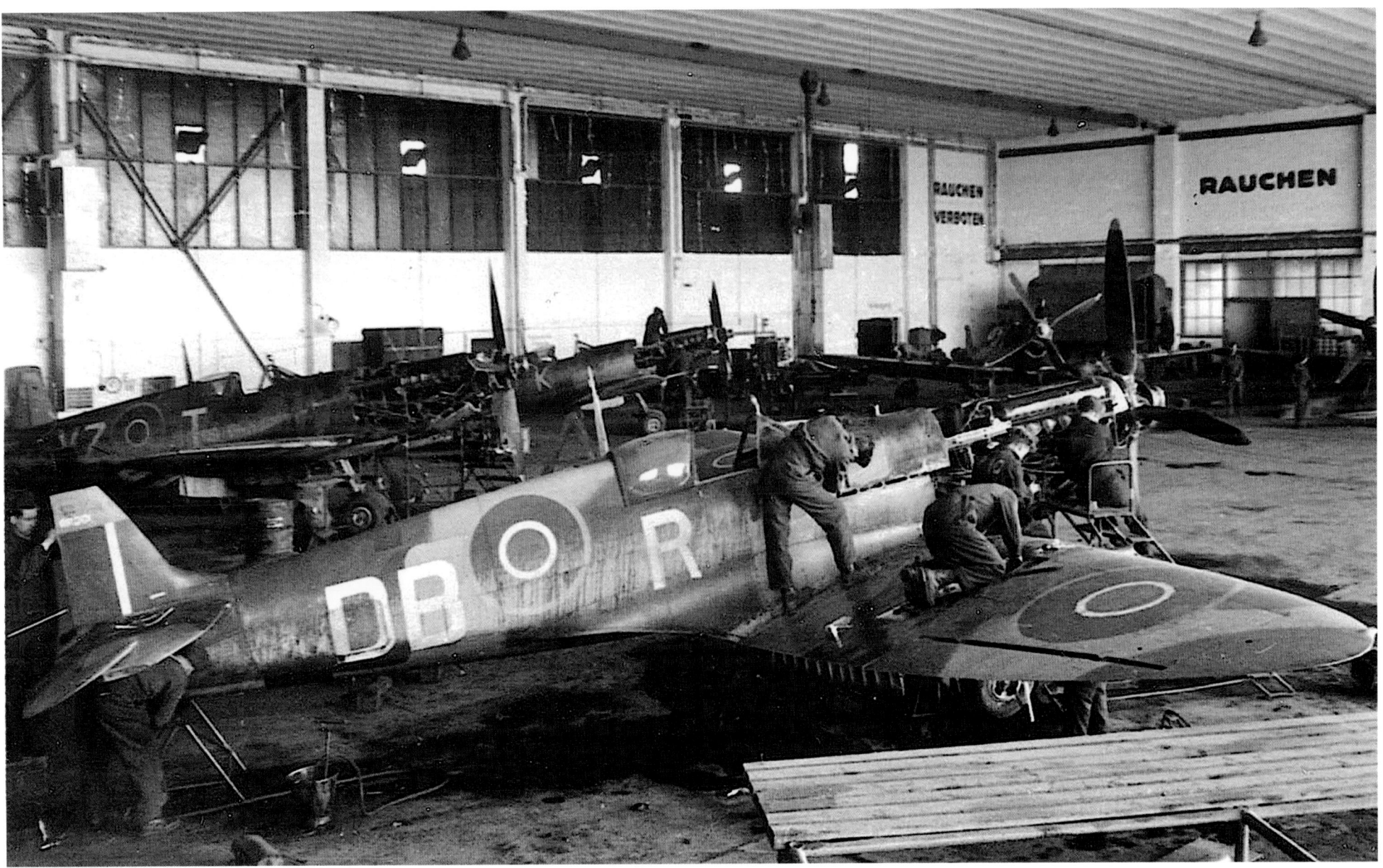

Spitfire IX RR201 of No 411 Sqn was used by Audet to claim seven of his ten aerial victories. He also destroyed an Me 262 on the ground during a strafing attack in this fighter, having shot one down earlier in the same mission. Previously assigned to No 66 Sqn, RR201 was coded DB-A when flown by Audet. It was written off on 30 April 1945 following a forced landing after being hit by flak.

Two Spitfire IXs from No 411 Sqn warm up their engines before departing on another mission from Heesch (B88) in early 1945. The GM2 gunsight, seen silhouetted against the windscreen of MJ334 in the foreground, was larger than its predecessor and restricted forward visibility. Unlike the combat novice Dick Audet, veteran Spitfire aces were not enamoured with it, having by then mastered the art of air-to-air gunnery and deflection shooting.

feat in February. That same month he was forced to bale out of his Spitfire IX (PL430) when it was hit by flak. The Operational Summary recorded:

On February 8, Flt Lt R J Audet and Flg Off R C McCracken went on the first Rhubarb [low-level operation in search of targets of opportunity to strafe] to Twente Aerodrome. They made the trip over on the deck. When they reached the 'drome they found only a handful of workmen about. A well-camouflaged gun position opened up on them. Flg Off McCracken returned the fire with all he had, and although no claims are submitted, he must have made it quite warm for them.

Flt Lt Audet received some flak from the northern end of the 'drome and his aircraft was hit, and badly damaged, by the first few bursts. He thought he would have to bale out, but by careful nursing he was able to bring the aircraft back to base. He could not land, however, as the aircraft refused to remain straight and level when he cut the speed. Audet ended up climbing to a safe altitude and baling out well in sight of all ground personnel, who saw both the aircraft and Dick come down. He was very lucky to hit a soft field, being picked up immediately by a chap on a motorcycle, transferred to a jeep and driven back to Intelligence in time for interrogation.

Audet's luck did not last, however, for on 3 March, in wet and stormy weather, he attacked a train near Coesfeld, Germany, and was shot down by flak. While other Spitfire units in the area that day had reported seeing 'a lot of stuff on the ground but we were not allowed to attack it', Audet's No 411 Sqn had either disobeyed the order or had not received it for they shot up the train. During the attack, Audet – who had just returned from a week's leave – was hit. His aircraft (MK950) started trailing glycol and quickly burst into flames, diving into a wood from a height of 500ft and exploding. Audet was killed instantly. His death was a tremendous blow to No 411 Sqn, for at just 22 years of age he had amassed an impressive score of 10.5 victories and one damaged in only 83 sorties. This moving epitaph to Audet (who was posthumously awarded a Bar to his DFC) appeared in No 411 Sqn's record book: 'Modest and unassuming, he was just one of the boys, and a real credit to Canada and her RCAF. His daring and keenness led to his presumed death. He was a leader, respected and admired by all. Just one swell guy.

Audet's body was never recovered.

Spitfire IXE RR201/DB-A of Flt Lt Dick Audet, No 411 Sqn, Heesch (B88), the Netherlands, 29 December 1944

Flt Lt Audet was one of the few Allied pilots during World War Two to become an 'ace in a day', a feat he achieved in the space of just two minutes, despite having never seen an enemy fighter before. On 29 December 1944, he claimed three Fw 190s and two Bf 109s destroyed in this aircraft, which he also used to down an Fw 190 on 14 January and an Me 262 nine days later. Delivered new to No 66 Sqn in October 1944, RR201 was subsequently passed on to No 411 Sqn. Aside from Audet, two other pilots from his unit also claimed victories with the fighter prior to it being damaged beyond repair on 30 April when Flt Lt S M McClarty force-landed near Scharesbeck after RR201 had been hit by flak, knocking out its engine.

DOUGLAS BADER

Arguably the RAF's most famous wartime pilot, Douglas Bader overcame the loss of both legs in a pre-war flying accident to become an ace with 24 victories to his name.

Although born in St John's Wood, North London, on 21 February 1910, Douglas Bader spent his early years in India, where his father worked as a civil engineer. Sent home once he had reached schooling age, the somewhat unruly Bader excelled at sport and also did well enough in his final exams to receive an offer of a place at Oxford University, although he chose Cambridge instead. He was the recipient of one of six annual prize cadetships offered by RAF Cranwell, Lincolnshire, enrolling as an officer cadet in 1928. Bader undertook his first flight (in an Avro 504) on 13 September that year, and flew solo five months later.

In July 1930, following the completion of his flying training, Bader was commissioned as a pilot officer and joined No 23 Sqn at Kenley, Surrey. Charged with defending London, the unit was equipped with the Gloster Gamecock biplane fighters, which were replaced by Bristol Bulldogs from July 1931. Aside from learning his craft as a fighter pilot, Bader followed his passion for sport by playing rugby for the RAF, Harlequins, Surrey and the Combined Services team, and cricket for the RAF. His natural aptitude for flying saw him successfully represent No 23 Sqn in RAF Fighter Command's pairs aerobatic competition at Hendon in the summer of 1931.

Bader's promising career in the RAF came to an abrupt end on 14 December 1931 when he crashed his Bulldog while attempting low-altitude aerobatics at Woodley, in Reading. Once extricated from the wreckage of his fighter, he was taken to the Royal Berkshire Hospital, where both of his legs were amputated. Following many months recuperating, Bader worked tirelessly to regain his mobility with the aid of artificial legs. He was eventually able to drive a suitably modified car, play golf and, in June 1932, fly. Nevertheless, Bader was invalided out of the RAF in May 1933.

He soon obtained work with the Asiatic Petroleum Company (later renamed Shell Oil) and remained with the firm until accepted back into the RAF in October 1939 following the outbreak of war. With the successful completion of a series of flight tests at the Central Flying School (CFS) at Upavon, Wiltshire, Bader was cleared for operational flying.

Flanked by fellow aces Flt Lt Eric Ball and Plt Off Willie McKnight at Duxford in October 1940, Sqn Ldr Douglas Bader admires the rather apt personal insignia he had applied to his Hurricane I V7467 while CO of No 242 Sqn. Bader had made seven claims in this aircraft the previous month, with four of them credited as victories.

He quickly progressed through a refresher course on modern aircraft types before receiving orders to Spitfire-equipped No 19 Sqn at Duxford, Cambridgeshire, in January 1940. Bader joined co-located No 222 Sqn, also flying Spitfires, as a flight commander on the eve of the Dunkirk evacuation, and he claimed his first successes off the French Channel coast on 1 June.

In July he was given command of battle-weary No 242 Sqn at Coltishall, Norfolk, the unit having been withdrawn from France in mid-June in a state of disarray. Staffed mainly by demoralised Canadian pilots that lacked aircraft, the squadron was reinvigorated by Bader – leading by example, he whipped his men back into shape after getting hold of sufficient Hurricanes. No 242 Sqn was declared operational again as part of No 12 Group

As a Wing Leader, Wg Cdr Bader was permitted to use his initials on his aircraft in place of unit code letters. Spitfire IIA P7966 was duly marked D-B at Tangmere after he became the airfield's Wing Commander Flying in March 1941. His fighter, which had been issued new to No 616 Sqn shortly after Bader's arrival at the West Sussex airfield, also bore a rank pennant. P7966 later served with Nos 412 and 154 Sqns before being relegated to OTU service.

in August, and Bader led the unit throughout the Battle of Britain. During the campaign, he was credited with 11 victories between 11 July and 27 September.

Aside from leading No 242 Sqn, Bader also convinced his Air Officer Commanding No 12 Group, Air Vice-Marshal Trafford Leigh-Mallory, that fighter units could inflict significantly more damage on the Luftwaffe's bomber formations if 'big wings' comprised of aircraft from several squadrons were grouped together before attacking the enemy. The adoption of this controversial tactic led to heated clashes between staff officers in Nos 11 and 12 Groups over the time it took for such wings to be assembled. Despite 'big wings' being shunned by Nos 10 and 11 Groups during the Battle of Britain, Bader frequently led a mixed Spitfire and Hurricane wing comprising up to five squadrons into action through to the end of the campaign.

In January 1941, Bader received a DFC, and in March he was promoted to wing commander and became one of the first wing leaders when he took charge of the newly formed Tangmere Wing, on the Sussex coast. In just seven weeks from 21 June 1941, he claimed 11 victories, five probables and five damaged. All of his victims were Bf 109s. This success earned him a Distinguished Service Order (DSO) and Bar in July, and a Bar to his DFC would follow in September. By then, however, Bader was a PoW, his outstanding run of success having come to an end on 9 August (during his 62nd sweep over France since 24 March) when he was either shot down by a Bf 109 from *Jagdgeschwader* (JG) 26 or, in error, by a Spitfire from No 616 Sqn.

Bader believed that he had, in fact, been involved in a mid-air collision with a German fighter, and he wrote as much in a story that was published by the North American Newspaper Alliance in December 1945:

Bader was a great advocate of 'goon-baiting' during his years as a PoW, and he is seen here doing his best to express his displeasure about something while being held at *Stalag Luft IIIB* in Sagan, in western Poland, in 1942. He escaped from here for several days in August 1942, and upon his recapture, Bader was sent to *Oflag IV-C* – better known as Colditz Castle.

Our target was the neighbourhood of Lille, where we met some of our bombers who were due to blow the daylights out of a French factory. We were well over France when about 18 Me 109s appeared below us. Four of us in front dived down on to the leading four German fighters and each took his opposite number. The normal method of making such an attack was to close behind the Me 109, give him a quick squirt and then, from one's superior speed with the dive, pull up and so maintain the height advantage for further attacks.

This time, unfortunately, my judgement was very bad. I nearly collided from behind with my opposite number and I was compelled, instead of pulling up, to go on behind and down underneath him. On getting underneath this collection of Huns, I saw, a couple of thousand feet below and a short distance in front, four more Huns. I thought I might as well have a swing around with them, which I did. As I turned away, I collided with an Me 109 on my right.

It was entirely my fault. The Spitfire's nose dropped very abruptly and the stick and rudder had no feeling in them. The aeroplane was pointing straight downwards and twisting very slowly in a left-hand direction. There appeared to be no fuselage behind my seat at all. In fact, the complete tail assembly had been removed. Immediately I realised I was out of control I cut the engine, and the next thing was to get out at

Strapped into the cockpit of a suitably marked Spitfire IX at North Weald on 15 September 1945, Wg Cdr Bader awaits the order to start the engine of his fighter and taxi out. He would lead 12 Spitfire IXs flown by fellow Battle of Britain veterans over central London some two minutes ahead of a 300-aircraft flypast, this event being part of the nationwide Thanksgiving Week to mark the end of World War Two.

about 18,000ft. The cockpit hood was a little obstinate before it finally came away. Having undone the harness, I lifted myself up in the seat with my hands to get out. I was surprised to feel as though I was being assisted out of the cockpit. Other pilots who have baled out at high speed have told me there is a kind of suction, which helps to pull the pilot out – rather like drawing a cork out of a bottle. Just when everything appeared to be going smoothly and I was nearly clear, my legs became stuck.

My only clear memory was of being held to the aeroplane by my right leg. We parted company at about 4,000ft, and I seemed to shoot upwards from the aeroplane, leaving

Newly promoted Gp Capt Bader sits in the centre of the front row for a formal photograph of the staff and students – and a Tempest V – at the Fighter Leader's School at Tangmere in the summer of 1945. More than half of these men (some of whom are from the Fleet Air Arm, PAF, RAAF, *Armée de l'Air* and the SAAF) have medal ribbons on their service dress tunics.

Looking every inch the fighter ace, Gp Capt Bader poses for the camera in his service dress uniform on the eve of his retirement from the RAF in July 1946.

my right leg behind. I released my parachute. Just before passing through a cloud layer about 1,000ft from the ground an Me 109 seemed to be rushing towards me, and it passed about 50 yards away. The last few hundred feet I remember very clearly, seeing three rustic French figures leaning on a fence beside the field into which I was about to arrive. I do not remember striking the ground because I was knocked out for a couple of minutes. My left leg must have struck me in the chest because I broke two ribs. This, apart from a cut hand and a cut throat, was the only damage I suffered. Three members of the Luftwaffe removed my parachute harness before carrying me to a car. I was driven, bleeding rather profusely from the throat, to a hospital in St Omer.

Bader would spend the rest of the war as a PoW, during which time he made several escape attempts that eventually saw him sent to Colditz Castle. Liberated in April 1945, he was made commanding officer (CO) of the Fighter Leader's School at Tangmere and subsequently led the 1945 Battle of Britain flypast over London in September of that year.

Bader left the RAF in February 1946 and returned to Shell Oil. His flying exploits in both war and peace reached a worldwide audience following the release of the motion picture *Reach for the Sky* in 1956, and he used his growing celebrity status to further the cause of limbless people. Bader, who was knighted for this work in 1976, made his final flight at the controls of an aircraft in June 1979. He passed away on 3 September 1982 after suffering a heart attack.

Spitfire IIA P7966/D-B of Wg Cdr Douglas Bader, Officer Commanding (OC) Tangmere Wing, Tangmere, West Sussex, March 1941

This aircraft was one of the first to feature the Wing Leader's initials on the fuselage – it was also a presentation Spitfire, adorned with the legend *Manxman* below the cockpit on its starboard side. Issued new to No 616 Sqn (part of Bader's Tangmere Wing), the aircraft subsequently served with Nos 412 and 154 Sqns. P7966 was then passed on to No 61 OTU, before transferring to No 52 OTU in 1942. It was destroyed in a crash while still assigned to the latter unit in October 1942.

GEORGE BEURLING

Both a crack shot and a loner, Canadian George Beurling was the highest scoring ace of the Malta campaign.

The son of a Swedish father and an English mother, George Frederick Beurling was born in Montreal, Canada, on 6 December 1921. Taking to the air for the first time in 1930, he went solo some eight years later at the age of 16 while at the controls of a Curtiss-Reid Rambler biplane. Beurling was, however, too young to be granted a pilot's licence. Leaving high school shortly after, Beurling was initially employed as a co-pilot with an airfreight company in Gravenhurst, Ontario. He soon grew bored of this, however, and after reading an article in a newspaper describing how a small number of American volunteers were heading to China to fight the Japanese, he resigned. Unfortunately for Beurling, he was arrested when he attempted to enter the US illegally.

Following Germany's invasion of Poland in September 1939, and with Europe now at war, Beurling went straight to his local RCAF recruiter, which was unprepared for such a large

During a pause in the action, pilots from No 249 Sqn pose for a group photograph in front of a Spitfire VB at Takali in August 1942. Sgt Beurling is standing tenth from the left in the back row, directly beneath the nose of the Spitfire. He had already claimed 18 victories by the time this photograph was taken. Note the 51° *Stormo* emblem in front of Sqn Ldr R A Mitchell (OC No 249 Sqn) and Gp Capt W K Le May (Takali Station Commander), taken as a souvenir from a downed Macchi C.202.

influx of volunteers, and Beurling, along with many others, was turned away. Unperturbed, he tried to enlist in the Finnish Air Force in an attempt to help the Scandinavian country defend itself from Soviet invasion. Beurling was accepted, but his father refused to sign the necessary papers as he was still under-age. In May 1940, Beurling managed to work his way across the Atlantic to join the RAF, but he had failed to take his birth certificate with him so he was turned away yet again. Returning home to find the required paperwork, Beurling was soon on board a ship back to Scotland. Finally, in September 1940, he was accepted for service in the RAF.

After completing a year of training, Sgt Beurling was posted to the RCAF's No 403 'Wolf' Sqn, equipped with Spitfire VBs, at Debden, Essex. However, a decision that RCAF units should be manned exclusively by RCAF personnel resulted in Beurling, who was serving with the RAF, being posted to No 41 Sqn (also flying the Spitfire VB) at Merston, West Sussex. On 1 May 1942, he claimed his first victory when he shot down an Fw 190 over the Channel. Expecting to be congratulated on his success, Beurling was reprimanded instead for deliberately breaking formation to chase after his foe.

Considered a lone wolf by his squadronmates, and unpopular with his superiors for continually leaving formation to attack German fighters, Beurling was readily granted a transfer when he requested a posting to Malta, which he believed was 'the fighter pilot's paradise'. He duly flew a Spitfire from the carrier HMS *Eagle* to the island on 9 June 1942, his aircraft being one of 32 participating in Operation *Salient*. Once on Malta, Beurling joined No 249 Sqn. Those who flew with him in defence of the island were stunned by his phenomenal eyesight, and many felt safe knowing that they would never be bounced by enemy fighters. Beurling had worked hard on improving his vision during his training in Britain, having been one of the few aviators of his generation to understand the need for sound aircraft recognition at an early stage in his career as a fighter pilot. He explained to a reporter who interviewed him while on Malta, 'I would pick out a hill in the distance, then a tree on that hill, then a branch of that tree and bring my eyes to focus on it and try to make out the details as quickly as possible. By doing that again and again, I found I could spot aircraft in the sky and distinguish what they were quicker than other fellows.'

This is thought to be the only photograph in existence of the highest-scoring Spitfire of the Malta campaign, Mk VC BR301/UF-S. Assigned to No 249 Sqn following its delivery to Takali on 9 May 1942 as part of Operation *Bowery* (involving 64 Spitfires flown in from USS *Wasp* (CV-7) and HMS *Eagle*), the fighter was credited with eight and two shared victories, one and one shared probables and seven damaged. Sgt Beurling claimed five victories and two damaged in just two engagements in BR301 on 27 and 29 July.

Beurling's ability to see enemy aircraft before anyone else became legendary on Malta. Neither a smoker or a drinker, he was never heard to swear either – his prime expletive was 'screwball'.

The month after he arrived on Malta, Beurling claimed 15 aircraft destroyed and six damaged. His first successes came on 6 July, and the trio of victories he achieved that day gave him ace status. The second of these kills took the form of an Italian Reggiane Re.2001, which Beurling misidentified as a 'Macchi 202' in the following combat report:

As the bombers turned to run I saw a Macchi 202 boring up Smitty's [Flg Off John Smith] tail. I did a quick climbing turn and bored in on the Eyetie, catching him unawares. A one-second burst smacked him in the engine and glycol tank. He burst into flames and went down like a plummet. The same performance followed with another Macchi. Like the first one, this baby picked on Smitty, and I on Smitty's 'friend'. He saw me coming, however, and I broke away, diving. We went down vertically together from 20,000ft to about 5,000ft, and I let him have it as he pulled out from about 300 yards and slightly to starboard. God knows where I hit him, but he exploded into a million pieces.

Beurling was somewhat dismissive of his opponents in the *Regia Aeronautica*, explaining during a 1943 interview that 'The "Eyeties" are comparatively easy to shoot down. Oh, they're brave enough. In fact, I think the "Eyeties" have more courage than the Germans, but their tactics aren't so good. They try to do clever aerobatics and looping. But they will stick with it even if things are going against them, whereas the "Jerries" will run.'

After his eighth victory, Beurling was awarded the Distinguished Flying Medal (DFM), followed by a Bar to this at the end of July. In October, with his score standing at 20.333 victories, Beurling (who had reluctantly accepted a commission to pilot officer the previous month) received the DFC. The October 'Blitz', which saw Ju 88s and their

Groundcrew from No 249 Sqn flank the scoreboard applied to Spitfire VB EP706 at Takali in late September 1942. This tally was exclusively the work of Flt Sgt Beurling, who would claim four Bf 109s destroyed and one damaged in EP706.

Bf 109 escorts mount a series of attacks on RAF airfields and naval installations, provided Beurling with another target-rich environment. In just five days he shot down eight aircraft, three of them falling to him on the 13th. His combat report for that date read as follows:

As 'Tiger Red 3', I attacked eight Ju 88s, taking a straggler from slightly above to the right with a two-second burst of cannon and machine guns. Pieces came off the starboard wing. I then broke to port and down and saw one Messerschmitt closing in from port above. I broke left and then turned into him. At 50 yards astern I fired a one-and-a-half-seconds burst of cannon and machine guns. The enemy aircraft burst into flames. A second Messerschmitt came down from the starboard quarter above. As the enemy aircraft pulled out ahead at 250–300 yards, I gave him a four-second burst with machine guns; I observed no strikes but the pilot baled out. At this time, I saw my first enemy aircraft strike the sea.

Some of the bombers targeted Luqa airfield, before fleeing north for Sicily. Beurling quickly caught one. 'I attacked a Ju 88 from the starboard quarter above, 300 yards, with cannon and machine guns, firing a two-second burst and observing strikes on the root of the starboard wing, and black, oily smoke pouring out. I fired the remainder of my ammunition into the fuselage. The enemy aircraft did a diving turn to the right, striking the sea.'

Beurling repeated this success on 14 October, when he claimed what proved to be his final three victories in the defence of Malta. That same day he was shot down while attempting to intercept a large enemy formation. Hit in the right heel by a cannon splinter and peppered in the left leg by shrapnel, Beurling baled out at 1,000ft and came down in the sea. He was rescued within 20 minutes and subsequently spent two weeks in hospital. While convalescing, Beurling was awarded a DSO, and was sent back to Britain, via Gibraltar, on 31 October. He was one of 24 tour-expired or wounded pilots and ten civilians who were evacuated from Malta on that date aboard a Liberator that had flown in from Alexandria, Egypt.

Unfortunately, the transport arrived at Gibraltar in a severe storm, causing the pilot to overshoot the runway. Attempting to go around again, he stalled and crashed into the water 100 yards from shore. Eight civilians and six pilots died either from drowning or injuries sustained in the crash. Beurling, despite having his leg in plaster, managed to swim ashore.

Flg Off Beurling hams it up for press photographers after visiting Buckingham Palace on 25 May 1943. According to a Canadian Press report on this date, 'The first fighting man to be given four decorations at once at a royal investiture, Flg Off George Beurling received a DSO, DFC and DFM and Bar from the King at a recent ceremony at Buckingham Palace. Beurling, Canada's leading fighter pilot who is credited with 29 enemy planes destroyed, drew such a crowd when he left the palace grounds that traffic was blocked in and out of the palace gate.'

Possibly the most highly decorated flying officer in the RCAF, Beurling is seen here buying war bonds with fellow No 249 Sqn Malta veteran Flg Off Bob Middlemiss (who made seven claims in Spitfires, three for aircraft destroyed), having just been assigned to No 403 Sqn at Headcorn Advanced Landing Ground (ALG) in Kent. This photograph was taken shortly after Beurling had transferred from the RAF to the RCAF on 1 September 1943.

GEORGE BEURLING

The most impressive scoreboard ever seen on a Spitfire IX was applied to MH883/VZ-B of No 412 Sqn, the fighter featuring the 30.333 scalps then credited to Flt Lt Beurling. The ranking Allied ace of the Malta campaign briefly served with the unit as a flight commander at Biggin Hill from late November 1943 until February 1944, claiming his final victory – in this aircraft – on 30 December.

Having finally made it back to Britain, he was posted home to Canada (while on temporary loan to the RCAF) on leave in November.

Returning to England in mid-1943, Beurling became an instructor at No 61 Operational Training Unit (OTU) in July. Transferring to the RCAF, he was posted to No 403 Sqn and claimed another victory on 24 September. Later sent to No 412 'Falcon' Sqn, Beurling would achieve his final victory on 30 December 1943, for a total of 31.333 kills and nine damaged.

A maverick who was never able to come to terms with authority, Beurling was allowed to retire from the RCAF on 16 October 1944. Restless in civilian life, he volunteered for service with the newly formed Israeli Air Force. On his way to the Middle East, Beurling was tasked with ferrying a Norduyn Norseman utility aircraft across Europe to Israel. However, he and his co-pilot were killed when the aeroplane blew up as it departed Rome on 20 May 1948. Sabotage was suspected but never proven.

Spitfire VB EP706/T-L of Plt Off George Beurling, No 249 Sqn, Takali, Malta, October 1942

This aircraft was delivered to the RAF in July 1942 and flown to Malta from the carrier HMS *Furious* during one of the August reinforcement operations (either *Bellows* or *Baritone*). High-scoring ace Plt Off George Beurling used a number of Spitfires while defending Malta, and he claimed four Bf 109s destroyed and one damaged in EP706 in separate engagements on 25 September and 10 October 1942. It is depicted here with 20 victory symbols, denoting Beurling's score at the end of September. EP706 remained with No 249 Sqn until it was lost due to engine failure while on a patrol over the Mediterranean on 3 March 1943.

ROBERT FINDLAY BOYD

Scotsman Robert Findlay Boyd was one of the most successful pilots during the Battle of Britain with 14 victories in Spitfires.

Born in East Kilbride, Scotland, on 8 June 1916, Robert Findlay Boyd was the son of a colliery owner who found employment as a mining engineer during the late 1930s. Having joined the Royal Auxiliary Air Force in 1935, he quickly earned his wings and was posted to his local unit, No 602 'City of Glasgow' Sqn, at Abbotsinch the following year. Boyd initially flew Hawker Hart and Hind light bombers through to November 1938, when the squadron was re-tasked with the army co-operation/liaison role and issued with Hector biplanes. They were kept for just two months, as No 602 Sqn was assigned the fighter role in January 1939 and equipped with Gauntlet IIs.

In May, the unit became the first Auxiliary squadron to receive Spitfire Is. The fact that it had been issued with the aircraft ahead of most regular units in RAF Fighter Command was an official acknowledgement of No 602 Sqn's prowess in its assigned role. The unit was embodied into the RAF on 24 August 1939 – just a week before Germany invaded Poland.

Despite flying myriad coastal and convoy patrols from Abbotsinch, Grangemouth, Drem and Dyce in the early months of World War Two, Boyd only got to fire his guns twice during this period. On 30 November, he spotted an enemy aircraft heading for cloud cover. Rapidly closing on it, Boyd fired a two-second burst from 400 yards but his quarry disappeared, apparently undamaged. The future ace had greater success on 7 July 1940, when he led two other Spitfires from A Flight's 'Yellow' Section in the interception of a lone Ju 88 off St Abb's Head, Scotland. Boyd was credited with a third of a victory.

On 13 August, No 602 Sqn was urgently sent south to Westhampnett, which was a satellite airfield for Tangmere in West Sussex. Now a flight commander, Boyd would lead both A Flight and, on a number of occasions, the entire squadron into action during the climax of the Battle of Britain. From 15 August to

With his hands firmly buried in the pockets of his 1930 pattern flying suit, Plt Off Boyd (at bottom left) joins other aviators and groundcrew from No 602 Sqn for a group photograph with the unit's newly delivered Hinds at Abbotsinch in June 1937.

Occasionally flown by Flg Off Boyd in 1939–40, Spitfire IA K9964 prepares to taxi out from the No 602 Sqn dispersal at Drem in March 1940. Among the first Spitfires delivered to the unit in May 1939, K9964, christened *BOGUS* (it wore the codes ZT-B/LO-B), remained with No 602 Sqn until the fighter was damaged when it was hit on the ground by a Miles Master on 16 May 1940 at Dyce. Later issued to No 64 Sqn, the aircraft fell into German hands virtually intact when it force landed in France on 15 August 1940.

The pilot cadre (and the squadron adjutant) and their dogs pose for a formal photograph at Drem in March 1940. Six of these pilots, including Flt Lt Boyd sitting at the far right, would become aces before the year was out.

Boyd had just tightened his straps [in the cockpit of his Spitfire] and waved his fitter, Smithy [LAC W H Smith], away. As he gunned the engine, the Spitfire raced across the field, and hardly had he felt the drumming of the wheels stop when a Ju 87 appeared over the trees, having completed a dive on Tangmere. Boyd, his undercarriage only half pumped up, automatically corrected his aim as the Stuka curved across from the left. One burst put the dive-bomber into the ground, almost intact, just at the side of the airfield. The Spitfire banked round, completed its circuit, dropped its wheels and landed; Boyd nipped over to the Ju 87 and collected his first trophies of battle – a Luger pistol and a Leica camera. He'd been in the air for almost exactly a minute; surely the quickest 'kill' of the war.

2 October, he made 17 claims, 14 of them credited to him as victories. Two of his successes came against Ju 87s when the *Stukageschwader* targeted Tangmere and other sites in West Sussex on 16 and 18 August. The first of these victories, on the 16th, was described by Douglas McRoberts in his No 602 Sqn history, *Lions Rampant*:

Later that same day Boyd shared in the destruction of an He 111 with the rest of Blue Section, which he had led on a patrol from Westhampnett. The solitary Heinkel bomber had been sighted over Worthing, on the West Sussex coast, and Boyd led his section in the subsequent interception, as he recounted in his very brief combat report. 'Took off at 16.20 hrs. Sighted enemy aircraft approximately 1,000ft above and coming towards us. "Blue 1" [Boyd] did a climbing turn and delivered a beam attack, followed by "Blue 2", who stopped one motor. Successive attacks were delivered by the section until the enemy aircraft crashed in waste ground approximately four miles north of Worthing.'

No 602 Sqn had been heavily involved in the defence of key military installations on the south coast following its switch to No 11 Group, and after making 11 claims in less than one month, Boyd was given leave by his CO, Sqn Ldr Sandy Johnstone. However, as Johnstone explains in his wartime diary entry for 12 September, this break from operations had to be cut short due to incessant Luftwaffe attacks, and the attrition they caused on the unit:

The sector as a whole is desperately short of aircraft. Although 602 might find five serviceable aircraft at a pinch, the two Tangmere squadrons can only raise seven between them, and the shortage of qualified aircrew is even more acute. Indeed, I have had to recall Boyd from leave, and was expecting to see him yesterday, only to find he was caught up in the air raids on London, where the entire transport system is in a state of near chaos. Waterloo and Victoria stations are out of action and many bus services have been suspended because of the difficulty of driving through the streets of the city. In fact, Boyd said the only way he was able to get about was by Underground, but that, as he pointed out, does not yet run as far as Chichester.

Boyd was awarded a well-earned DFC on 24 September, with the citation to the medal noting that he had, 'led his flight into action on all possible occasions, and by his initiative and accurate shooting had personally destroyed nine enemy aircraft. He had displayed cool judgement and a keen desire to engage the enemy irrespective of the odds against him.' A Bar for his DFC followed on 25 October, and its citation noted, 'His fine leadership has enabled his squadron to attain many successes with few losses to themselves. Flt Lt Boyd has distinguished himself by his cool bearing and capable leadership.'

Boyd's impressive victory tally during the campaign led No 602 Sqn's historian, Wg Cdr Hector MacLean, to liken the ace to two legendary 'knights of the air' in his unit history *Fighters in Defence*. 'Like Manfred von Richthofen and Mick Mannock, the two aces of the Great War who ran up the highest score of victories for their respective sides, Robert Findlay Boyd regarded a fighter aeroplane as a gun platform. In the air, he tended to wait for his opportunity. Then he would move in with rapid and devastating effect.' Boyd's success, according to Douglas McRoberts, was due to the distance from which he opened fire and the type of ammunition he used. His preference for explosive shells made him unpopular with the armourers serving with No 602 Sqn, however:

The armourers had mixed feelings about 'Boydey', or 'Boyd the Bastard' as some called him. Findlay Boyd, by now the professional killer, had his guns tested every week, and harmonised to only 50 yards. If he came that close, the Germans in his sights would take the full weight of the eight Brownings at one concentrated spot. He insisted on a higher proportion of De Wilde explosive ammunition in his gunbelts – one De Wilde to every two of ball ammunition. The armourers called it a 'dirty' loading – the heavier De Wildes had a tendency to foul the barrels – but they were much more effective at destroying aircraft. Whenever Boyd was in combat, the barrels ended up in a mess and the armourers could weep. His last 50 rounds would contain tracers – a warning the guns were about to run out. But Boyd didn't usually need all his ammunition.

Boyd left No 602 Sqn in December 1940 after being given command of No 54 Sqn, and he led the unit into action during early offensive sweeps across the Channel as part of the recently formed Hornchurch Wing at Hornchurch, Essex. Initially flying Spitfire IIs, before switching to the Mk VA, he made seven claims (five of which were victories) with the squadron between 17 April and 17 July 1941. Posted as an instructor to

This studio portrait of Flt Lt Boyd was taken just prior to him heading south with No 602 Sqn to the No 11 Group airfield at Westhampnett on 13 August 1940. He would make 17 claims, 14 of them credited to him as victories, during the Battle of Britain. His prowess in aerial combat had earned Boyd a DFC and Bar by the end of October 1940.

This Spitfire was one of a number of Mk IIAs left at Hornchurch by No 41 Sqn for No 54 Sqn, which was led south to the Essex airfield by Sqn Ldr Boyd in February 1941. P7666/KL-Z, christened *OBSERVER CORPS*, was shot down into the Channel on 20 April after being hit during an engagement with Bf 110s – Spitfire ace Plt Off Jack Stokoe had claimed his seventh victory with the aircraft just minutes earlier.

No 58 OTU at Grangemouth, Scotland, in mid-summer 1941, Boyd returned to operations in December when he was made wing leader of the Kenley Wing. He achieved four more claims over the next three months, and was awarded a DSO on 10 April 1942 while still at Kenley. The citation for the decoration stated, 'Wg Cdr Boyd has led the wing on many operational missions. Much of the outstanding success obtained by the wing can be attributed to the leadership, skill and fighting spirit of this officer.'

Boyd was posted to India in 1943, where he served as a staff officer with the newly formed FEAF until being given command of Spitfire VC-equipped No 166 Wing at Chittagong, in what was then Bengal. Seeing action on the Burma front through to the end of the war, Boyd chose to leave the RAF as a group captain in late 1945. Initially working for Scottish Aviation as a charter flight pilot, he eventually turned his back on flying to run a pig farm but soon encountered financial difficulties. Switching to herring fishing, Boyd then settled on the Isle of Skye and became the hotelier of the *Ferry Inn* in the port village of Uig. He passed away on 22 February 1975.

An RAF photographer took this shot of Sqn Ldr Boyd (on the wing of a Spitfire II), unit mascot 'Crash' and a number of pilots from No 54 Sqn at Hornchurch in May 1941. Among these aviators is future Spitfire ace Plt Off Jack Charles, standing fifth from right. Boyd made seven claims (including five victories) while CO of the unit, with both he and Charles enjoying success on 17 April when the latter was credited with No 54 Sqn's 100th victory of the war.

Spitfire IA X4162/LO-J of Flt Lt Robert Findlay Boyd, No 602 Sqn, Westhampnett, West Sussex, September 1940

This aircraft was first flown on 8 August 1940, and it was issued new to No 602 Sqn as an attrition replacement eight days later. Boyd achieved only a solitary success in the fighter when he was credited with a sixth of a victory over a Ju 88 that was downed ten miles south of Brighton on 21 September. His usual mount was LO-K, but the serial of this aircraft has remained elusive. X4162 later served with Nos 124 and 340 Sqns and No 52 OTU prior to being converted by Heston Aircraft into a photo-reconnaissance Spitfire PR VII Type G (which meant it retained its eight machine guns despite being fitted with two F24 cameras in the rear fuselage) in late 1942. The aircraft's final fate is unrecorded.

PETE BROTHERS

Pete Brothers was already a high-scoring Hurricane ace from the fighting in France and the Battle of Britain by the time he switched to Spitfires on the Channel Front in mid-1941.

Born in Prestwich, Lancashire, on 30 September 1917, Peter Malam 'Pete' Brothers was subsequently educated at North Manchester School. He had learned to fly by the age of 16, and he joined the RAF in January 1936 on a short-service commission as an acting pilot officer. Brothers initially received tuition at No 4 Elementary and Reserve Flying Training School (E&RFTS) at Brough, Hull, where he accumulated 110 hours in the Blackburn B2 biplane to add to his civilian flying experience. In April, he was posted to No 9 Flying Training School (FTS) at Thornaby-on-Tees, where he duly completed a six-month course of intermediate and advanced flying training. In October, having been given an 'above average' rating, Plt Off Brothers received orders to join Gauntlet II-equipped No 32 Sqn at Biggin Hill, Kent.

Exactly two years later, the unit replaced its obsolescent Gloster biplanes with Hurricanes. By then Brothers had been promoted to flight commander. His many hours in fighters would hold him in good stead during the spring and early summer of 1940, when No 32 Sqn saw considerable action over France and southern England. Credited with his first victory (a Bf 109E) on 18 May, Brothers' tally steadily rose over the following months.

In late August, when No 32 Sqn was posted to Acklington, Northumberland, for a rest following serious losses, Brothers was transferred to No 257 Sqn at Coltishall to serve as a flight commander under newly promoted Sqn Ldr Bob Tuck. His first victories with the unit came on 15 September, when he downed a Ju 88 and Do 17 over southwest London. Forty-eight hours earlier, Brothers had been awarded a DFC, the citation to which read:

Plt Off Pete Brothers flies in close-line abreast formation with other Gauntlet IIs of No 32 Sqn while at the controls of K5330 during aerobatics training in the summer of 1937. This aircraft had joined the unit at Biggin Hill directly from Glosters on 24 July 1936, some three months before Brothers arrived at the Kent fighter station. K5330 was later passed on to the SAAF.

Above left: This shot of Flt Lt Pete Brothers was taken by a Fox Film Unit photographer at Hawkinge on 29 July 1940 – the very day he claimed a Bf 109E off the Kent coast for his fifth victory.

Above right: Pilots from No 32 Sqn's A Flight sit in their dispersal area at Hawkinge on 29 July 1940 awaiting the call to scramble after flying in from Biggin Hill and being placed on immediate readiness. In this Fox Film Unit photograph, Flt Lt Brothers is sat fourth from the left.

During an offensive patrol on 18 August 1940, this officer's flight encountered about 100 enemy aircraft. He led the flight in an attack against them, but before this could be pressed home, he was himself attacked by a number of Messerschmitt 110s. Turning to meet them, he found himself in a stalled position; he spun out of it and immediately sighted and engaged a Dornier 215, which he shot down. Later in the day he destroyed a Messerschmitt 109. Altogether, Flt Lt Brothers has destroyed seven enemy aircraft. He has at all times displayed great courage and initiative.

In January 1941, Brothers was at last rested from frontline flying when he was posted as an instructor to recently formed No 55 OTU at Aston Down, Gloucestershire. Following his promotion to squadron leader in June, he was immediately given the job of forming No 457 Sqn of the Royal Australian Air Force (RAAF) at Baginton, Warwickshire. Equipped with Spitfires, the unit would be led into action by Brothers from Redhill, Surrey, in March 1942 – he claimed No 457 Sqn's first victory on the 26th of that month, as recorded in the following combat report:

At 1602 hrs I was leading No 457 Sqn in a Circus [bombers or fighter-bombers heavily escorted by fighters – the purpose of these sweeps was to draw enemy fighters into combat] operation five miles off Le Havre when enemy aircraft were reported above and at three o'clock (up sun). I turned right through 360 degrees and enemy aircraft were reported at six o'clock. As I turned left, I saw a Spitfire going down smoking. Ahead, an Me 109E was diving down sun. He saw me and pulled up into a steep climb. I pulled up after him and gave him a six-second burst at 200 yards from quarter astern. Pieces flew off, and then half the starboard wing broke off. The enemy aircraft turned over on its back and dived down into the sea, pieces still coming off. The pilot did not leave the aircraft.

Brothers was given command of No 602 Sqn three months later after No 457 Sqn was posted to

Having just got out of the cockpit of his Spitfire VB at Redhill following a sweep over northern France, Sqn Ldr Brothers gives a verbal account of the operation to No 457 Sqn's Intelligence Officer in the spring of 1942.

This is almost certainly the only photograph ever taken of Sqn Ldr Brothers in his Spitfire VB, BM143, while CO of No 457 Sqn – an Australian-manned unit which he helped form in June 1941. The fighter, seen here with Brothers strapped into the cockpit at Redhill in April 1942, was marked with both his victory tally and rank pennant.

Australia, and he made four claims flying Spitfire VBs with the unit. One of the pilots he led during this period was future ace 'Sammy' Sampson, who noted in his autobiography *Spitfire Offensive*:

> I was very fortunate to serve under Pete. When it came to leading, first his squadron and then his wing, he had what can only be described as an instinctive feel for the battle. Pete typically led us into an advantageous position before joining combat. He was an outstanding fighter pilot and a veteran of well over 20 aerial combats in which he was invariably at the right end, with the Hun at the receiving end.

Having consecutively led two squadrons in No 11 Group, Brothers was promoted to wing commander in October 1942 and made wing leader of the Tangmere Wing. He claimed an Fw 190 destroyed in January 1943 for his 15th victory and received a Bar to his DFC six months later. The citation for the decoration noted, 'This officer has displayed outstanding keenness and efficiency. Within recent months he has led a wing in many operations and, by his skilful work and personal example, has contributed in a large measure to the high standard of operational efficiency of the formation. He has displayed great devotion to duty.'

Following a second spell off operations, initially in command of No 61 OTU and then as a staff officer with HQ, No 10 Group, Brothers was given command of the Exeter Wing in early 1944. He had switched to commanding the Culmhead Wing in Somerset by D-Day, and on 7 August, while flying a Spitfire VII during a Rodeo [a mass fighter sweep] along the valley of the River Loire, Brothers claimed his 16th and final victory. He subsequently recalled the one-sided action as follows:

> As I closed the range, I was surprised to see my '190 start a gentle climb, weaving equally gently to the left and the right, offering a perfect target. 'Oh, my God, you poor sucker. You must be straight out of training school', I thought. It seemed so unfair and spoilt the exhilaration of the chase. This was not to be an exciting duel, but a massacre. Worse was to

A No 457 Sqn Spitfire VB sits at readiness, a trolley accumulator plugged into the electrical socket in front of the starboard wing root, ready to supply power to start the fighter's engine. Behind the aircraft, another Mk VB from the unit is on short finals to Redhill's grass runway.

follow. I opened fire and was horrified and sickened to see my cannon shells not knock off a wing or tail of the aircraft, but blast straight into the cockpit, instantly killing the pilot. The aircraft flipped over and hit the ground. 'I am sorry, I didn't mean that', I said out loud.

Brothers received a DSO three months later, with the following citation that accompanied the decoration appearing in the *London Gazette* on 3 November 1944:

> Since being awarded the Distinguished Flying Cross, this officer has participated in very many sorties, during which much damage has been inflicted on the enemy. Shipping, radio stations, oil storage tanks, power plants and other installations have been amongst the targets attacked. On one occasion he led a small formation of aircraft against a much superior force of enemy fighters. In the engagement, five enemy aircraft were shot down. This officer is a brave and resourceful leader whose example has proved a rare source of inspiration. He has destroyed 16 hostile aircraft.

By the time Brothers received his DSO, he had been posted to US Command and General Staff School at Fort Leavenworth, Kansas. By war's end, Pete Brothers had flown on operations for 44 months – a record equalled by few RAF pilots in World War Two. He had accumulated 875 operational flying hours during four frontline tours and been credited with 16 victories, one probable and three damaged. Despite engaging the enemy on countless occasions, and having had to limp home in damaged aircraft, he was never forced to take to his parachute.

Not offered a permanent commission post-war, Brothers joined the Colonial Service in Kenya, before returning to the RAF in 1949. He would see further action as CO of No 57 Sqn, equipped with Lincoln four-engined bombers, during the Malayan Emergency in 1952, and subsequently flew Valiant jet bombers as Wing Commander Flying at Marham, Norfolk. By the time he retired from the RAF in 1973, Brothers had attained the rank of air commodore. Serving as Chairman of the Battle of Britain Association for a number of years, he passed away on 18 December 2008.

Spitfire VII MD188/PB of Wg Cdr Pete Brothers, Wing Leader Culmhead Wing, Culmhead, Somerset, August 1944

First flown on 21 May 1944, this aircraft was one of the last Spitfire VIIs built. It joined No 131 Sqn at Culmhead on 25 June, finished in the standard RAF high-altitude scheme of the period – PR blue upper surfaces and deep sky type S undersides – to which D-Day stripes were quickly added. The fighter (depicted here with a long-range slipper tank) was immediately seconded to the Culmhead Station Flight and assigned to veteran ace Wg Cdr Pete Brothers, who had his initials applied as per standard practice. He claimed his 16th, and last, victory in MD188 during a Rodeo over France with No 131 Sqn on 7 August 1944. The aircraft was sent to RAF Colerne, Wiltshire, in early October 1944, where it participated in high-altitude trials. The fighter was struck off charge in December 1948.

CLIVE CALDWELL

Given the nickname 'Killer' by the press due to his clinical effectiveness as a fighter pilot, Clive Caldwell was the highest-scoring Australian ace of World War Two.

Having been born in the Sydney suburb of Lewisham on 28 July 1911, Clive Robertson Caldwell was educated at Sydney Grammar School and Trinity Grammar School. Employed as a commission agent during the 1930s, he joined the Aero Club of New South Wales in 1938 and 'went solo' after just three-and-half hours of tuition. Caldwell enlisted in the RAAF in May 1940 after having persuaded a pharmacist friend of his to alter the details on his birth certificate so that he was 'young enough' to fly fighters. However, having not wanted to become an instructor after completing his flying training, he resigned his commission and became one of the first pilots to enrol in the Empire Air Training Scheme (EATS) in Australia – graduates of the scheme were usually sent to frontline units. Caldwell was commissioned upon receiving his wings in January 1941.

Initially posted to Hurricane-equipped No 73 Sqn in North Africa in May, Caldwell was transferred to recently re-formed No 250 Sqn shortly thereafter. The unit was equipped with the first Tomahawk IIBs in-theatre, and on 26 June, the Australian claimed his first success with the aircraft when he downed a Bf 109 over Libya. He would go on to destroy 30 enemy aircraft, 20.5 of them in North Africa to make him the highest-scoring Allied pilot of the Western Desert campaign.

Caldwell's prowess in aerial combat, and aggression towards the enemy, earned him the nickname 'Killer', which he personally detested, as fellow Australian ace Bobby Gibbes recalled. 'Clive was given the nickname "Killer" – which was not of his choosing, or liking – due to his habit of shooting up any enemy vehicle which he saw below him when returning from a sortie. Invariably, he landed back at his base with almost no ammunition left.'

Caldwell's most successful day in combat came on 5 December when he was credited with downing five Italian Ju 87 Stukas in a single mission while supporting the Allied Operation *Crusader* offensive. By now a flight commander, he was simultaneously awarded a DFC and Bar following this success. In January 1942, Caldwell, having been

Sqn Ldr Caldwell (closest to the camera) became CO of No 112 Sqn on 6 January 1942, shortly after the unit had re-equipped with Kittyhawk IAs at Msus, in eastern Libya. He was already a 16-victory ace by then. Among the pilots in his squadron was ace Flt Lt Neville Duke, seen here standing third from left. Both men would survive the war with more than 25 aerial victories apiece.

promoted to squadron leader, was given command of No 112 Sqn just weeks after it had received Kittyhawk Is in place of its Tomahawk IIs. The first EATS graduate to lead a British squadron, he would claim 3.5 victories with the aircraft prior to Australian authorities requesting that he be sent home to help with the nation's defence against Japan. Having flown 300 combat sorties totalling 550 hours, engaging German and Italian fighters and dive-bombers over the North African desert, Caldwell returned home via Britain, where he familiarised himself with the Spitfire V by participating in a handful of operations with the Kenley Wing.

Reaching Australia in September 1942, Caldwell was promoted to wing commander and made wing leader of newly created No 1 Fighter Wing on 20 November. Flying a Spitfire VC marked with his wing commander's pennant and the codes CR-C, he was credited with his first successes against the Japanese in the defence of Darwin on 2 March 1943. Showing remarkable coolness under fire, Caldwell set about evaluating the relative performance of his Spitfire and the A6M2 Zero-sen that he was fighting while in actual combat:

> [The Spitfire] was a superior aircraft generally, though less manoeuvrable at low speeds. In straight and level flight and in the dive, the Spitfire appears faster. Though the angle of climb of the Zeke is steeper, the actual gaining of height seems the same, the Spitfire going up at a lesser angle but at a greater forward speed – an advantage. I believe that at altitudes above 20,000ft the Spitfire, in relation to the Zeke, is an even more superior aircraft.

Nine pilots from Nos 452 and 457 Sqns pose with No 1 Fighter Wing's Wing Commander Flying, Wg Cdr Caldwell (wearing the white shirt in the back row, and with the obligatory cigarette in his right hand) at Strauss, in the Northern Territory, in April 1943. To the right of Caldwell is high-scoring Spitfire ace Flg Off Adrian 'Tim' Goldsmith, who was credited with 16 and one shared destroyed, two probables and seven damaged in the defence of Malta and northern Australia.

Caldwell also gave an account detailing how he claimed one of two victories credited to him on this date:

> I commenced firing at 400 yards and pressed the attack home until I was within 100 yards. One burst only was fired of approximately two to two-and-a-half seconds duration. Strikes were observed on the fore section of the fuselage near the wing roots. At this juncture the enemy aircraft broke formation by making a gentle turn to starboard. Being in danger of attack from escorting Zekes, I disengaged by making a steep climbing turn to port, during which time I lost sight of the enemy aircraft. Shortly afterwards I observed an aircraft strike the water below the position in which the attack had taken place.

No 54 Sqn Spitfire VC BS164 served with Wg Cdr Caldwell's No 1 Fighter Wing during the height of operations in the Northern Territory in mid-1943. Here, the fighter is being wheeled back into its camouflaged bay at RAAF Base Darwin on June 22, shortly after the IJAAF had attacked the airfield – note that the groundcrew are all still wearing steel helmets. BS164 was routinely flown by No 54 Sqn CO Sqn Ldr Eric Gibbs, who made 11 claims (including six credited as victories) in the aircraft between 2 March and 6 July 1943.

Caldwell would take a steady toll of enemy aircraft over the next five months as the Japanese continued with their bombing campaign against targets in northern Australia. He would be credited with his final aerial victory on 17 August, when he downed a Ki-46 'Dinah' reconnaissance aircraft over the Arafura Sea. Having been scrambled to intercept the intruder while in the middle of afternoon tea, Caldwell engaged the 'Dinah' at 26,000ft, 20 miles off the coast of Darwin. He hit it several times, and then called in his wingman, Flt Sgt 'Paddy' Padula, to finish off the Ki-46. Despite some 'coaching' over the radio, Padula kept missing the target, so Caldwell opened fire once again. His combat report details what happened next:

> The pilot continued to fly on his course but there were signs he was having difficulty in maintaining control. I flew behind it for several miles – it was now burning at three points and trailing white smoke. Height at this juncture was 24,000ft. Pulling behind, I opened fire again from about 200 yards in a rear quarter attack. This attack was made for practice purposes, and I was certain that it was only a matter of time before it would be completely burnt. From the attack I observed strikes on the starboard wing and fuselage and on the wing root back.
>
> A fourth attack was made with machine guns only, and I observed tracer entering the port side of the fuselage, following which the enemy aircraft staggered badly, lost 3,000ft and recovered. I pulled out and flew in a position 400 yards to starboard to

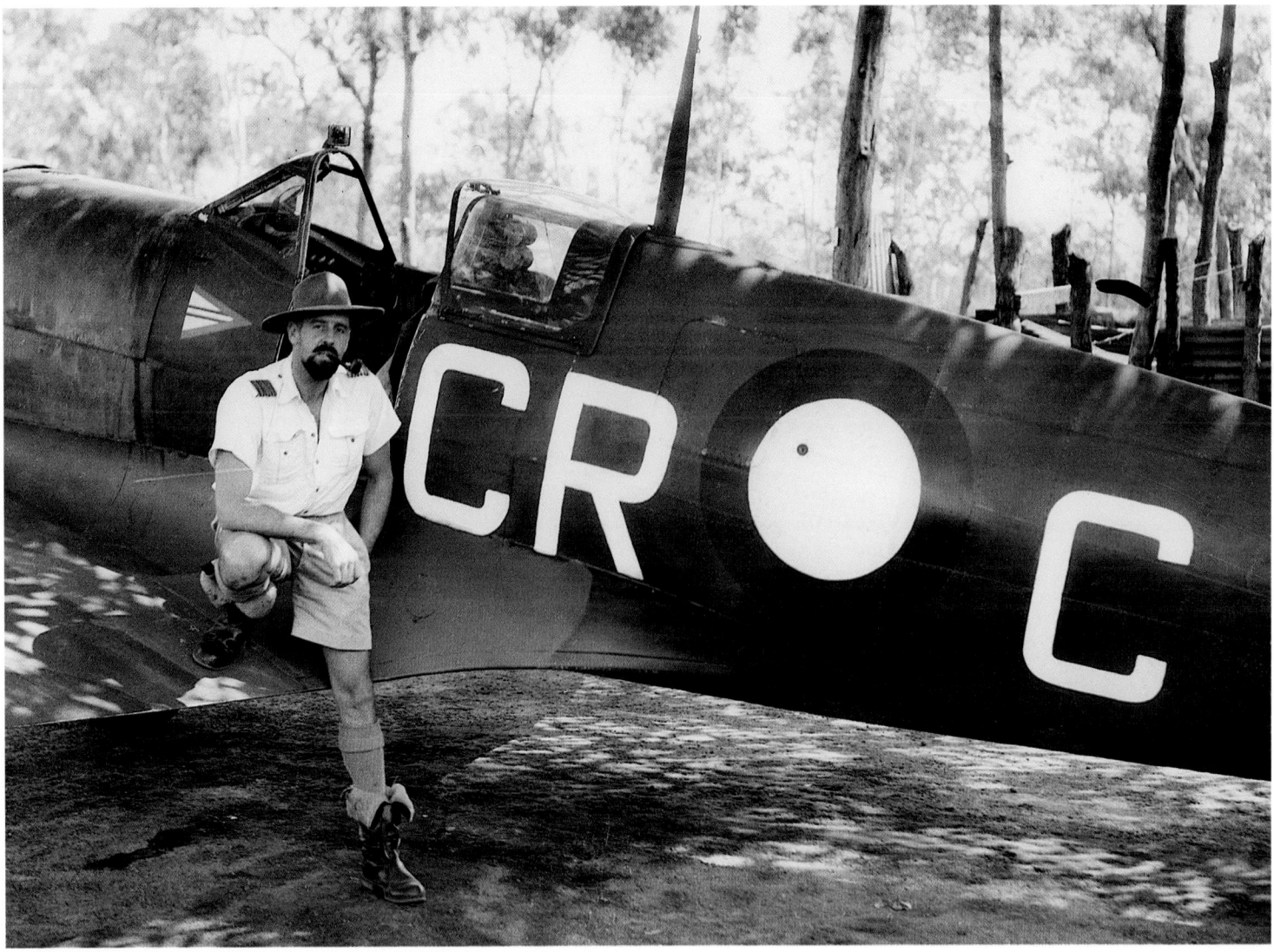

Wg Cdr Clive Caldwell, complete with pipe, unzipped flying boots and piratical beard, which he grew because the tropical heat caused a skin irritation, poses with his Spitfire VC, BS295. Photographed in June 1943, this aircraft is marked with the codes CR-C, for Clive Robertson Caldwell. Caldwell had claimed his first success over a Japanese aircraft in this Spitfire on 2 March 1943, and he also flew it during two raids in late June when he was credited with shooting down a pair of Zero-sens and probably destroying two 'Betty' bombers. Note the wing commander's pennant to the left of Caldwell's head.

By now CO of the RAAF's No 80 Fighter Wing on Morotai, Gp Capt Caldwell stands next to one of several Spitfire VIIIs that he was allocated while flying from the Netherlands East Indies in the final months of the Pacific War. This aircraft was marked up with his final victory tally.

watch the final results. Shortly afterwards it again began losing height, first gradually and then steeply, until I was obliged to dive at 360mph in order to retain my position abreast. The enemy aircraft appeared to make an attempt to level out momentarily and hit the water at a point 20 miles due west of Cape Fourcroy. I photographed the splash with my camera gun.

The 'Dinah' proved to be the last victory claim credited to the leading Australian ace of World War Two, and it also made him the most successful Spitfire pilot against the Japanese. The following month Caldwell was posted to No 2 OTU in Mildura, Victoria, as chief flying instructor. Awarded a DSO in November 1943 for his service during the defence of Darwin, he returned north to command Spitfire VIII-equipped No 80 (Fighter) Wing in the spring of 1944. Promoted to group captain in August, Caldwell led the unit to Morotai, in the Dutch East Indies, at year-end. Four months later, he became one of the ringleaders of the 'Morotai Mutiny' that saw eight senior officers seek to hand in their resignations as a protest against No 80 Wing's lack of meaningful participation in operations in the Southwest Pacific Theatre.

A subsequent investigation into the mutiny resulted in three officers being relieved of their commands, although Caldwell was cleared of any wrongdoing. However, prior to

The beard had gone by the time Wg Cdr Caldwell was photographed in his flying gear with his Spitfire VC at Strauss in late July 1943.

this incident, he and his Wing Leader, Wg Cdr Bobby Gibbes, had been charged after it was found that they had traded alcohol with US engineers in exchange for equipment that was urgently need to improve No 80 Wing's basic living facilities on Morotai. Liquor was being flown in by RAAF transport aircraft and then sold in sizeable quantities to American servicemen on the island. Caldwell was found guilty, in January 1946, and court martialled, resulting in him being reduced in rank to flight lieutenant. His service with the RAAF was terminated the following month.

Post-war, Caldwell found employment importing surplus military aircraft (primarily transport types) acquired from the US Foreign Liquidation Commission in the Philippines into Australia. He later became managing director of a Sydney-based cloth import/export company, becoming a partner in the firm in 1953. Four years later he went into business for himself when he established Clive Caldwell (Sales) Pty Ltd, which again specialised in the sale of fabrics. Following a successful career in business, Caldwell retired and eventually passed away in Sydney on 5 August 1994.

Spitfire VC BS234/CR-C of Wg Cdr Clive Caldwell, OC of No 1 Fighter Wing, Strauss, Northern Territory, March 1943

Wg Cdr Caldwell was assigned several Spitfire VCs marked with his personal CR-C code letters and rank pennant while leading No 1 Fighter Wing. It is believed that he was flying this particular aircraft when he claimed two victories on 2 March 1943, having engaged A6M2s in a series of dogfights off the coast of the Northern Territory. BS234 had arrived in Australia (where it was given the RAAF serial A58-95) from Britain in November 1942 and was allocated to No 457 Sqn upon reassembly. Seeing aerial combat with Japanese aircraft on several occasions between March and July 1943, the fighter remained with No 457 Sqn until May 1944. Subsequently serving as a training aircraft with Nos 2 and 8 OTUs, BS234 was sold for scrapping in November 1945.

BRIAN CARBURY

Little known New Zealander Brian Carbury was one of the RAF's leading Spitfire aces during the Battle of Britain.

The son of a veterinary surgeon, Brian John George Carbury was born in Wellington, New Zealand, on 27 February 1918. His family later moved to Auckland, where Carbury was schooled at New Lynn and King's College. While at the latter establishment, he excelled at rugby, cricket and tennis. Carbury was also a strong swimmer and having grown to a height of 6ft 4in, he was a formidable water polo player. Finally, and most importantly in light of his future career as a fighter pilot, he was an excellent marksman with a rifle.

Following brief employment as a shoe salesman for the Farmers Trading Company in Auckland, he travelled to England in June 1937 and secured a short-service commission in the RAF after having been denied entry into the Royal Navy for being too old. Undertaking his flying training at No 10 E&RFTS, Carbury was subsequently posted to No 41 Sqn at Catterick, North Yorkshire, in June 1938, where he flew Fury II biplanes.

The unit converted to Spitfire Is in January 1939, and in October of that same year, he was temporarily reassigned to No 603 'City of Edinburgh' Sqn at Turnhouse, Scotland, to help with the unit's transition from Gladiators to Spitfires. Carbury was permanently assigned to the Auxiliary squadron shortly thereafter, and he first saw action on 7 December 1939 when he damaged an He 111 near Arbroath. No 603 Sqn had engaged a formation of seven Heinkels heading for the airfield at Montrose, Scotland, and the unit's Operational Record Book (ORB) noted, 'P/O B J G Carbury carried out a frontal attack on the port aircraft of the first enemy formation, and on completing this, white smoke was observed issuing from both engines.' He followed this up with shares in the destruction of a second Heinkel bomber off Aberdeen on 7 March 1940 and a Ju 88 near Montrose on 3 July.

On 28 August, No 603 Sqn was sent south from Scotland to Hornchurch to relieve battle-weary No 65 Sqn. From then through to year-end, the unit would claim 67 enemy

After Plt Off Carbury completed flying training with No 10 E&RFTS, he was posted to Fury II-equipped No 41 Sqn at Catterick in June 1938. K7265 was one of the aircraft that he routinely flew as he learned his craft as a fighter pilot in the RAF.

Spitfire I XT-H (serial unknown), nicknamed 'Hell', was among the early Supermarine fighters delivered to No 603 Sqn from September 1939. The following month, Plt Off Carbury, who had been flying Spitfires with No 41 Sqn since January, was temporarily reassigned to No 603 Sqn at Turnhouse, where this photograph was taken, to assist pilots with their transition from the Gladiator to the new monoplane fighter.

aircraft destroyed for the loss of 30 Spitfires. Four of its pilots were credited with five or more Bf 109Es destroyed, with Carbury emerging as No 603 Sqn's 'ace of aces' by downing eight of the fighters in the first week of the unit's operations with No 11 Group. His opening encounter with Bf 109s came just hours after No 603 Sqn had arrived at Hornchurch on the 28th when the unit was bounced during a high-altitude interception at 30,000ft over Hawkinge, on the Kent coast. His combat report for this action read as follows:

Approximately over Dover I sighted the enemy aircraft (six Me 109s). As they attacked leading sections [of B Flight], we kept in a vic, but broke as Me 109s came down. I followed two through the clouds, with three following. I fired a short two-second burst at one Me 109 from 300 yards closing to 200 yards. Smoke emitted from in front of the cockpit and the fighter carried on in a 45-degree dive for France, so I left him. I sighted another Me 109, gave a full deflection burst but lost him in the cloud. I lost the rest of the Squadron so returned to base.

The following day, Carbury claimed his first Bf 109 destroyed while in search of a bombing raid approaching Manston, Kent. The ORB noted, 'Ten aircraft of 603 Squadron left Rochford [Essex] at 1810 hrs. When at 27,000ft over Manston they saw about 24 Me 109s in line astern, weaving over their heads. The 109s made no attempt to attack, so 603 climbed and attacked. A dogfight ensued.'

Carbury's combat report stated, 'I was leading Green Section when enemy aircraft were sighted. We went into line astern. Green 2 and 3 attacked individual enemy aircraft. I climbed and saw two Me 109s climbing below, so I carried out a frontal attack with slight deflection. A long burst and the enemy aircraft smoked and then blew up. I returned to base, having lost the rest of the formation.'

Having destroyed another Bf 109E on 30 August, he became one of only two Spitfire pilots to claim five victories in one day during the Battle of Britain on 31 August (the other was No 610 Sqn's Sgt Ronnie Hamlyn, who claimed four Bf 109Es and a Ju 88 destroyed on 24 August). Carbury's squadronmate Flg Off Richard Hillary also downed a Bf 109 that same day on his way to becoming an ace. He described the New Zealander in the following passage from his famous wartime autobiography *The Last Enemy*:

Then there was Brian Carbury, a New Zealander who was 6ft 4in with crinkly hair and a roving eye. There was little distinctive about him on the ground, but he was to prove to be the Squadron's greatest asset in the air.

I thought of the men I had known, of the men who were living and the men who were dead, and I came to this conclusion. It was to the Carburys and the Berrys [Alan Berry, also a Spitfire ace with No 603 Sqn] of this war that Britain must look, to the tough practical men who had come up the hard way, who were not fighting this war for any philosophical principles or economic ideals; who, unlike the average Oxford undergraduate [including Hillary], were not flying for aesthetic reasons, but because of an instinctive knowledge that this was the job for which they were most suited. These were the men who had blasted and would continue to

Very few photographs exist of Brian Carbury, despite his outstanding scoring record during 1940. At 6ft 4in, he was tall for a Spitfire pilot. Although cramped for room in the cockpit of his fighter, Carbury was one of the most effective pilots in No 11 Group from late August 1940 through to year-end.

Spitfire I X4277 of No 603 Sqn is surrounded by aircraft from No 222 Sqn at Hornchurch on 1 September 1940. Just 24 hours before this photograph was taken, Flg Off Carbury had been credited with the destruction of five Bf 109s (two of which he erroneously identified as 'He 113s') and Plt Off Richard Hillary had also downed a Messerschmitt fighter in X4277. Both pilots would enjoy more success against Bf 109s on 2 September, and Hillary would claim his fifth victory in X4277 just minutes before he was shot down in flames.

blast the Luftwaffe out of the sky while their more intellectual comrades would, alas, in the main be killed.

Carbury wrote post-war that he had not expected to live through the Battle of Britain, as he viewed every operation that he flew during the campaign as:

> ... tantamount to a suicide mission. Once in contact with the enemy there were frequently so many of them it was a matter of fighting your way out and knowing when to break off – 'He who turns and flies away lives to fight another day'. It was often a case of flying full tilt through the formation and shooting at anything in range, before pulling away from the initial attack and not being tempted to stay and 'mix it' from a vulnerable position.

AC1 J B S MacKenzie, who served as groundcrew with No 603 Sqn throughout the Battle of Britain, revered Carbury's abilities as a fighter pilot and the tactics he employed in combat. 'The "Carbury Trick" was the expression we gave to his tactic of getting in very close to the enemy before firing. He didn't mess around firing from distance. He could also push the Spitfire to its limits if the enemy fighters got on his own tail, thus shaking off all but the most experienced German pilots.'

When Carbury received a DFC and Bar in September and October 1940, he became one of only a handful of pilots to be awarded both decorations during the Battle of Britain period.

Like Carbury, No 603 Sqn's Spitfires were also camera-shy during the Battle of Britain. Indeed, the best photographed aircraft from the unit was X4260, which was the subject of numerous shots after the fighter fell into German hands on 6 September 1940. Its pilot, Plt Off Jim Caister, was forced down near Guînes, northern France, after being attacked by veteran ace Hauptmann Hubertus von Bonin, *Gruppenkommandeur* of I./JG 54. X4260 was soon on its undercarriage, fitted with a replacement propeller and repainted light blue overall, after which it was transported back to Germany for flight testing at Rechlin. The Spitfire had been with No 603 Sqn for just 15 days prior to its loss, having flown 9.55 hours in that time.

X4260 proved to be a source of great fascination for the personnel of I./JG 54, the fighter being towed into the unit's wooded dispersal area at Guînes so that it could be kept out of view of RAF reconnaissance aircraft.

His citation for the Bar read, in part, 'Flying Officer Carbury has displayed outstanding gallantry and skill in engagements against the enemy. His cool courage in the face of the enemy has been a splendid example to other pilots of his Squadron.' By the end of 1940, Carbury's victory tally stood at 15 and two shared destroyed, two probables and five damaged.

As with many pre-war fighter pilots who survived the Battle of Britain, he was posted to RAF Flying Training Command as an instructor in December 1940, initially being sent to the CFS and then on to No 58 OTU. Carbury's time as an instructor ended abruptly in October 1941 when he was found guilty of fraud after being accused of passing 17 false cheques. These had been written in an attempt to cover his wife's 'opulent' lifestyle, which Carbury could not sustain on a flight lieutenant's pay. Dismissed from the RAF, he remained in Britain, and in 1949 he had his pilot's licence suspended and was fined £100 for ferrying a surplus Beaufighter to Palestine (which was not allowed at the time). Eventually finding work as a salesman for a heating and ventilation company in London, Brian Carbury was diagnosed with leukemia and died on 31 July 1961 in High Wycombe.

Spitfire IA R6835/XT-W of Flg Off Brian Carbury, No 603 Sqn, Hornchurch, Essex, August 1940

Possibly the most successful pilot/aircraft combination in RAF Fighter Command in the summer of 1940, Carbury used R6835 to down eight Bf 109s between 29 August and 2 September, with five of these victories being scored during the course of three flights on 31 August. In his final combat on this date, which saw No 603 Sqn engage Bf 109Es from I./JG 3 over the Thames Estuary, R6835 was hit by a 20mm shell after Carbury had despatched two fighters earlier in the action. Badly damaged by an exploding oxygen bottle, the Spitfire took ten months to repair. Eventually reissued to No 457 Sqn in June 1941, the fighter had been relegated to No 53 OTU by October of that year. After spending 19 months training would-be Spitfire pilots, the aircraft was passed on to the Fleet Air Arm in May 1943.

JACK CHARLES

One of the pilots credited with claiming Biggin Hill's 1,000th victory in World War Two, Canadian ace Jack Charles downed 16 German fighters in 1941–43.

Edward Francis John 'Jack' Charles was born to English parents (his father had been a pilot in the Royal Flying Corps) in Coventry on 6 February 1919, although his family moved to Saskatchewan, south-central Canada, two years later. Charles enlisted as a trooper in the Saskatchewan Horse Militia in June 1937 and joined the RAF four months later. He completed his provisional pilot officer training with the RCAF, having learned to fly in Fleet Finch biplanes at Trenton, Ontario. Charles' graduation was, however, delayed by five months when he suffered injuries in a Tiger Moth crash while attempting a forced landing approach at an unfamiliar airfield.

He departed Canada for Britain in May 1939 and subsequently undertook courses with Nos 5 and 3 FTSs prior to being posted to the School of Army Cooperation in September. Charles' first operational posting came at year-end when he joined Tiger Moth-equipped No 81 Sqn. He was posted to No 2 Sqn upon its return from France in June 1940, where he flew Lysanders. Responding to the urgent call for pilots issued by RAF Fighter Command during the early weeks of the Battle of Britain, Charles was posted to No 7 OTU on 21 August to convert to the Spitfire.

Joining No 54 Sqn at Hornchurch on 3 September, he would remain with the unit for more than a year. His flight commander, seasoned Battle of Britain ace Flt Lt Al Deere, said of him,

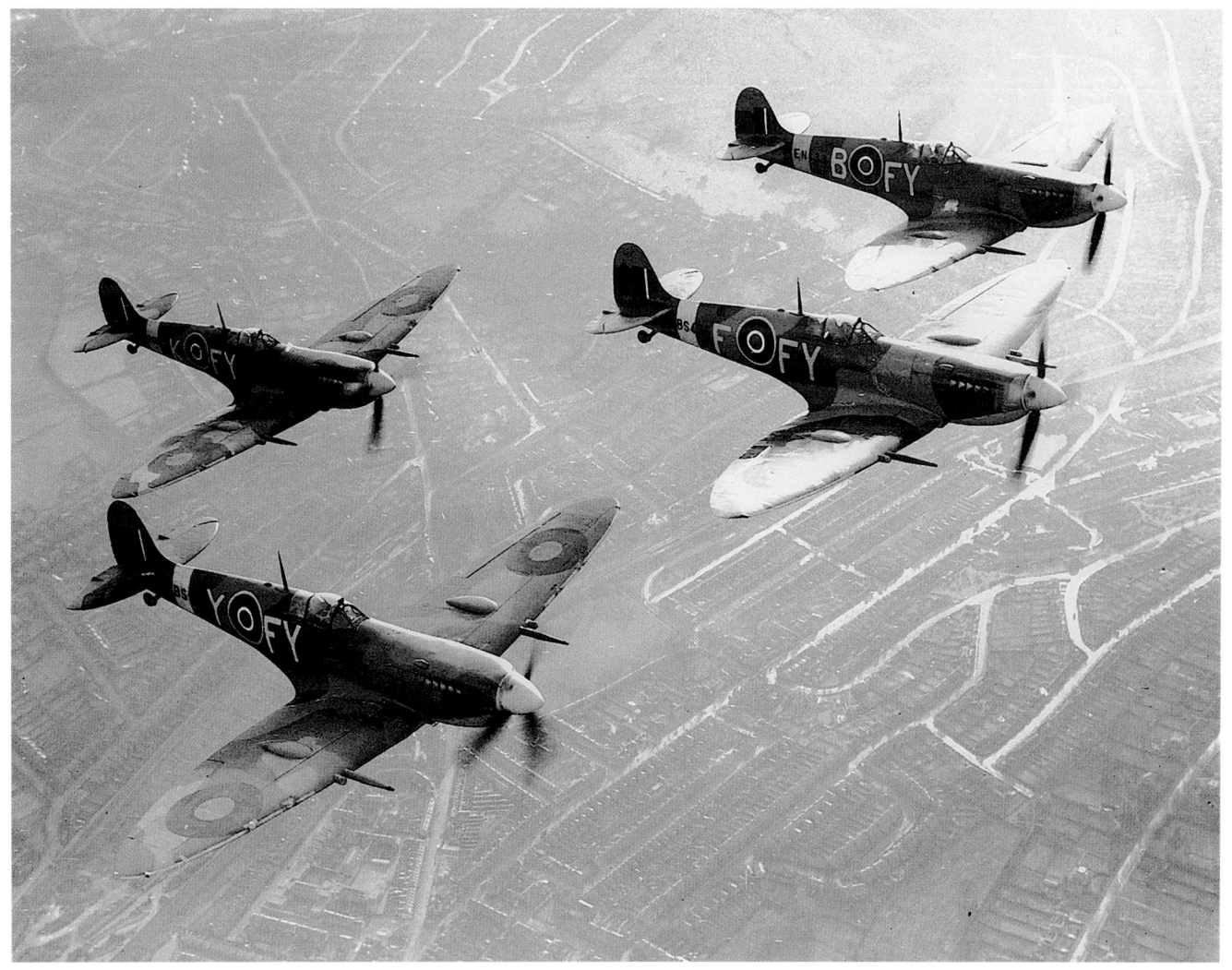

Four Spitfire IXs from No 611 Sqn fly in close formation over Kent on 8 December 1942. The following month Flt Lt Jack Charles joined the unit at Biggin Hill as a flight commander, and he routinely flew BS547 FY-Y. The formation is being led by the then CO of No 611 Sqn, Australian Sqn Ldr Hugo 'Sinker' Armstrong, in BS435 FY-F. He claimed 11 victories in Spitfires, three of them in this aircraft, prior to being shot down into the Channel in BS435 on 5 February 1943. Armstrong's body was never found.

'He was a likeable chap, but did keep pretty much to himself. He was a bit of a loner – his only interest, outside of flying, was for the fairer sex.' Charles had to wait until 17 April 1941 to make the first of his 14 claims with No 54 Sqn. While flying a Spitfire II on a convoy escort east of Manston, he was vectored towards an intruder, as he subsequently reported:

> I followed Red Leader, being vectored on to bandits being reported at Angels Ten [10,000ft]. I sighted and reported one aircraft at 1200 hrs and subsequently saw three more. I took my section to the south, Red Leader approaching on the left. As I saw I had speed on them, I decided to approach from below, from which position I ascertained them to be [Bf] 110s. I fired my first burst of 50 rounds at the leading aircraft and then broke off to attack the rear one, and he did not see me until I fired at him in a quarter-cum-astern attack.
>
> I opened fire at 300 yards, closing to 50 yards, and silenced the rear gunner before the Messerschmitt pulled vertically into the thin cloud. I throttled back, and following, had a line astern burst of two seconds above cloud at a range of 50 yards. Bits were coming off; black smoke was coming from the port engine and white smoke from the other. I followed it through cloud and watched it smash into the Channel.

Charles' first victory was also No 54 Sqn's 100th. Having failed to make a single claim during his first seven months with the unit, he made up for lost time by attaining ace status on 4 July – he received a DFC 11 days later.

Sgt George Mason flew Spitfires with No 611 'West Lancashire' Sqn from Hornchurch during this period, and the unit regularly undertook sweeps with No 54 Sqn. On the ground, he routinely encountered Flg Off Charles:

> He made a name for himself that year [1941]. I got to know Jack and respected him as a fighter pilot: good eyesight, a clear R/T [radio transmission] voice, plenty of courage. He was also an open-hearted fellow. Got along with everyone, a great one for the girls and apparently irresistible! Not much respect for authority as such, but loyal to those he respected as men. Capable of cold and ruthless behaviour in the face of the enemy – his record proves that!

In October, Charles was posted to the CFS to learn to become an instructor, subsequently serving in this capacity with No 9 Service Flying Training School (SFTS) and Nos 9 and 5 (Pilot) Advanced Flying Units. After more than a year off operations, he was sent on a refresher course to No 52 OTU in December 1942 and then joined Spitfire IX-equipped No 64 Sqn the following month. Charles damaged an Fw 190 in March 1943, shortly after which he was transferred to No 611 Sqn at Biggin Hill as a flight commander. On 22 April, he was made CO of the unit, his appointment having been personally requested by his old flight commander from No 54 Sqn, now Wg Cdr Al Deere, Wing Leader at Biggin Hill, who said, 'Operationally, as a squadron leader on Spitfires, he was second to none. He had very pale blue eyes, which served him well because he had the ability to spot enemy aircraft at great distances; a tremendous asset in sweeps over occupied Europe.'

May 1943 would prove to be a memorable month both for Sqn Ldr Charles and Biggin Hill airfield, for one of the quartet of Fw 190s he claimed shot down over France

Spitfire IXs are seen here between operations in the No 611 Sqn dispersal area at Biggin Hill in the early spring of 1943. On 22 April that year, newly promoted Sqn Ldr Charles became CO of this unit.

in the space of just four days proved to be the fighter station's 1,000th aerial victory. This success came on 15 May in a location southeast of Caen, when Charles was credited with a brace of Fw 190s. A 'colourful' news report by Canadian Press staff reporter Alan Randal, titled 'Charles Gets Four Nazis in Four Days', detailed the event:

> Young Johnny Charles did a wing-over-wing roll over his airfield in southern England again Tuesday. He did it with an easy grace. It's getting to be old stuff for him. The groundcrew, waiting in the noon sunshine for his return, were pop-eyed when they saw the aerobatics. They had been about ready to see the RAF squadron leader from Lashburn, Saskatchewan, make a normal landing instead of coming in signalling his fourth kill in as many days.
>
> Today's kill brought Charles' score to 11½ destroyed and 6½ probables, and followed a busy weekend in which Charles shared with a fighting French squadron commander a sweepstakes purse of approximately $1,500 for shooting down the 1,000th enemy plane in his sector. Each destroyed a Nazi aircraft so close together it was impossible to tell which was the 1,000th and which was number 999, so the pilots split the prize money.
>
> Operations in the last four days boosted the sector's total to 1,012 aircraft destroyed. Friday morning, Charles scored the first of his run of four kills, bringing the sector's total to 966. 'I was leading the squadron and saw this Jerry below me,' said the 24-year-old pilot. 'I dived under him and then came up and opened fire at about 220 yards, closing to almost 50. The enemy aircraft turned on its back and I last saw him going straight down.'

Charles' wingman on that mission was future Spitfire ace Flg Off Johnny Checketts, who had great respect for his CO:

> Jack was not one to suffer fools, and he could be outspoken to a degree. He was, however, easy to get along with, had a good sense of humour and liked company. He could be very difficult after imbibing, and in those few instances I saw him like this he was aggressive and pugilistic to a degree. Even so, Jack really had a happy nature, and was liked by those who served with him.
>
> Jack had great eyesight and could shoot, too. His aerial discipline was very strict, and woe betide anyone who transgressed. I became one of his flight commanders, and I felt safe in his company when in combat. This feeling is hard to explain, and there is only

Sqn Ldr Jack Charles sits strapped into his Spitfire IX prior to departing on a mission with the Biggin Hill Wing in April 1943. Having made 14 claims (seven of which were victories) with No 54 Sqn in 1941, he achieved his first kill with No 611 Sqn on 18 April 1943 when he downed an Fw 190 in a head-on pass. Charles fired just 24 cannon shells and 160 0.303in rounds during this fleeting engagement, the German fighter crashing into the mouth of the Baie d'Authie, on the French Channel coast.

Above: Having claimed two Fw 190s from 2./JG 2 destroyed (one of which was flown by 98-victory ace Oberleutnant Horst Hannig, who was killed) on 15 May 1943 during Circus 297, Sqn Ldr Charles was credited with almost certainly scoring Biggin Hill's 1,000th aerial victory of the war. He marked this achievement up in chalk on the propeller blade of his Spitfire IX, EN554 FY-F, for the benefit of the attendant press photographers.

Right: Commandant René Mouchotte and Sqn Ldr Jack Charles shake hands on 15 May 1943, both men having claimed victories at virtually the same time that day. Charles shared the sweepstakes purse of £300 (raised by raffles over the previous few months) awarded to the claimant of the 1,000th victory with Mouchotte, CO of Biggin Hill-based No 341 Sqn. The Frenchman was subsequently killed in action on 27 August 1943 during Ramrod S8 while escorting USAAF B-17s.

one other man to whom it applies, and that is Al Deere. The confidence he inspired in us made No 611 Sqn a top-scoring one and a superbly happy one.

Promoted to wing commander, Charles was sent to Middle Wallop, Hampshire, as wing leader in August 1943, before transferring to Portreath, Cornwall, to lead the wing there the following month. He remained in this position for just ten days, as he was sent to No 10 Group HQ to undertake staff duties on 26 September – 48 hours after he had claimed his final victory. By then his tally stood at 15 and one shared destroyed, six and one shared probably destroyed and five damaged.

Sqn Ldr Charles is seen here with his Biggin Hill Wing Leader, Wg Cdr Al Deere, in June 1943. Both men were great friends, with Deere later being the godfather of Charles' first-born child.

Having received a Bar to his DFC in July 1943, Charles was awarded a US Silver Star the following month and a DSO in October. The citation to the latter decoration read:

Wing Commander Charles is an inspiring leader whose great skill and tenacity have contributed materially to the successes obtained by the formations with which he has flown. In September 1943, he led a formation of fighters that acted as escort to a bomber force detailed to attack an airfield in northern France. During the operation 12 enemy fighters were engaged and in the ensuing combat four of the hostile aircraft were shot down, one of them by Wing Commander Charles. This officer, who has destroyed at least 15 enemy aircraft, has displayed great courage and unflagging devotion to duty.

Transferring to the RCAF in May 1944 and given command of the Tangmere Wing the following month, Charles subsequently filled various staff postings from August 1944 through to VE Day. Remaining in the service post-war, he was diagnosed with acute schizophrenia in 1949 and spent the rest of his life in the Shaughnessy Veterans' Hospital in Vancouver. Jack Charles died on 5 November 1986.

Spitfire IX PT396/EJC of Wg Cdr Jack Charles, Wing Leader Tangmere Wing, Tangmere, West Sussex, August 1944

Wg Cdr Charles was assigned this brand new Spitfire IX upon its arrival at Tangmere in late July 1944, the aircraft having originally been allocated to No 602 Sqn, which had recently been transferred to Normandy from Ford, West Sussex. Marked with Charles' rank pennant, initials and the RAF Tangmere station crest, the aircraft was subsequently issued to the Mediterranean Air Force in April 1945 and eventually acquired by the Italian Air Force in June 1947.

JOHNNY CHECKETTS

Although Kiwi ace Johnny Checketts took some time to make his mark in combat on the Channel Front, he eventually enjoyed great success at the controls of a Spitfire in 1943–44.

John Milne Checketts was born in Invercargill on New Zealand's South Island on 20 February 1912. Educated at Invercargill South School, he subsequently studied engineering at Southland Technical College in the late 1920s. Checketts completed an apprenticeship as a motor mechanic in 1934 and also worked on the family farm. Having joined the Civil Reserve for the Royal New Zealand Air Force (RNZAF) in August 1939, he was eventually called up in October of the following year. Checketts completed his flying training locally and was commissioned as a pilot officer in the RNZAF upon receiving his wings in June 1941. He sailed for Britain the following month.

Although Checketts was taught to fly the Hurricane with No 56 OTU at Sutton Bridge, Lincolnshire, he was posted to Spitfire VB-equipped and New Zealand-manned No 485 Sqn at Kenley. Undertaking his first mission on 7 January 1942, he managed to register a few hits on three Fw 190s over the next six months but submitted no claims. Checketts helped to sink an E-boat on 12 February when the battleships *Scharnhorst* and *Gneisenau* steamed from France to Germany during the Channel Dash. On 4 May, he was attacked by six Bf 109s and shot down for the first time, baling out over the Channel. He was picked up by a rescue launch less than an hour after taking to his parachute.

Promoted to flying officer in June 1942, Checketts undertook a course at the Central Gunnery School (CGS) at Sutton Bridge and then returned to No 485 Sqn the following month. In mid-August, after accumulating 220 operational flying hours in nine months, he was posted to No 1488 Fighter Gunnery Flight at Martlesham Heath, Suffolk, as an instructor, specialising in deflection shooting. Checketts returned to operational flying in January 1943 with a posting to Spitfire IX-equipped No 611 Sqn at Biggin Hill. Made a flight commander in the spring,

Plt Off Johnny Checketts (squatting, second from left) and other pilots from No 485 Sqn at Kenley in the spring of 1942. He had joined the unit in January of that year, serving alongside several high-scoring Kiwi Spitfire aces including Plt Off Evan Mackie (standing, second from left), Flt Lt Bill Crawford-Compton (standing, fourth from left) and Sqn Ldr E P 'Hawkeye' Wells (standing, fourth from right).

Spitfire VB W3528, in the foreground, was serving with No 485 Sqn when Plt Off Checketts joined the unit at Kenley, and it is seen here at the unit dispersal in February 1942. The fighter parked immediately behind it is marked with the squadron commander's pennant, No 485 Sqn then being led by Sqn Ldr Marcus Knight. He was replaced by 'Hawkeye' Wells shortly after this photograph was taken, while W3528 was passed on to No 118 Sqn in early April.

he finally claimed his first victory during a bomber escort Ramrod (short-range bomber attacks to destroy ground targets, similar to Circus attacks that saw bombers attacking with a heavy fighter escort) mission to Caen on 30 May. The first of his 14 victories was also No 611 Sqn's 100th success. Checketts' combat report read:

While flying as Blue 3 to Sqn Ldr [Jack] Charles, we saw numerous enemy aircraft, including FW 190s and ME 109s. When Sqn Ldr Charles warned me, we broke into two sections as the top squadron was attacked, and flew inland and up sun. Two FW 190s attacked Blue 4 and myself, but we outclimbed them and they lost sight of

Above: In this unusual shot, Plt Off Checketts peers through the armoured windscreen of a Spitfire Mk VB. The fighter's Mk II reflector gunsight can be clearly seen, as can the bulging sides of the Spitfire's 'blown' canopy and the round external rear-view mirror.

Right: Plt Off Checketts looked after Flt Lt Al Deere's Scottish Terrier 'Stevie' (named for a friend killed in the Battle of Britain) at Kenley after its owner was sent to the US in late January 1942 on a fighter tactics lecture tour. When Deere returned in May and took charge of No 403 Sqn at Southend, Checketts sat 'Stevie' on his knee in a Spitfire and flew him over to the Essex airfield from Kenley.

us, evidently mistaking Blue 1 and 2 for us because they manoeuvred to attack them. I warned Blue 1 and he flew in front of me, and I attacked the FW 190 from behind and below with a great overtaking speed. I opened fire from 200 yards with an angle off of from ten degrees to nil and saw heavy strikes on the fuselage and wings. The enemy aircraft appeared to stop and shed cowlings and pieces and smoke rose in dense clouds. I broke upwards and saw him spin down, smoking. Blue 4 saw the combat and Sqn Ldr Charles also, and both saw the enemy aircraft burst into flames. Blue 4 warned me that the second FW 190 was firing at me, and I steep-turned to port and Blue 4 flew up behind the Hun and shot him down.

Although Checketts had damaged a number of German fighters prior to this engagement, the modest Kiwi had been reluctant to make more than three claims. Another victory followed on 11 June, with a probable 12 days later.

In July, Checketts was made CO of No 485 Sqn, which had replaced No 611 Sqn at Biggin Hill. The unit had also inherited its Spitfire IXs. It was while leading No 485 Sqn during the summer of 1943 that he really made his mark, with 16 claims (ten of which were victories), between 14 July and 6 September. He scored multiple victories on two occasions during this period, including a pair of Fw 190s on 27 July while his unit was providing high cover to USAAF B-26s. No 485 Sqn became embroiled in a running battle over Rouen at 20,000ft that lasted eight minutes and resulted in the unit being credited with four Fw 190s destroyed without loss. Checketts, having quickly shot a fighter down in flames, then became separated from his section in the subsequent melee. As he flew over the French coast he sighted three more Focke-Wulfs

A quartet of Spitfire IXs from No 611 Sqn, each fitted with a 30-gallon underbelly slipper tank, perform a flypast at Biggin Hill airfield in January 1943. That same month Flg Off Checketts joined the unit fresh from a spell instructing at No 1488 Fighter Gunnery Flight at Martlesham Heath. He would make his first six claims (all Fw 190s, two of which were confirmed as destroyed) with the squadron between 13 January and 23 June, after which he moved to No 485 Sqn as its new CO.

below him, so he dived on them. 'They were at about 25,000ft. I attacked the rear one from about 300 yards astern and saw strikes on the port wing. I then hit him just as he rolled over, and he went down steeply with flames streaming from the fuselage and cockpit.'

These two victories gave the 31-year-old New Zealander ace status and started a successful run for him, as by the end of August he had more than doubled his total – including three Bf 109s destroyed, and a fourth as a probable, over Lille on 9 August. His combat report for this mission stated:

While leading Green Section 485 (NZ) Squadron, I sighted four enemy aircraft 5,000ft below approximately, in the Lille–Merville area, and I led my section down to attack. When I got there, there were eight ME 109s, and I attacked the port one of the line abreast formation. This enemy aircraft was fired at from 200/250 yards at 10,000ft and blew up. I shifted over to the starboard one, because the Hun formation turned 45 degrees to port without seeing us. I opened fire at 200 yards and he blew to pieces, and I had trouble avoiding the debris. I then closed on the next enemy aircraft, and I fired from about 250/300 yards and observed only machine gun strikes, so I gave him another burst and he also shed pieces and burst into flames. I called frantically to my Nos. 2, 3 and 4 to help me and I closed on the extreme starboard one, the others selecting their targets.

Just then, one Hun saw us and dived away; I closed on my target and was almost line abreast of Flg Off Rae's target when I fired. I observed heavy strikes and pieces flew off, and just then, Flg Off Rae's Hun blew up beside me. Flg Off Gibb's one, which was about 20 yards from the port side of Flg Off Rae's, shed cowlings and turned over on his back with his flaps down and started to burn. I looked round for Flg Off Tucker, and saw a Hun going down in flames. I presume he shot it down. I called my section together and we returned to base. Green Section reported fires on the ground.

Eight days later, Checketts received a DFC for his early exploits, the citation for the award stating, 'This officer has led the squadron and, on occasions, the wing with great skill. He has invariably displayed great keenness to engage the enemy and has destroyed two enemy aircraft and damaged several more. In addition, he has destroyed two E-boats and successfully attacked military installations.'

With his battledress tunic boasting ribbons including a DFC and DSO, Sqn Ldr Checketts, pipe in hand, poses with a well weathered Spitfire VA at the CGS at Sutton Bridge in early 1944 while serving as CO of the Air-to-Air Combat Squadron. Checketts would send autograph hunters this photograph on request, usually with the comment, 'Poor old girl, she looks more battered than me.'

Checketts' run of success came to an abrupt end on 6 September during a high-cover escort mission for USAAF B-26 Marauders bombing railway marshalling yards in France. Bounced by Fw 190s from above, he managed to down one, probably destroy a second and damage a third prior to being shot down himself. Landing near the enemy airfield at Abbeville, he was rescued by the Resistance and, seven weeks later, smuggled out to a Royal Navy launch off the Brittany coast along with four other RAF pilots.

In November, Checketts was sent to the CGS at Sutton Bridge as CO of the Air-to-Air Combat Squadron, and the following month he received a DSO. After six months as an instructor, he was given command of Typhoon-equipped No 1 Sqn, although his tenure lasted just six weeks. Promoted to wing commander and put in charge of the Air Defence of Great Britain's No 142 Wing, equipped with Spitfire VBs, at Horne, Surrey, Checketts completed four sorties during Operation *Overlord* on 6 June 1944.

The German V1 offensive commenced shortly thereafter, and he was credited with two 'flying bombs' destroyed over Caterham, Surrey, on 16 and 18 June. The day after downing his second V1, Checketts led his wing firstly to Westhampnett and then to nearby Merston. No 142 Wing's squadrons were issued with Spitfire IXs in July, and Checketts claimed his final two victories (both Bf 109s) with the aircraft on 1 August and 25 September. Taken off operations a short while later, he spent six months at the newly formed Central Fighter Establishment before being posted to the Empire CFS.

Returning to New Zealand in September 1945 and transferring to the RNZAF, Checketts served in various positions until he resigned his commission in 1954. Taking full retirement in 1982, he helped with the development of the RNZAF Museum at Wigram, which opened in 1987. Checketts succumbed to cancer on 21 April 2006, aged 94.

Spitfire IX EN572/FY-H of Flt Lt Johnny Checketts, No 611 Sqn, Biggin Hill, Kent, June 1943

Originally ordered as a Spitfire VB, EN572 (depicted here with a long-range slipper tank) was completed as a Mk IX and issued to No 611 Sqn at Biggin Hill just 11 days after its first flight on 19 April 1943. Having scored his first two victories with the aircraft, Checketts retained it when No 485 Sqn replaced No 611 Sqn within the Biggin Hill Wing in July of that year. He would make a further 13 claims in the fighter up until 6 September, when he was shot down over Normandy in EN572 by five Fw 190s after he had exhausted his ammunition destroying a Focke-Wulf, claiming a second as a probable and damaging a third.

PIERRE CLOSTERMANN

The most famous French ace of World War Two thanks to his bestselling post-war autobiography *The Big Show*, Pierre Clostermann scored his early victories in the Spitfire IX.

Pierre Henri Clostermann was born to French diplomat parents in Curitiba, Brazil, on 28 February 1921. Sent to France to complete his secondary education, he obtained his private pilot's licence in November 1937. Back in Brazil when war broke out in Europe, Clostermann attempted to join up but had his application refused by the French ambassador. Unperturbed, he travelled to California to train as a commercial pilot with the Ryan Flying School in San Diego. Clostermann eventually joined the Free French Air Force in March 1942, after which he made his way to Britain. Here, he attended the RAF College at Cranwell, Lincolnshire, and then No 61 OTU at Rednal, in Shropshire.

In January 1943, Sgt Clostermann was transferred to newly formed, Spitfire VB-equipped, No 341 'Free French' Sqn at Turnhouse. Three months later, the unit moved to Biggin Hill, where it re-equipped with Spitfire IXs. Clostermann made five claims with the fighter during a summer of intensive action, with his first victories coming on 27 July. His combat report noted:

I was flying as Yellow 2. Going northwest out of the sun at 21,000ft, I saw two FW 190s, followed by four more. My No 1 engaged the first while I fired a short burst at the second from 600 yards, with no observed results. By now, the first FW came into my sights, my No 1 having gone over to attack the second. Giving him three short bursts from 30–10 degrees deflection from 300 to 200 yards, I saw strikes all around the cockpit, with volumes of black smoke issuing from him.

As the Boche went down in a dive, upside down, completely out of control, I broke away and fired a quick burst at another FW 190 but saw nothing, and came up above another on which I dived, firing a series of short bursts using 1½-ring deflection and closing to within ten yards when I passed behind him. By now thick black smoke was coming from him. Pulling out of the dive, I flew parallel with him and saw the pilot jettison the canopy and bale out.

These specific successes, and his performance generally, earned Clostermann a commission to the rank of aspirant in October. That same month he was posted to No 602 Sqn at Detling, Kent, when No 341 Sqn

No 602 Sqn pilots congregate both on and in front of Spitfire IX MH909 at Detling in mid-January 1944. Future ace Aspirant Pierre Clostermann is in the cockpit, the Frenchman having by then made six claims (two of which were victories). He would achieve ace status on 26 June.

was sent to Perranporth, Cornwall, for a rest. Aside from numerous sweeps and escort missions, Clostermann also flew high-altitude patrols over Scapa Flow in Spitfire VBs when No 602 Sqn was posted north to Skeabrae, Orkney, in January 1944. Upon returning south to Detling in March, the unit was heavily committed to providing close escort for USAAF B-17 Flying Fortresses and B-24 Liberators returning to airfields in England after attacking targets in occupied France in the lead up to D-Day. Clostermann described one such mission in *The Big Show*:

> Here and there in the Fortress formations were gaps. From close to, you could see machines with one, sometimes two stationary engines and feathered propellers. Others had lacerated tailplanes, gaping holes in the fuselages, wings tarnished by fire or glistening with black oil oozing from gutted engines.
>
> Behind the formation were the stragglers, making for the coast, for the haven of refuge of an advanced airfield on the other side of the Channel, flying only by a sublime effort of will. You could imagine the blood pouring over the heaps of empty cartridges, the pilot nursing his remaining engines and anxiously eyeing the long white trail of petrol escaping from his riddled tanks. These isolated Fortresses were the Focke-Wulfs' favourite prey. Therefore, the squadrons detached two or three pairs of Spitfires charged with bringing each straggler back safe – an exhausting task, as these damaged [aircraft] often dragged along on a third of their total power, stretching the endurance of their escort to the limit.
>
> On this occasion [Flt Lt] Ken [Charney] sent [Flg Off J O] Carpenter and I to escort a Liberator, which was only in the air by a miracle. Its No 3 engine had completely come out of its housing and hung on the leading edge, a mass of lifeless ironmongery. Its No 1 engine was on fire, the flames slowly eating into the wing and the smoke escaping through the aluminium plates of

Spitfire IX MH709 has its engine run up at Ford in the spring of 1944, this aircraft having been with No 602 Sqn from early October 1943. The fighter remained with the unit throughout Clostermann's time with No 602 Sqn, and it was eventually downed by a German fighter over Normandy on 4 July 1944 with the loss of its pilot, Flt Sgt Harry Chalice.

the upper surface, buckled by the heat. Through the tears in the fuselage, the surviving crewmen were throwing overboard all their superfluous equipment – machine guns, ammunition belts, radio, armour plates – to lighten the machine, which was slowly losing height. To crown it all, there was a split in the hydraulic system, freeing one of the wheels of the undercarriage, which hung down and increased the drag still further.

At 1,800 revs, -2 boost and 200mph, we had to zigzag to keep level with him still over France, 12 miles behind the main formation. Ten Focke-Wulfs began to prowl around us, at a respectful distance, as if suspecting a trap. Anxiously, 'Carp' and I kept an eye on them. Suddenly they attacked, in pairs. Short of juice as we were, all we could do was face each attack by a very tight 180-degree turn, fire a short burst in the approximate direction of the Hun, and immediately resume our position by another quick 180-degree turn. This performance was repeated a dozen times, but we succeeded in making the Focke-Wulfs keep their distance.

Over Dieppe the fighters gave way to the flak. We were flying at about 10,000ft. The German light flak opened fire with unbelievable ferocity. An absolute pyramid of black puffs charged with lightning appeared in a fraction of a second. Violently shaken by several well-aimed shells, 'Carp' and I separated and gained height as fast as we could with our meagre reserves of petrol. The poor Liberator, incapable of taking any sort of violent evasive action, was quickly bracketed. Just when we thought it was out of range, there was an explosion and the big bomber, cut in half, suddenly disappeared in a sheet of flame. Only three parachutes opened out. The blazing aluminium coffin crashed a few hundred yards from the cliffs in a shower of spray, taking with it the remaining members of the crew. With heavy hearts, we landed at Lympne [on the Kent coast], our tanks empty.

Spitfire IX MJ586 was assigned to Sous-Lieutenant Clostermann following its delivery to No 602 Sqn at Ford on 15 June – just ten days prior to the unit moving to Normandy. Following Clostermann's multi-claim engagement on 2 July in MJ305, MJ586's scoreboard was updated to feature seven victories (top two rows), three probables (third row) and seven damaged (bottom row).

Sous-Lieutenant Clostermann shakes hands with his flight commander, Flt Lt Ken Charney, at Longues (B11) after they both downed Fw 190s on 2 July 1944. This proved to be the final victory credited to Malta veteran Charney, taking his tally to six destroyed, four probables and seven damaged, all in Spitfires. For Clostermann, who also damaged four more Focke-Wulfs during this engagement five miles south of Cabourg on the Normandy coast, this was his final success in a Spitfire.

Luckily, we were often more fortunate than this and succeeded in bringing our charges back to our airfield at Detling, where our arrival always caused the greatest agitation – ambulances, fire service, curious onlookers. We felt fully repaid by the gratitude in the eyes of the poor exhausted fellows. In many cases it was only the moral support of the presence of a pair of Spitfires that gave them the courage to hold out to the end, to resist the temptation of baling out and waiting for the end of the war in some Oflag [prison camp] or other.

Aside from these missions, Clostermann also increasingly undertook strafing and dive-bombing operations with the Spitfire IX after No 602 Sqn moved to Ford in mid-April in preparation for Operation *Overlord*. Attacking V1 launch sites on the French coast as part of Operation *Noball* in the weeks immediately prior to D-Day, Clostermann flew several beachhead patrols on 6 June, before moving with No 602 Sqn to Normandy 19 days later. Attaining ace status on 26 June, he made the last of his 17 claims in Spitfires on 2 July and was awarded a DFC later that same month. Clostermann was posted to the French Air Force HQ shortly thereafter.

In December, he undertook a conversion course on to the Tempest V and joined No 122 Wing in the Netherlands in January 1945. By now a lieutenant, Clostermann was sent to No 274 Sqn at Volkel (B80). He made four claims with this unit, before transferring to No 56 Sqn as a flight commander. A move to No 3 Sqn followed in early April, and he was in the thick of the action through to war's end. Indeed, Clostermann made no fewer than 17 claims in the Tempest V

Lieutenant Clostermann, now serving as a flight commander with Tempest V-equipped No 3 Sqn at Hopsten (B112) in Germany, lights a cigarette between missions in late April 1945. Behind him, on the wing of his fighter, are his parachute, maps, flying helmet and gloves. Clostermann was credited with two aerial and six strafing victories with No 3 Sqn between 20 April and 4 May 1945.

Wearing his *Armée de l'Air* service dress uniform, Lt Clostermann poses for a formal portrait in the summer of 1945. He would receive ten French decorations and ten foreign orders and medals for his service in World War Two.

between 5 March and 4 May, this success earning him a Bar to his DFC, together with French, Belgian and US decorations. Officially credited with 33 victories (although post-war analysis has revised this tally to 11), he also claimed 225 motor vehicles, 72 locomotives, five tanks and two E-boats destroyed.

Having survived almost two-and-half years of near-constant action, during which time he had flown 432 combat missions, Clostermann was forced to bale out for the first time on 12 May when his fighter was hit by another Tempest V during a victory flypast to mark the end of the war in Europe. Although four aircraft were lost and three pilots killed, the French ace survived when his parachute deployed just above the ground.

Released from the RAF in August 1945, he subsequently wrote *Le Grand Cirque* in 1948. One of the first post-war autobiographies, the book was translated into English as *The Big Show* in 1954. A huge commercial success, its various editions have sold almost three million copies. Clostermann also wrote a second book in 1957 detailing the exploits of both Allied and Axis pilots. Aside from his writing, Clostermann pursued a career as an aeronautical engineer, helping to establish Reims Aviation, acting as an advisor for Cessna in France and working for Renault. He was also a successful politician, serving eight terms as a Member of Parliament in the French National Assembly from 1946 through to 1969. Alarmed by the growing crisis in Algeria, Clostermann joined the *Armeé de l'Air* in 1956 and flew ground-attack missions in North Africa.

Serving as vice-president of the National Defence Commission for a number of years, Clostermann eventually retired from public service and spent much of his time ocean fishing. He also presented a number of television programmes. Pierre Clostermann died on 22 March 2006 at his home in the French Pyrenees.

Spitfire IX MJ586/LO-D of Sous-Lieutenant Pierre Clostermann, No 602 Sqn, Longues (B11), France, July 1944

Marked with a No 602 Sqn 'Lion Rampant' insignia on the nose, partially removed D-Day stripes and Clostermann's victory tally as of early July 1944, MJ586 is depicted here just after the unit was transferred to Longues (B11), inland from the Normandy beachhead, 19 days after Operation *Overlord*. Clostermann made two claims in this aircraft on 29 and 30 June.

AL DEERE

One of the earliest Spitfire aces, Kiwi Al Deere made ten claims during the Battle of France and Operation *Dynamo* (the evacuation of Dunkirk) in late May 1940.

Born in Auckland, New Zealand, on 12 December 1917, Deere had attended Wanganui High School and then worked as a sheep farmer and in a solicitor's office prior to travelling to England in September 1937 to join the RAF on a short-service commission. Undertaking his basic training at the de Havilland Flying School, he then progressed to No 13 E&RFTS. Deere was presented with his wings after completing the course at No 6 FTS and was posted to Gladiator-equipped No 54 Sqn at Hornchurch in August 1938. The unit received Spitfire Is six months later, Deere noting in his autobiography *Nine Lives*:

On 6 March 1939, I flew my first Spitfire. The transition from slow biplanes to the faster monoplanes was effected without fuss, and in a matter of weeks we were nearly as competent on Spitfires as we had been on Gladiators. Training on Spitfires followed the same pattern as for Gladiators, except that we did a little more cine-gun work to get practice on the new reflector gunsight with which the aircraft was fitted.

No 54 Sqn was committed to operations over the French coast from 21 May 1940 as the British Expeditionary Force fell back to Dunkirk and nearby Calais. Deere's first victories came on 23 May when he and Plt Off Johnny Allen escorted their flight commander, Flt Lt James Leathart, who was at the controls of the squadron's Master trainer, across the Channel to Calais-Marck airfield to rescue the CO of No 74 Sqn. Deere and Allen were engaged by a larger formation of Bf 109s while the Master was on the ground, the pair claiming six German fighters destroyed between them. Deere later recalled:

This was my first real combat, and the first recorded combat of a Spitfire with a Bf 109. My abiding memory was the thrill of the action – there was no sense of danger at that early stage in the war. So much so that I stayed behind the second of the two

The charred remains of No 54 Sqn Spitfire I N3180 on the beach at De Panne, in Belgium, on 28 May 1940. The fighter was assigned to Plt Off Al Deere, and he had made ten claims (including seven victories) with the Spitfire prior to it being hit by return fire from a Do 17. The aircraft caught fire after he force-landed on the beach, and an unconscious Deere (who had knocked himself out on the gunsight as the Spitfire rapidly decelerated upon hitting the sand) had to be dragged clear by a soldier.

Bf 109s that I encountered after I had run out of ammunition just to see if I could do so. I only broke off when petrol became a factor. My prolonged fight with this Bf 109 allowed me to assess the relative performance of the two aircraft.

In early engagements between the Hurricane and Bf 109 in France, the speed and climb of the latter had become legendary, and were claimed by many to be far superior to that of the Spitfire. I was able to refute this, and indeed was confident that, except in a dive, the Spitfire was superior in most other fields, and was vastly more manoeuvrable. My superior rate of climb was, however, due mostly to the type of Spitfire with which my squadron was equipped. We had the first Rotol constant-speed airscrews [propellers] on which we had been doing trials when the fighting started. Other Spitfires were, at that stage, using a two-speed (either fully fine pitch or fully course) airscrew, which meant they lost performance in a climb. The constant-speed unit changed its pitch as the engine revs went up.

There was a great deal of scepticism about my claim that the Spitfire was the superior fighter, but the big thing for me was that we shouldn't have any fear of the Bf 109 in combat.

Deere would continue to enjoy success against Bf 109s, Bf 110s and Ju 88s until 28 May, when his fighter was hit by return fire from a Do 17 bomber and he was forced down on a Belgian beach. Despite suffering a head injury while crash-landing, he managed to reach Dunkirk via a British Army lorry and board a boat back to Dover.

Deere was one of a handful of fighter pilots awarded decorations by His Majesty King George VI on 27 June 1940, the citation that accompanied his DFC read, in part:

During May 1940, this officer has, in company with his squadron, participated in numerous offensive patrols over northern France, and has been engaged in seven combats often against superior numbers of the enemy. In the course of these engagements, he has personally shot down five enemy aircraft and assisted in the destruction of others. Throughout these engagements this officer has displayed courage and determination in his attacks on the enemy.

Deere would also see plenty of action during the Battle of Britain, colliding with a Bf 109 on 9 July, being forced to take to his parachute on 15 and 28 August, and being bombed in his aircraft when he attempted to scramble from Hornchurch in the midst of a Luftwaffe raid on 31 August. The Spitfire ended up on its back, although Deere escaped relatively unscathed. No 54 Sqn had been in the vanguard of operations undertaken by No 11 Group since the third week of May, and according to Deere the strain of combat was beginning to tell by early September:

Our morale was getting a bit low because there were only three of us – George Gribble, Colin Gray and me – left in the squadron who had any combat experience. We had been there the whole time and were pretty tired. Each time we went up, there seemed to be more and more Germans up there. We'd gone through two squadron commanders.

Flt Lt Al Deere, then serving as a flight commander with No 602 Sqn at Kenley, is introduced to a packed audience consisting primarily of '2,000 girls' (according to the Kiwi ace) at the HMV gramophone factory in Hayes, Middlesex, on 22 July 1941. Company workers, who made radios for Spitfires and other RAF aircraft throughout World War Two, were regularly addressed by high-profile aircrew charged with making morale-boosting speeches.

The new pilots who came in – they just went up and came down! You'd say to them, 'Now, look, don't get yourself lost. Stick with us. Don't bother about shooting to start with.' But, of course, they couldn't resist peeling off, and some of them didn't come back and some had to crash land.

One day, the adjutant rang me up and said, 'There are two new pilots reporting to No 54 Sqn.' I said, 'Thank God. Send them over.' They turned out to be two New Zealanders, like me, who had been three months at sea coming over. They'd only flown Vildebeests, a very old-fashioned biplane, in training. They'd been sent to an operational training unit and given five or six hours on Spitfires. And that was it! They hadn't even seen a reflector gunsight. They both got shot down on their second day of operations and were fished out of the Channel and ended up in hospital together.

No 54 Sqn was withdrawn for a rest shortly thereafter, by which time Deere had 14 victories to his name. Removed from active flying in January 1941, he eventually returned to operations as flight commander of No 602 Sqn five months later. Promoted to CO of the unit in late July, he had made four claims flying Spitfire VBs by the time he was despatched to the USA on a lecture tour in January 1942. Deere was given command of No 403 Sqn at North Weald, Essex, in May of that year, although he only led the unit for three months.

Sent to RAF Staff College, Deere eventually became wing leader of the Biggin Hill Wing in March 1943. In the weeks prior to this, he had flown as a supernumerary squadron leader with No 611 Sqn as he eased himself back into operations. On 16 February, he claimed his first victory since November 1941 while participating in a Rodeo to Hardelot, in France, with the Biggin Hill Wing. When Deere spotted 15 Fw 190s at 10,000ft, No 340 Sqn remained above to provide high cover while No 611 Sqn dived down to intercept the German fighters, allowing the Kiwi ace to follow an Fw 190 into a dive:

It was some time before I could get within firing range, and there was 480mph IAS [indicated airspeed] on my clock when I opened fire with a short burst from dead astern at 200 yards. Pieces flew off the fuselage, and two further bursts produced many more pieces. By this time I had struck the bumps near cloud, and being unable to hold

Deere had joined No 602 Sqn in Ayr, Scotland, in May 1941, just prior to the unit heading south again to No 11 Group. Sent to Kenley, it would receive Spitfire VBs two months later.

Promoted to squadron leader and made CO of No 602 Sqn on 1 August 1941, Deere made an unfortunate start to his spell in command of the unit when he shot down a Hurricane II of No 242 Sqn in error over the Channel on 1 August 1941. Its pilot, Sgt M C A Chase-Cosgrain, was killed.

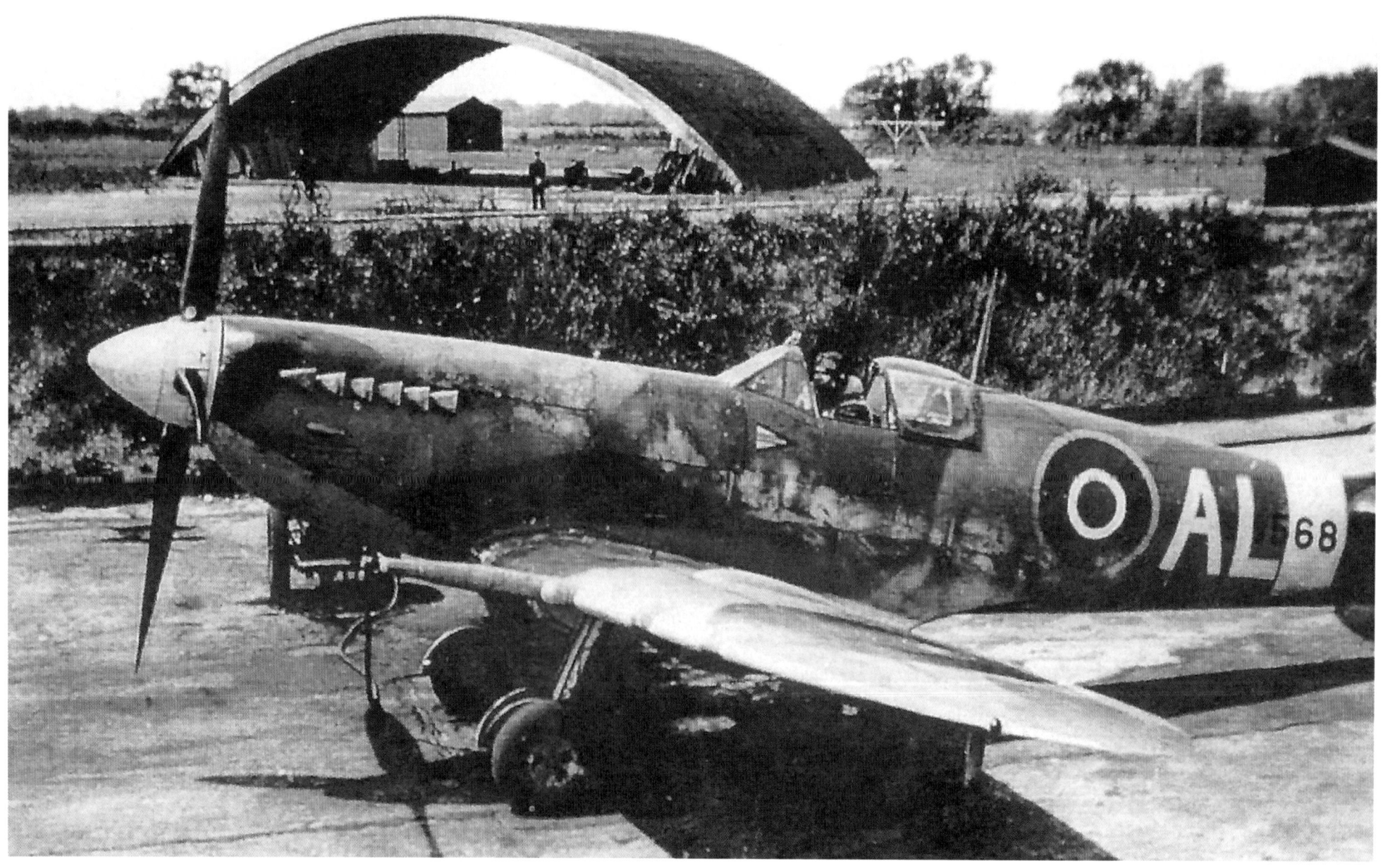

Wg Cdr Deere's personal Spitfire IX, EN568/AL, marked with his command pennant, sits in a blast pen at Biggin Hill in the spring of 1943. Flying it during June and July of that year, he shot down an Fw 190, probably destroyed a second and damaged a third – these were his final claims.

In August 1943, Biggin Hill was visited by New Zealand's High Commissioner in London, Bill Jordan (civilian), to congratulate No 485 Sqn on recent successes in combat over France. Here, the unit's pilots and Biggin Hill Wing staff officers have congregated around, and on, a Spitfire IX to mark the occasion. Standing to the right of Jordan is Sqn Ldr Johnny Checketts (then CO of No 485 Sqn), while Wg Cdr Deere (Biggin Hill Wing Leader) is second from the right and Spitfire ace Flg Off Jack Rae is to his left.

him in my sights any longer, broke to one side and followed the enemy aircraft down. He continued in his dive and went straight into the sea off Calais.

Deere's final victory came on 23 June (when he failed to fire a single round) while leading the Biggin Hill Wing on a Ramrod. He noted in his combat report:

I was leading Green Section, 611 Squadron on Ramrod 100. When at 11,000ft just north of Berck I saw two FW 190s coming up behind and made a sharp turn to port to engage. The enemy aircraft broke violently up and to port and the No 2 went into a high-speed stall and spun violently to starboard. He did not recover from the spin and hit the ground about three miles north of Rue.

He followed this up with a probable on 14 July, taking his victory tally to 17 and one shared destroyed, two and one shared unconfirmed destroyed, four probables and seven and one shared damaged. Awarded a DSO later that month, Deere led 121 missions prior to being taken off operations in September 1943 due to illness. Spells with the CGS and the staff of No 11 Group followed until he was given command of No 145 Free French Wing in May 1944. Shortly after D-Day he led his pilots on their return to France.

Remaining in the RAF post-war, Deere commanded several airfields and performed a number of staff roles (including being Aide de Camp to Her Majesty The Queen) before eventually retiring in December 1967 with the rank of air commodore. He passed away on 21 September 1995.

Spitfire I N3180/KL-B of Flg Off Al Deere, No 54 Sqn, Hornchurch, Essex, May 1940

This aircraft was the first of Deere's fighters to bear his personal *KIWI* titling and insignia below the cockpit. Delivered to the RAF in November 1939, N3180 had been assigned to No 54 Sqn in early 1940. Deere used it to make eight claims in five days over northern France between 23 and 28 May, and on the latter date the fighter was brought down by return fire from a Do 17. He force-landed on a Belgian beach and the aircraft burned out.

NEVILLE DUKE

Neville Duke was the leading Allied ace in the Mediterranean theatre, and he used several marks of Spitfire to claim the majority of his 28 victories.

Neville Frederick Duke was born in Tonbridge, Kent, on 11 January 1922 and educated locally at the Convent of St Mary and The Judd School. After graduating, and while waiting to turn 18, he worked as an auctioneer and estate agent. When Duke's attempts to get into the Fleet Air Arm met with failure in early 1940, he enlisted in the RAF as a cadet instead in June of that same year. Commissioned as a pilot officer while learning to fly the Spitfire at No 58 OTU in February 1941, he was posted to No 92 Sqn at Biggin Hill two months later. Flying some of the earliest Spitfire VBs to reach RAF Fighter Command, Duke was credited with two Bf 109Fs destroyed and two damaged during his six months of operations on the Channel Front.

When No 92 Sqn was posted north to No 13 Group for a rest in October 1941, he was transferred to North Africa to join No 112 Sqn, equipped with Tomahawk IIBs. Having survived being shot down twice in six days by Bf 109Fs from II./JG 27, Duke had taken his tally to eight victories by the end of February 1942. No 112 Sqn had switched to Kittyhawk IAs by then, and he continued to fly the Curtiss fighter through to the end of his operational tour in April – Duke had been awarded a DFC the previous month. He was able to impart his hard-earned combat experiences to would-be Kittyhawk pilots while serving as an instructor with the Fighter School at El Ballal in the Canal Zone.

In November 1942, Duke re-joined No 92 Sqn, which had been sent to North Africa earlier in the year. He hit his scoring stride with the unit, claiming 14 victories (both German and Italian aircraft) between 8 January and 16 April 1943. His first success in a Spitfire took the form of an Italian C.202 fighter downed over Tunisia, the action being described by Duke as follows:

Barely 19 years old, Plt Off Neville Duke poses with a No 92 Sqn Spitfire VB at Biggin Hill in the spring of 1941. Flying some of the first Mk VBs to enter frontline service, he made four claims (including two victories) during his six months with the unit. While on operations with the Biggin Hill Wing, Duke occasionally flew as wingman for Wg Cdr 'Sailor' Malan.

Spitfire VB R6923 had seen brief service with No 19 Sqn as a cannon-only Mk IB during the Battle of Britain. Withdrawn from use when its twin Hispano 20mm weapons suffered repeated jamming in combat, the aircraft was eventually fitted with the improved B-type wing that featured two cannons and four 0.303in machine guns. R6923 was on strength with No 92 Sqn from late April 1941 until the fighter was shot down into the Channel by a Bf 109 on 21 June that year – its pilot, Sgt G W Aston, was rescued. The fighter appeared in Plt Off Duke's logbook just once, on 25 May.

Scrambled in the morning and came across *Stukas* and 109s bombing our forward troops. Got stuck into the top cover of Macchi 202s at 13,000ft. The boys had a pretty hard fight as the Macchis stayed and fought. I dived on two slightly below, with Flt Sgt Sales. We were well placed and in the sun – they never saw us until it was too late, and when they put their noses down for home we were on them. The one I chased went down almost vertically from 10,000ft to the deck, and I drew smoke from him with a cannon shell in his radiator and oil cooler. He finally hit the ground and burst into flames after some more hits from my cannons, which were working well this day! The aircraft dissolved into flames and small pieces. Quite a scrap.

Having been promoted to flight commander soon after re-joining No 92 Sqn, Duke received a DSO in March 1943. Although the vast majority of his claims in the Spitfire were against Axis fighters, he was credited with downing two Italian three-engined SM.82 transports on 16 April during a sweep of the Cape Bon Peninsula, in Tunisia. Leading three Spitfires from No 92 Sqn, he spotted the aircraft flying low over the sea:

When we were over the Cape, I saw a large number of transport aircraft low down, and I called the 'Wingco' and dived after them. They were Savoia 82s, large three-engined jobs – about 18 of them. The first one I attacked, I was going so fast I couldn't get more than a short burst in. I attacked another after throttling right back, letting him have everything as I closed right up. I skimmed over the top of him, having seen my shells explode on him. He flew into the sea with a terrific splash, and I had a fleeting vision of pieces of cowling, etc. flying up with a sheet of spray.

Duke finished his second tour in June 1943, after which he was promoted to squadron leader and sent to No 73 OTU at Abu Sueir, Egypt, as its Chief Flying Instructor. He eventually commenced his third tour in March 1944 when he took command of Spitfire VIII-equipped No 145 Sqn in Italy. Although the unit predominantly flew fighter-bomber missions, Duke nevertheless managed to down three Bf 109s and two Fw 190s to confirm his position as the leading Allied ace in the Mediterranean theatre. The first of these came on 13 May during a sweep over enemy-held territory:

Great things at last! We met up with six Me 109s over Arezzo, the other side of Perugia (near Florence). There were six of us and we had a good dice. I got a burst at one and saw

Photographed at the start of his second tour with No 92 Sqn, but this time in North Africa, Flg Off Duke had his then extant score of eight victories recorded beneath the cockpit of his aircraft, Spitfire VC ER220/QJ-R. Between 8 January and 16 April 1943, he would add 14 victories to his tally – two of them in this fighter.

Now with 12 victories recorded, ER220 suffered the indignity of nosing over on a rough Tunisian airstrip – possibly Ben Gardane South – in early March 1943. It was Duke's regular mount between November 1942 and February 1943, and he used ER220 to claim a C.202 destroyed on 8 January, followed by a Stuka 13 days later. Quickly repaired, ER220 later served with No 601 Sqn until it was shot down by a Bf 110 off Cape Bon on 17 April 1943.

strikes under its belly before he rolled down and off. Stayed up and dodged and turned for a bit, finally fixing on to one up above, whom I climbed and turned with, easily out-climbing and out-turning him. I could see him flicking on the stall – he throttled back and straightened out, kicking his tail and skidding violently. Observed strikes in the fuselage and forward around the engine cowl. Pieces started coming off as the enemy aircraft went down in a wide spiral. I lost sight of it, but saw an explosion where the aircraft had hit the ground.

Duke claimed his final successes, against Bf 109 night fighters, on 3 September near Ravenna:

Closed in, after a long chase. Took the left-hand chap and fired at long range and got a strike in the first burst behind the cockpit. Closed, firing another burst, and the hood flew off and the pilot baled out. I chased after two more 109s, easily closing on the leader. I fired, and after a couple of bursts got hits in the fuselage and he caught fire. Later the pilot baled out.

This brace of Bf 109s made Duke the top-scoring Allied fighter pilot in the Mediterranean theatre, the 22-year-old being credited with a total of 27 and two shared victories, one probable and six damaged during the course of 486 operational sorties totalling 712 hours.

Upon returning to Britain, Duke became a production test pilot for Hawkers in January 1945. The following year he was a student on the No 4 Course at the Empire Test Pilots' School at Cranfield, Bedfordshire. Upon graduation, Duke joined the RAF High Speed Flight in June 1946 and then undertook test flying in 1947–48 with the Aeroplane and Armament Experimental Establishment (A&AEE) at Boscombe Down, Wiltshire. He received an Air Force Cross in 1948 for his exploration of aircraft performance at high Mach numbers and high altitudes with the A&AEE.

Duke resigned from the RAF in June 1948 and joined Hawkers, becoming the company's Chief Test Pilot three years later. He also retained his military links by serving in the Royal Auxiliary Air Force, leading No 615 'County of Surrey' Sqn in 1950–51. Flying all the early Hawker jets, Duke will forever be associated with the Hunter. Indeed, on 7 September 1953, he set a new World Air Speed Record of 727.63mph in all-red Hunter WB188. Twelve days later, he followed this up with a 100km closed-circuit record when he averaged 709.2mph in the aircraft.

Now-Sqn Ldr Duke would commence his final operational tour in March 1944 as CO of Italy-based No 145 Sqn, which had been equipped with Spitfire VIIIs since June of the previous year. Although the unit primarily used the aircraft as a fighter-bomber, as seen here, Duke still managed to make seven claims (six of which were for victories) while leading No 145 Sqn through to 21 September, when he completed his tour.

In June 1948, Sqn Ldr Duke resigned from the RAF to join Hawkers as a test pilot. Having become the company's Chief Test Pilot three years later following the death of ace T S 'Wimpy' Wade, he gained worldwide fame on 7 September 1953 when he set a new world air speed record of 727.63mph in all-red Hunter WB188. Duke followed this up 12 days later with a 100km closed-circuit record when he averaged 709.2mph in the aircraft.

Duke injured his back in two separate crash landings in 1955–56, forcing him to resign from Hawkers in October 1956. He then took up freelance flying of less powerful civil aircraft until 1960, when he formed Duke Aviation. He sold the company in 1982 to concentrate on freelance testing and consultancy, and five years later he became involved with Edgley Aircraft and the Brooklands Aerospace Group, testing the Optica, Fieldmaster and Firemaster.

Continuing to fly well into his 80s, Duke became ill while at the controls of his Grumman AA-5B light aircraft on 7 April 2007 en route to Popham Airfield, Hampshire, with his wife Gwen. Although he managed to land safely, Duke collapsed as he climbed out of the aircraft. Diagnosed as suffering from an aneurysm, he passed away in St Peter's Hospital in Chertsey, Surrey, later that same evening following an emergency operation.

Spitfire VC ER220/QJ-R of Flg Off Neville Duke, No 92 Sqn, Hamraiet and Wadi Sirru, Libya, late January 1943

On the morning of 8 January 1943, Flg Off Neville Duke was scrambled from Hamraiet in this aircraft, which was his regular mount until February 1943. He and his wingman, Flt Sgt Sales, soon encountered a large formation of Bf 109s and C.202s at 13,000ft. Diving almost vertically on a pair of Macchis 3,000ft below them, Duke and Sales chased the fighters to ground level. Managing to get hits on his target, Duke saw the Macchi break up and crash. He was also at the controls of ER220 on 21 February when, near Castel Benito, he intercepted a formation of Ju 87s flying at 1,000ft. As the Stukas went into a dive, Duke got ahead of the formation and fired, hitting one in the starboard wing root and causing it to spin down in flames. ER220 later served with No 601 'Country of London' Sqn until it was shot down by a Bf 110 off Cape Bon on 17 April 1943.

WILFRED DUNCAN SMITH

High-scoring ace Wilfred Duncan Smith saw action in the Spitfire on many occasions between 1940 and 1951.

The son of an officer in the Indian Civil Service, Wilfred George Gerald Duncan Smith was born in Madras on 28 May 1914. At the age of eight he was sent to Scotland in order to complete his education, before returning to India in 1933 and obtaining employment as a coffee and tea planter. Within three years Duncan Smith was back in England, and he decided to join the RAF Volunteer Reserve (RAFVR). Called up for full-time service in May 1939, he undertook flying training the following year. Duncan Smith flew a Spitfire for the first time with No 7 OTU in September 1940.

Posted to Spitfire I-equipped No 611 Sqn at Digby, Lincolnshire, in early October 1940, Duncan Smith participated in operations on the Channel Front through to November 1941 while primarily flying from Hornchurch. He scored his first confirmed victory during a Circus on 18 June:

Off Gravelines we ran into two formations of eight Me 109s. 611 as bottom squadron had a perfect bounce, with 54 and 603 Sqns guarding from above. The first attack by [Wg Cdr] Eric [Stapleton] produced a flamer, which spiralled down into the sea. I got on the tail of one German and, closing on him from dead astern, opened fire. To my satisfaction his tailplane disintegrated, bits flying everywhere, whereupon he did a most extraordinary upward corkscrew before spinning vertically down. I followed and watched with wonder as the enemy fighter broke up piece by piece.

Duncan Smith would claim six Bf 109s destroyed, five probably destroyed (along with a Do 17) and one damaged between 29 December 1940 and 27 August 1941. This success resulted in him being awarded a DFC in July 1941, followed by a Bar to this decoration five months later. The citation accompanying the latter read as follows:

During 1941, this officer has carried out 190 operational patrols, 98 of which have been over enemy territory. By his skill, coolness and strong sense of duty, Flight Lieutenant [Duncan] Smith has set a splendid example to all. He has always devoted himself unselfishly to the success of his squadron, thereby contributing materially to its achievements. Flight Lieutenant [Duncan] Smith has destroyed at least five enemy aircraft.

Serving as a flight commander with Spitfire VA/B-equipped No 603 Sqn from August 1941, Duncan Smith contracted double pneumonia in November 1941 and was forced off operations for two months. After a brief spell as a flight commander with No 411 Sqn, Duncan Smith was promoted to squadron leader and made CO of No 64 Sqn in March 1942. Flying principally from Southend and Hornchurch, he led the unit during five

Delivered new to No 64 Sqn at Southend in April 1942, BM476 was assigned to Sqn Ldr Duncan Smith, who had assumed command of the unit on 20 March. He had his rank pennant applied to the fighter, as well as the name *ATCHASHIKAR*, which meant 'good hunting' in Hindi. The fighter is seen here having its flight controls checked in a two-bay revetment at Hornchurch in the early summer of 1942. Duncan Smith claimed one victory, one probable and one damaged (all Fw 190s) in BM476 in May–June before his unit transitioned to the Spitfire IX.

action-packed months of combat. A highlight of this period was the squadron's transition to Spitfire IXs in July, making it the first unit to fly the new mark in RAF Fighter Command. Duncan Smith claimed his first victory with the potent new fighter on 30 July during a Circus over Saint-Omer:

I was leading the Squadron as Red 1, and midway between Gravelines and the target at 14,000ft, I was told that a formation of enemy aircraft were following the wing and slightly above them. On looking back, I sighted enemy aircraft, took the Squadron in a right-hand turn round, slightly up sun, and gave the order to follow me down to attack.

A recently delivered Spitfire VB of No 64 Sqn is refuelled at Hornchurch in May 1942. Note the oxygen bottle on the grass in front of the aircraft. Fitted on the starboard side of the fuselage aft of the seat, its contents were critically important to the pilot when flying above 10,000ft. Groundcrews found that replacing the bottle after every sortie posed numerous problems. Swapping them out involved removing the armour plate behind the pilot's seat, undoing the pipework and making sure no oil or grease got on it in order to prevent spontaneous combustion on contact with oxygen in flight, taking out the empty bottle and replacing it with a full one and, finally, reinstalling the armour plate. This all had to be done as quickly as possible in order for the aircraft to be ready in time for its next sortie.

There were about 15 enemy aircraft in various formations. I took the left-hand one, opening fire at 300 yards, closing to 200 yards, giving it a six-second burst and observing no results. After further two-second bursts, there was a violent explosion in the port wing root, followed by a puff of black smoke. The enemy aircraft turned slowly on its side, diving, and then spiralled down, with flames coming from underneath the port wing.

I pulled up into the sun and orbited, climbing to 14,000ft, and then made my way to the target with Red 2, where I saw the main formation on its way home, and followed behind it. Midway across the Channel I observed dogfights below and went down to investigate with Red 2. I saw a FW 190 being chased by a Spitfire, which fired at it and broke away. I dived after it, giving a two-second burst before overtaking very fast. I observed a puff of white smoke from the port side of the cockpit and a thick stream of white vapour. I broke to the left and saw Red 2 attacking this aircraft, which took fire, and disappeared in a steep dive.

Duncan Smith would make a total of nine claims while with No 64 Sqn, five of them in the Spitfire IX – including three over Dieppe on 19 August during Operation *Jubilee*. At the end of that month, he was promoted to Wing Commander Flying at North Weald, and he received a DSO in early September, the citation to the decoration noting, 'Since being awarded a Bar to the Distinguished Flying Cross, this officer has completed a great number of sorties. He is a brilliant pilot and a fine leader whose skill has proved a source of inspiration to all. Squadron Leader [Duncan] Smith has destroyed ten and probably destroyed several other enemy aircraft.'

From December 1942 through to March 1943 Duncan Smith served as Wing Commander Tactics at HQ, RAF Fighter Command, after which he completed an eight-week course at RAF Fighter Command's School of Tactics. He was then posted to Malta, where he briefly took charge of the Luqa Wing. Leading by example, Duncan Smith made six claims in two months in Spitfire IXs prior to becoming Wing Commander Flying of the Desert Air Force's No 244 Wing. He was in the vanguard of the action during the invasion of Sicily, making his 31st claim during a dawn patrol over Augusta on 29 August 1943:

I chased after the enemy and was immediately shot at by a second FW 190, which dived in over my left shoulder. Tracers streaked past my port wing, and it shot past very close.

Made Wing Commander Flying of No 244 Wing in July 1943, Wg Cdr Duncan Smith continued to add victories to his tally flying Spitfire IXs in the lead up to the invasion of the Italian mainland. He is seen here with 'Bonzo', a mascot of one of the squadrons in No 244 Wing, on the wing root of Duncan Smith's recently 'acquired' Saiman 202 communications aircraft at Tortorella, in Italy.

Above: Wg Cdr Duncan Smith smiles for the camera prior to undertaking an operation from Sicily with No 244 Wing squadrons in August 1943. He would make three claims while leading the wing, one of which resulted in the destruction of an Fw 190.

Right: From July 1950, Sqn Ldr Duncan Smith commanded Spitfire FR 18-equipped No 60 Sqn at Tengah, in western Singapore. His unit was heavily committed to Operation *Firedog* as part of the Malayan Emergency. Indeed, on New Year's Day 1951, Duncan Smith led four FR 18s in a strike on a target near Kota Tinggi. This proved to be the last operation where an RAF Spitfire fired its guns. Here, he is seen with Flt Lt 'Jimmie' James, who was one of his flight commanders. James had seen action, and made 11 claims, in Hurricanes and Spitfires with No 607 Sqn over Burma in 1942–44.

The pilot unwisely straightened up, giving me an excellent opportunity to open fire on him from slightly below on a fine quarter. I saw strikes on his wing root and the bottom of the cockpit, and with smoke trailing he disappeared into a thick cloud.

Duncan Smith was forced to take to his parachute over the sea four days later when his fighter ran out of fuel following a tank switch failure. After spending five hours in a dinghy, he was rescued by a Walrus amphibious biplane, which survived being strafed by a German fighter moments after it had alighted to pick Duncan Smith up. Having been promoted to group captain in November 1943, he was given command of No 324 Wing in Italy and

When Sqn Ldr Duncan Smith led the RAF's final Spitfire strike on 1 January 1951, he was flying his personal aircraft, NH850/Z, which was adorned with colourful nose and spinner stripes and a No 60 Sqn badge on the fin.

continued to fly whenever possible. Duncan Smith made four more claims with the wing, taking his final tally to 17 and two shared destroyed, six and two shared probables and eight damaged. He left the wing in March 1945, receiving a Bar to his DSO that same month.

Although Duncan Smith left the RAF at war's end, he remained in the RAFVR until he was given a permanent commission in March 1948. Serving initially with No 61 Group, he became CO of Spitfire FR 18-equipped No 60 Sqn in Malaya in July 1950. The unit was heavily committed to Operation *Firedog* as part of the Malayan Emergency at the time, and on New Year's Day 1951, Duncan Smith led four FR 18s in a strike on a target near Kota Tinggi. This proved to be the last mission where an RAF Spitfire fired its guns in anger, as the unit converted to Vampires shortly thereafter. Duncan Smith would receive a second Bar to his DFC in September 1952 for his service in the Malayan Emergency.

Remaining in the RAF until 1960, Duncan Smith spent his final years in service undertaking staff duties and also completing an exchange posting with the USAF. Once out of uniform, he worked as aviation sales and commercial manager for Triplex Glass until taking full retirement. The father of Conservative politician Iain Duncan Smith, Wilfred Duncan Smith passed away on 11 December 1996, aged 82.

Spitfire VB BM476/SH-Z of Sqn Ldr Wilfred Duncan Smith, OC No 64 Sqn, Hornchurch, Essex, May 1942

This aircraft was delivered new to No 64 Sqn in April 1942 and assigned to Sqn Ldr Duncan Smith, who had his rank pennant applied forward of the cockpit. He claimed one victory, one probable and one damaged (all Fw 190s) in BM476 in May–June before his unit transitioned to the Spitfire IX. The fighter went on to see further frontline service with Nos 154, 165, 122, 234, 303 and 26 Sqns, before finally being destroyed in a crash landing at Hawarden, Wales, following an inflight engine fire on 28 April 1945 while assigned to No 58 OTU.

DON FINLAY

Don Finlay was an Olympic medallist, Battle of Britain veteran and Spitfire ace, fighting on the Channel Front and in the Far East.

Born in Bournemouth, Dorset, on 27 May 1909, and with Osborne as his surname and Finlay as a given name, Don was educated at Taunton's School in Southampton, Hampshire, from 1920 through to 1925, following which he joined the RAF as a Halton Apprentice. Passing out as a fitter of aero engines in 1928, he subsequently re-mustered as an airman six years later. Completing his flying training, Finlay was granted a permanent commission upon graduating from RAF Cranwell in April 1935. He was posted to Bulldog II-equipped No 17 Sqn at Kenley the following month.

Finlay had been captain of the college's athletics squad while at Cranwell. He also played football and rugby for the RAF and was its long jump champion. Finlay had, in fact, represented Great Britain at the 1932 Summer Olympics in Los Angeles, where he won a bronze medal in the 110m hurdles, and was also a member of the 4 x 100m relay team, which finished sixth. Four years later, Finlay competed in the 1936 Summer Olympics in Berlin, coming second in the 110m hurdle.

Long before Don Finlay became a Spitfire ace, he had represented Great Britain at international level in the 110 metre hurdles. Seen here at an England versus France meeting in 1931, he went on to win bronze at the 1932 Summer Olympics in Los Angeles and silver at the 1936 event in Berlin. Finlay was also British Team Captain for the 1948 Summer Olympics in London.

That same year, he joined No 54 Sqn at Hornchurch just as the unit replaced its Bulldog IIAs with Gauntlet IIs. In August 1937, Finlay commenced a two-year course at the RAF School of Aeronautical Engineering at Henlow, Bedfordshire, after which he remained out of the cockpit with the Pilotless Aircraft Section until he was posted to No 7 OTU at Hawarden for conversion on to the Spitfire in August 1940. Finlay was then sent to No 54 Sqn at Hornchurch as a supernumerary squadron leader in order to gain experience of frontline flying prior to being given his own unit to command.

Sqn Ldr Finlay would lead high-scoring No 41 Sqn from September 1940 through to August 1941, with the unit being assigned to No 11 Group for much of that time. Aside from Finlay, Kiwi Flg Off John Mackenzie (left) and Flt Lts Tony Lovell (second from left) and Norman Ryder (second from right) achieved ace status with No 41 Sqn in 1940. Finally, newly commissioned Plt Off Roy Ford served with the unit from December 1939 through to April 1941. This photograph was taken at Hornchurch in December 1940.

On 28 August, just 24 hours after returning to operations, Finlay was shot down over east Kent by a Bf 109 while patrolling the Canterbury–Manston–Ramsgate line at 25,000–30,000ft. According to No 54 Sqn flight commander Flt Lt Al Deere, 'I had told him [Finlay] that at height it was very difficult to keep position, and if he got behind he'd had it. Well, he got behind and was shot down by a 109.' Finlay provided details of this incident in a letter he wrote to his friend, and athletics correspondent, Harold Abrahams while convalescing in hospital:

Much has happened since I was posted to lead a squadron in the big battle for London. I was almost immediately shot down near Canterbury. I don't quite know what happened. I heard a boom and saw a plume of smoke as my aeroplane was set on fire, an explosive bullet having exploded near my head – I have no idea where it came from. I sustained small shrapnel injuries to my head and to my right buttock, plus a black eye. The trouble is, Harold, I have never in my life allowed a German to get in front of me. In this game, however, the rear position is the one to aim at, and I must readjust my ideas. However, I am now back again [on operations] and itching to even the score.

Having returned to operational flying on 14 September, Finlay took command of No 41 Sqn at Hornchurch. Between then and late November, he made eight claims, seven of them for Bf 109s. Following 11 months as CO of No 41 Sqn, Finlay was promoted to the rank of wing commander in August 1941 and posted to No 11 Group as its Engineering Officer. While serving in this role, he managed to perform a number of operational flights with various wings, and he was awarded a further victory on 3 March 1942 after engaging a Bf 109F while flying a Spitfire VB with No 485 Sqn (part of the Kenley Wing) on a 'feint diversion' to northern France:

Flying as Blue 3 with 485 Squadron, I became separated with Blue 4 after turning to meet an attack from the rear on Blue 4 by one ME 109F about ten miles off Dover. I was subsequently unable to regain the squadron owing to continual attacks from pairs of ME 109Fs from ten degrees above and ten degrees to port head-on, closing to about point blank range. Owing to the nature of the attack, I was unable to confirm any

No 41 Sqn pilots gather around a propeller blade from a downed German bomber that was used as a scoreboard by the unit at Hornchurch in late 1940. Sqn Ldr Finlay is holding the blade while an unidentified pilot adds a dot before his name. The dots were added whenever a victory was claimed.

result, but enemy aircraft appeared to fly through the burst without evasion. Attack was from the sun. Blue 4 remained in position behind, and I was able to disengage to the north after 15–20 minutes [of] evasive manoeuvres.

Finlay was awarded a DFC the following month, with his tally standing at four and two shared destroyed and three and one shared damaged. The citation that accompanied the decoration stated:

From September 1940 to August 1941, Wing Commander Finlay was the CO of No 41 Squadron. He participated in many sorties during which he destroyed at least three enemy aircraft in combat. On one sortie, he attacked a German ship, leaving it a mass of flames. During this period his squadron destroyed 66 enemy aircraft. Since joining his present unit, Wing Commander Finlay has participated in several sorties. On 3 March 1942, he destroyed a Messerschmitt 109 following a courageous head-on attack, thus bringing his victories to four. This officer has always shown great keenness and he has set a splendid example to all.

The introduction of the Spitfire IX into operational service with Hornchurch-based No 64 Sqn in July 1942 gave Finlay the chance to make his final combat claim. On 30 July he twice flew the fighter with the unit as he assessed the Mk IX from an engineering perspective as part of his job. Although he failed to engage enemy fighters while participating in Circus

Sqn Ldr Finlay and his brand new presentation Spitfire II P7666 were the subject of a number of photographs taken at Hornchurch in early 1941 after he had claimed two victories in the fighter on 23 and 27 November 1940. The fighter's construction costs (£5,000) had been paid for by members of the Observer Corps, hence the insignia and titling applied to the aircraft.

Spitfire II P7666 had been delivered new to No 41 Sqn on 21 November 1940, and just 48 hours later Sqn Ldr Finlay used it to down a Bf 109E from II./JG 51 near Tonbridge. The fighter was passed on to No 54 Sqn on 22 February 1941, and it served with the unit until lost off Harwich on 20 April following combat with Bf 109s from JG 51.

200, later that day Finlay managed to damage an Fw 190 during an early evening Ramrod in support of Hurricane fighter-bombers targeting the airfield at Saint-Omer:

I was flying as Red 3 with 64 Squadron. Sqn Ldr [Wilfred Duncan] Smith dived to starboard from about 16,000ft to attack a formation of FW 190s. I saw Red 1 (Sqn Ldr Smith) open fire and then attack two FW 190s, which went towards Dunkirk. I slowly overhauled these two, which took evasive manoeuvres. The rear one turned three-quarters over and lost height. I did not follow and he re-joined his No. 1. I got within 300 yards near Bergues according to my range bar but could not close. Height was now 18,000ft, and I realised I could not close at this height on a FW. I fired several bursts from dead astern, the FWs now climbing straight. After allowing more for the bullet drop, at least one hit was secured on the left-hand side of the fuselage or wing root, a small piece coming off. The FW dived steeply, and a moment later

Gp Capt Finlay dons his flying helmet after climbing into the cockpit of a Spitfire VIII of No 909 Wing at Palel in late 1944. He would frequently undertake both liaison flights and operational sorties in Mk VIIIs while in-theatre. Finlay also had a Tiger Moth at his disposal.

the other one further ahead attacked a Spitfire, which was simultaneously attacked from head on by three FWs. This turned out to be Red 4. In the ensuing melee I lost contact, climbed to 9,500ft and crossed the coast west of Dunkirk.

In December 1942, Finlay left No 11 Group to take command of the Air Fighting Development Unit (AFDU) at Duxford. Tasked with developing aerial warfare tactics for fighters and bombers, the AFDU flew both new Allied aircraft and captured enemy types. Finlay only led the unit for three months, as he was promoted to the rank of group captain in March 1943 and given command of RAF Rednal, as well as its nearby satellite station, RAF Montford Bridge. He was also CO of No 61 OTU, based at both sites and charged with training day-fighter pilots bound for Spitfire squadrons. Finlay was decorated with an Air Force Cross at the end of his 16 months at Rednal, the award citation stating that 'His pupils have always reached a very high standard of efficiency and have invariably been turned out on time. He has set a very high standard, and gets the best from his staff and pupils.'

Finlay's next posting took him to India, where he was given command of Wing Headquarters Palel in October 1944. This was redesignated No 909 Wing the following month, and it controlled five Spitfire- and Hurricane-equipped squadrons. Finlay flew numerous operations in Spitfire VIIIs over Burma while in-theatre, and he led the wing through to VJ Day.

Remaining in the RAF post-war, he reverted to the rank of wing commander and was posted to No 1 School of Technical Training at Halton, Buckinghamshire, as senior technical training officer. Made British Team Captain for the 1948 Summer Olympics in London, Finlay was chosen to take the Olympic oath. He failed to win any medals in the Games, however. He competed in the 1950 British Empire Games two years later, having won the 120 yards hurdles competition at the 1934 event.

Finlay eventually retired from the RAF with the rank of group captain in February 1959 and went into business. Severely injured in a car accident in 1966 and left a paraplegic, Don Finlay passed away in Wycombe General Hospital on 19 April 1970.

Spitfire IIA P7666/EB-Z of Sqn Ldr Donald Finlay, OC No 41 Sqn, Hornchurch, Essex, November 1940

Newly built presentation Spitfire IIA P7666 was issued to No 41 Sqn on 21 November 1940, its construction costs (£5,000) having been paid for by members of the Observer Corps. Forty-eight hours after the fighter's arrival at the airfield, Sqn Ldr Finlay used it to down a Bf 109 near Tonbridge, Kent. He claimed a second Messerschmitt off Dover in P7666 on 27 November. This aircraft was passed on to No 54 Sqn on 22 February 1941, and it was abandoned off Harwich on 20 April that year after being damaged by Bf 109s from JG 51. Its pilot, Spitfire ace Plt Off Jack Stokoe, had downed a Bf 110 just minutes earlier.

BRENDAN 'PADDY' FINUCANE

Irishman Brendan 'Paddy' Finucane was the youngest wing commander in the RAF when he was killed in combat on 15 July 1942, having by then been credited with more than 30 victories.

Brendan Eamonn Fergus 'Paddy' Finucane was born in Dublin on 16 October 1920 and raised as a devout Roman Catholic. Educated at O'Connell's Irish Christian Brothers School, he moved with his family (who had mixed Irish and English heritage) to England in 1936. Finucane had shown a keen interest in flying from the early 1930s, and he was accepted into the RAF in August 1938 and sent to No 6 E&RFTS at Sywell, Northamptonshire. Although he initially found the unit's Tiger Moths a challenge to fly, he eventually succeeded in going solo and was posted to No 8 FTS at Montrose.

Finucane again struggled to master the school's Hart and Fury biplanes, and only managed to obtain his wings thanks to a steady improvement in his flying skills and a dogged determination to succeed. From August 1939, he accumulated more flying experience at the controls of various second-line types ranging from Queen Bee drones of the RAF's Targeting Section to obsolete Virginia bombers of the Practice and Parachute Test Flight Centre. Finally, on 27 June 1940, he was posted to No 7 OTU at Hawarden to learn how to fly the Spitfire. Fifteen days later, Finucane joined No 65 Sqn at Hornchurch with 22 hours in the Spitfire in his logbook, these having been accumulated during 26 flights undertaken in just nine days.

Despite being a novice at air combat, Finucane more than held his own in the Battle of Britain. All five of the Irishman's claims during the campaign would come in just 24 hours

A trio of Spitfire Is from No 65 Sqn race across the grass at Manston during the afternoon of 13 August 1940, the unit having been sent here from Hornchurch in order to be closer to the action. The squadron's A and B Flights engaged 20–30 Bf 109s over the Channel off Dover that day, with some success. Among the pilots to make claims was Plt Off Finucane, who was credited with one destroyed and one probable. The previous day, again flying from Manston, he had claimed one Bf 109 destroyed, one probable and one damaged.

on 12–13 August when No 65 Sqn clashed with Bf 109s over the Channel. The combat report for his first success (on 12 August) read:

> At about 12.30 hrs, 65 Squadron was about to take off when the aerodrome [Manston] was bombed. I was Green 3. The squadron took off. I climbed into the clouds and when coming out the far side I saw an Me 109 slightly below me and about 350 yards ahead. Yellow 1 was on my starboard side and was shooting at the enemy aircraft. I closed on the Me 109 but he escaped into the clouds. I followed him around and next sighted the aircraft just ahead of me at about 3,000ft. I gave him a short burst and then we were in the clouds again. As we came out again at about 1,000ft over the sea I found myself in position for a further long burst. The enemy aircraft started to smoke and was diving towards the sea.
>
> I had to break away as I found myself being attacked, but I saw the enemy aircraft heading straight for the sea and apparently out of control when only 200ft from the water. Gaining height while evading my pursuers, I saw another Me 109 under the cloud base doing steep turns. At 30 degrees deflection, I gave him a short burst at a range of 200 yards and I saw my bullets striking the enemy aircraft. The enemy aircraft disappeared into the cloud and I followed him, but unfortunately I lost him. I then returned to base.

Finucane was credited with two destroyed, two probably destroyed and one damaged in the space of just 48 hours. No 65 Sqn moved north to Turnhouse for a rest at the end of August, and Finucane failed to improve his tally until the unit returned to No 11 Group on 4 January 1941. Now flying from Tangmere, he would steadily add to his score during patrols of the Channel coast and while participating in RAF Fighter Command's new Offensive Sweeps campaign that saw No 11 Group squadrons mounting 'hit-and-run' operations over Belgium and France. Finucane 'made ace' on 15 April 1941 when he downed a Bf 109 south of Dover. Awarded a DFC ten days later, he was posted to No 452 Sqn as a flight commander the following month.

The first RAAF unit to form in Britain, No 452 Sqn was transferred from Kirton-in-Lindsey, North Lincolnshire, to Kenley on 21 July. Ten days earlier, Finucane had claimed the unit's first victory while it was using West Malling, Kent, as an advanced base. Leading No 452 Sqn on a sweep of the French coast, he had shot down a Bf 109. 'I cut in on the inside of his turn and followed him down. When about 150 yards behind I gave him a short burst of three seconds. The enemy pilot baled out.' Finucane had used just 90 rounds to achieve the victory.

He would enjoy great success with No 452 Sqn, being credited with 16 victories, two probables and two damaged (all Bf 109E/Fs) while flying with the Kenley Wing. The squadron was initially equipped with Spitfire IIs, but these were replaced by Mk VBs during

Promoted to flight commander in mid-April 1941 and sent to newly formed No 452 Sqn, Flt Lt Finucane proved popular among the unit's primarily Australian pilots. Here, he is seen enjoying a 'smoko' with future Spitfire ace Sgt Keith Chisholm (left) and Sgt Ian Milne at Kenley in the summer of 1941.

August. That month, No 452 Sqn was RAF Fighter Command's top scoring unit with 22 victories. Finucane had claimed a remarkable eight and two shared kills (and a probable) in August, and he usually celebrated his success at mission-end with a 'beat up' of Kenley. The unit diarist recorded, 'The A Flight commander was known to come in with the motor full on at nought feet over dispersal and go up into a series of tight climbing rolls after a pass over the airfield. He was a good aerobatic pilot.'

Finucane's remarkable scoring run, which had received coverage in the national press (as well as in Australia), came to a painful halt in mid-October when he broke his heel bone jumping over a low wall in Croydon during a night of heavy drinking with the squadron. Off operations and recuperating until the new year, Finucane was awarded a DSO and two Bars to his DFC by King George VI at Buckingham Palace while convalescing. The citation to the DSO read:

> Recently during two sorties on consecutive days, Flight Lieutenant Finucane destroyed five Messerschmitt 109s, bringing his total victories to at least 20. He has flown with this squadron since June 1941, during which time the squadron has destroyed 42 enemy aircraft, of which Flight Lieutenant Finucane had personally destroyed 15. The successes achieved are undoubtedly due to this officer's brilliant leadership and example.

On 20 January 1942, recently promoted Finucane assumed command of No 602 Sqn at Redhill. The unit was heavily committed to offensive operations over the next six months, capably led by its young CO. Indeed, he would claim three and three shared victories, five probables and five damaged – all were Bf 109s and Fw 190s. However, prior to hitting his scoring stride with No 602 Sqn, Finucane was wounded in the leg while engaging Fw 190s mid-Channel on 20 February, and he was grounded for three weeks while recovering. By now one of the RAF's leading aces, he was asked during an interview about the key to his success. 'The first necessity in

No 452 Sqn flew Spitfire IIAs from Kenley during the first three months it was based in Surrey, with Flt Lt Finucane claiming eight victories in the aircraft between 11 July and 19 August. The unit had fully switched to Mk VBs by early September, however. Coming over the hedge at Kenley in the summer of 1941, Spitfire IIA P7786/UD-C was used by Sgt Keith Chisholm to share in the destruction of two Bf 109s on 9 August. He would subsequently become the first RAAF ace on the Channel Front.

Flt Lts Keith 'Bluey' Truscott, 'Paddy' Finucane and Ray 'Throttle' Thorold-Smith of No 452 Sqn were photographed together at Kenley on 10 November 1941. All three were by then Spitfire aces, the two Australians having been hand-picked by Finucane to become flight commanders. Finucane was still walking with the aid of a stick at this point, having broken a heel bone jumping over a wall in Croydon during a night out on 13 October. None of these men would survive the war.

Hornchurch Wing, Finucane, who was still four months short of his 22nd birthday, became the youngest pilot to hold this rank in the RAF. He lasted a little over two weeks in the role before being posted missing in action on a Ramrod targeting a Wehrmacht camp at Étaples, on the French Channel coast, on 15 July 1942.

Such missions were highly dangerous, as the heavily defended coastline bristled with German light flak batteries. Knowing how vulnerable the Spitfire's cooling system was to the slightest damage, Finucane had avoided undertaking Ramrods while with No 452 Sqn – he preferred his chances engaging Luftwaffe fighters at medium altitude. However, as a wing leader, he could no longer ignore it when he was instructed by No 11 Group HQ to carry out such an operation.

Despite leading his wing in across the beach at 'zero feet', Finucane's Spitfire was hit in the radiator by flak. He immediately turned for home in an attempt to glide his aircraft across the Channel. Ten miles from the French coast Finucane was forced to ditch. Although he successfully put the fighter down in a minimum-speed, nose-up ditching, the Spitfire quickly disappeared and no trace of Finucane

Wearing newly issued short-waisted battledress, Sqn Ldr Finucane lights his pipe at Kenley shortly after taking charge of No 602 Sqn in January 1942. The diminutive Irishman would claim six victories with the unit, making him the leading ace on the Channel Front by early June.

combat is to see the other bloke before he sees you – and I've been blessed with a good pair of eyes. The second is to hit him when you fire. You don't get a second chance in this game.'

By the end of June, Finucane had flown 108 operations over France, and his tally stood at 26 and six shared destroyed, eight and one shared probables and eight damaged. When, on 27 June of that month, he was promoted to wing commander and made wing leader of the

Finucane made 16 claims between 20 February and 8 June 1942 while leading No 602 Sqn, and 12 of them were in this Spitfire VB BM124. A presentation aircraft funded by the people of Tonga and named in honour of their long-serving Queen, the fighter was assigned to Finucane upon its delivery to Kenley fresh from the factory on 16 March. Although Finucane chose not to adorn his aircraft with a victory tally, he did add a green shamrock beneath the cockpit immediately aft of the *QUEEN SALOTE* titling. The Spitfire was also marked with No 602 Sqn's lion insignia.

was ever found. His demise was witnessed by his wingman, future Spitfire ace Plt Off Alan Aikman, who had first warned him that his fighter was trailing coolant vapour.

'He jettisoned the cockpit canopy. It was a textbook ditching, but the Spitfire suddenly disappeared in a wall of water – it nosed down and sank instantly. There was no sign of Finucane.'

It was a huge loss, for the Irishman had claimed 30 victories since the start of 1941, and he was to remain the most successful Allied ace on the Channel Front through to the war's end.

Spitfire VB BM124/LO-W of Sqn Ldr Brendan 'Paddy' Finucane, OC No 602 Sqn, Kenley and Redhill, Surrey, March–June 1942

The highest-scoring RAF pilot on the Channel Front, Sqn Ldr 'Paddy' Finucane became CO of No 602 Sqn in January 1942. After recovering from leg wounds suffered in combat with an Fw 190 on 20 February 1942, he adopted BM124 upon its delivery to Kenley on 16 March. The fighter, built at Castle Bromwich in the West Midlands, was a presentation aircraft funded by the people of Tonga. Finucane eschewed personal scores on his Spitfires, but in addition to No 602 Sqn's lion insignia, he adorned the fighter with a shamrock to show his Irish roots. He saw much action at its controls, and over France between late March and early June 1942, Finucane claimed four victories, four probable and four damaged with BM124. *QUEEN SALOTE* survived the war, having served with five operational squadrons. It was scrapped in 1946.

BOB FOSTER

A veteran of the Battle of Britain, Bob Foster became an ace defending Australia in 1943.

Born in Clapham, South London, on 14 May 1920, Robert William Foster attended a local school in Battersea prior to finding employment in the marketing departments of Shell-Mex and BP. Having joined the RAFVR in May 1939, he was called up on 2 September and sent to No 1 Initial Training Wing (ITW) in Cambridge in November. He was transferred to No 12 FTS at Grantham, Lincolnshire, the following month. After completing his flying training and being awarded his wings, Foster undertook Hurricane conversion with No 6 OTU at Sutton Bridge in June 1940.

Commissioned shortly thereafter, he was posted to No 605 'County of Warwick' Sqn at Drem, Scotland, and travelled south with the unit to Croydon on 7 September, just as the Battle of Britain reached its climax. Foster made his first claim (for a Bf 110 damaged) on 27 September, although his Hurricane I was also hit during this action and he force-landed at Gatwick, West Sussex. A further six claims followed through to 8 November, two of which were classified as victories. Foster's first confirmed success, on 7 October, was a Bf 109 that he bounced near Lingfield, Surrey, after having shaken off several other German fighters:

'I dived down as fast as I could to get out of the way [of the German fighters] and, as I pulled up, I saw a 109 ahead of me. Anyway, he'd had his battle and he was going home and not thinking. He didn't see me so I shot him down, just like that. You couldn't relax at all.'

Having been re-equipped with Hurricane IIAs in November 1940, No 605 Sqn was posted to Martlesham Heath, Suffolk, three months later. While flying a convoy patrol from here on 24 March, Foster damaged an He 111 80 miles east of Felixstowe, on the Suffolk coast.

A group of No 1 Fighter Wing pilots (from both the RAF and the RAAF) are seen at Laverton, Victoria, soon after their arrival in Australia in late 1942. Most are sporting summer uniforms. Battle of Britain veteran and No 54 Sqn flight commander Flt Lt Bob Foster is standing in the front row second from left. The tall individual in the back row is Spitfire ace Sqn Ldr Ray Thorold-Smith.

Following more than a year of operational flying, he was posted to No 55 OTU at Usworth, near Sunderland, in September 1941 to serve as an instructor.

In April 1942, Foster joined Spitfire VB-equipped No 54 Sqn at Castletown, Scotland, as a flight commander. Two months later the unit was posted overseas as part of No 1 Fighter Wing (dubbed the 'Churchill Wing'), which was tasked with defending northern Australia from Japanese air attack. Foster and his squadronmates embarked in the troopship *Highland Chieftain* and eventually arrived in Melbourne, Victoria, in August. It would take the wing a full five months to receive its tropicalised Spitfire VBs and train up on them. No 54 Sqn finally headed to Darwin, in the Northern Territory, on 25 January 1943.

A trio of pilots from No 54 Sqn practise formation flying near Sydney in January 1943, prior to moving north to Darwin, where all three aircraft were to be used to claim victories. Nearest is BS164/K, in which Sqn Ldr Eric 'Bill' Gibbs made all of his claims (five victories and one shared victory and five damaged). Next is BR544/A, which Flt Lt Robin Norwood was flying when he was credited with shooting down a Zero-sen on 15 March. The third Spitfire VC is BR539/X in which Flt Lt Bob Foster made most of his claims (three destroyed, one probable and two damaged).

Foster duly claimed No 1 Fighter Wing's first victory in the defence of Australia on 6 February 1943, describing the action that saw an Imperial Japanese Naval Air Force (IJNAF) Ki-46 'Dinah' photo-reconnaissance aircraft shot down as follows:

I had been on standby against another possible Jap raid and was scrambled from our base at Darwin with my No 2 and ordered out to the northwest over the sea after an unidentified 'plot'. After what seemed an interminable number of changes in direction, not helped by my aircraft suffering from radio problems, I spotted a lone aircraft and positioned us for a stern attack on what we thought was a Dinah 'recce job' – and this indeed proved to be so.

When I eventually opened fire, although I could see my cannon shells hitting the port engine, they had no effect – and neither did my next burst. Having closed in somewhat, my third burst struck both engines and the fuselage, and soon after I opened up again I saw flames shooting out of one of the engines. They rapidly spread to the rest of the aircraft, and we then watched as it dived away in a smoky arc until it hit the water, still burning furiously.

This victory was the first of eight claims that Foster would make through to 6 July. Four of his successes were over IJNAF G4M 'Betty' bombers, and their destruction gave him ace status. The first of these fell to Foster during the 15 March raid on Darwin, the No 54 Sqn pilot later recalling:

I fired a two- to three-second burst at the bombers, then dived to 14,000ft and climbed into the sun behind them. By then they were heading west. I got above and slightly to starboard behind the formation in line abreast. I caught them up about 50 miles northwest of Darwin when they were at about 20,000ft, with 'Zekes' all around them.

The wing tip from the Zero-sen downed by Flg Off Al Mawer on 15 March 1943 became the No 54 Sqn scoreboard, with victories illustrated by nips of whiskey. It is seen here with eight nips in May, two of which denoted kills by Flt Lt Foster on 6 February and 15 March. The No 54 Sqn crest is on the right, while the two black swans to the left are a reference to an official gift sent from Australia to Prime Minister Winston Churchill. The wing tip was photographed outside the unit's readiness hut on 10 May, with Sgt W H Eldred pointing at the tally. Standing next to him in the pith helmet is Flg Off F Quinn (No 1 Fighter Wing's Intelligence Officer), while the remaining pilots are Flg Offs J B Yerby (an American in the RAF), George Farries and Ian Taylor.

Weather-beaten No 54 Sqn Spitfire VC AR564/DL-L patrols over typical northern Australian terrain, its now-famous elliptical wings (a major factor in the aircraft's excellent performance characteristics as a fighter) being clearly visible from this angle. The fighter's original RAF roundels applied in the factory can also be seen beneath the distinctive blue and white markings used by RAAF aircraft in World War Two.

I went in on the starboard bomber and raked the formation to about halfway along the line, closing to 50 yards. Then, as two 'Zekes' were approaching from astern, I broke away and dived. I looked up and saw one bomber towards the starboard end of the line break formation and go down gently to port, with thick smoke coming from its port engine. Another bomber further along the line was also emitting thick smoke from its port engine, but it kept formation.

As Foster alluded to in his account, the A6M2 Zero-sen fighter escort for the IJNAF bombers always posed a threat to the unwary when attacking the 'Bettys'. 'As far as the Zero was concerned, the Spitfire VC had the advantage of speed and could out-climb and out-dive it', he noted. 'However, as with any other Allied aircraft, it could not match the Japanese fighter for manoeuvrability – one didn't try to "mix it" with the Zero. The escorting Zeros were always a menace, which meant that at least one squadron had to be detached to deal with them, leaving fewer to attack the bombers – hence the losses suffered by the latter were not as high as they might have been.'

Foster became only the third Spitfire pilot to claim five victories over Australia when, on 6 July, he engaged 'Bettys' for the last time as they targeted recently built Fenton airfield southwest of Darwin:

I took off with No 54 Sqn as leader of Blue Section and rendezvoused over Sattler at 6,000ft. We were informed that the enemy formation was approaching the target from a westerly direction, and had been detected at a range of 130 miles. As we neared Anson Bay, we were told that 30+ enemy aircraft were approaching Peron Island from due west, and moments later I sighted the formation crossing over Cape Ford at 'one o'clock' to us. We were in battle formation sections, line abreast at 32,000ft, while the bombers were at 25,000–26,000ft and flying in three main formations in vic. I observed no fighters, although they had been reported behind and above the bombers. 'Wingco' [Wg Cdr Clive Caldwell] detailed No 54 Sqn to attack the bomber formation.

In my first attack, I opened fire at the leading aircraft of the starboard formation of nine-plus aircraft, allowing just over one ring deflection from 300–400 yards and closing to 50–75 yards, using cannons and machine guns. Strikes were observed on its starboard engine, as well as to the fuselage of the bomber to the right of the one I attacked. As I broke down and away under the bomber formation, I noticed the latter aircraft smoking. At the same time, I observed another bomber move towards the centre of the formation – it too was smoking from the starboard engine.

Heavy return fire was experienced from the blisters – it bore a resemblance to large white flashes, and I am of the opinion that it was either 20mm cannon or 12.7mm cannon.

Breaking away to port underneath the bombers, I commenced climbing into the sun, and when up about a mile above the bomber formation, I observed a lone 'Betty' flying northwest at about 18,000–20,000ft in the opposite direction to the bomber formation. I dived after him and delivered a stern attack, opening up with a one-second burst from 300 yards. This bomber broke down. I eventually saw it crash on land, burning fiercely. As my petrol position was now rather serious, I returned to base.

Leaning on the trailing edge of the wing of a Spitfire VC at Winnellie, Flt Lt Bob Foster discusses his victory over a Japanese bomber on 20 June 1943 with Flg Off Tony Hughes. This success gave Foster ace status. Hughes was not so lucky, having to force land during the mission.

Foster was awarded a DFC six weeks later following his success in the defence of Darwin. Returning to Britain in February 1944, he joined the Air Information Unit and often worked as an escort for war correspondents who were interviewing service personnel in the frontline. In this role, Foster accompanied the press corps during the Normandy landings and witnessed the subsequent advance through France at first hand. Indeed, he is thought to have been the first RAF officer to enter Paris with the liberating French army, walking with Gen Charles de Gaulle down the Champs-Élysées on 26 August 1944.

Transferred to HQ Fighter Command two months later, Foster was subsequently posted to Bentwaters, Suffolk, as station adjutant. Released from the RAF with the rank of squadron leader in February 1947, he resumed his career with Shell Mex and BP. Foster remained in the Royal Auxiliary Air Force post-war, serving with No 3163 Fighter Control Unit until it was disbanded in 1958. By then he had been promoted to the rank of wing commander.

Retiring from the oil industry to the East Sussex coast in 1975, Foster eventually became chairman of the Battle of Britain Fighter Association in 2009. He passed away on 30 July 2014.

Groundcrew service a No 54 Sqn Spitfire VC between flights at RAAF Base Darwin. No 1 Fighter Wing struggled to keep its fighters serviceable due to their airfields being hundreds of miles from established engineering support facilities. Here, the airman standing on the wing root of the fighter is securing the filler cap for the fuel tank fitted immediately in front of the cockpit. His shirtless colleague perched atop the open cockpit hatch is checking the operability of the port aileron, which is raised at the trailing edge, by moving the control column.

Spitfire VC BR539/DL-X of Flt Lt Bob Foster, No 54 Sqn, Winnellie, Northern Territory, March–July 1943

This aircraft was regularly flown by Flt Lt Bob Foster, who used it to down a 'Betty' bomber and claim a second example damaged during the 15 March raid on Darwin. He flew it again during his next successful combat on 20 June, when he claimed another 'Betty' (this was almost certainly a Ki-49 'Helen' bomber from the Imperial Japanese Army Air Force (IJAAF)) destroyed and a 'Zeke' damaged – the latter was a Ki-43 'Oscar' from the IJAAF. Foster was again at the controls of BR539 on 6 July when he fought his final combat in the defence of Australia, claiming another 'Betty' destroyed and a second bomber as a probable. This aircraft was passed on to No 452 Sqn in June 1944, before being relegated to the role of training aircraft with Nos 2 and 8 OTUs. It was wrecked in a take-off accident in March 1945 and later scrapped.

IAN GLEED

One of the great RAF wing leaders during the 'hard years' on the Channel Front in 1941–42, Ian Gleed enjoyed notable success in Hurricanes and Spitfires.

Ian Richard Gleed was born in North London on 3 July 1916, the son of Seymour and Florence Gleed. His father had attained the rank of captain in the Royal Army Medical Corps during World War One, and had continued to practise medicine after leaving the service. Gleed learned to fly at Hatfield, Hertfordshire, in 1935 while studying at Epsom College. Having joined the RAF on a short-service commission in March of the following year, he had soon been nicknamed 'Widge', short for 'Wizard Midget', due to his modest 5ft 6in stature.

Upon the completion of his training on 25 December 1936, Gleed was posted to Gauntlet II-equipped No 46 Sqn at Kenley. The unit received Hurricanes in March 1939, and after flying the Hawker fighter for seven months, Gleed was promoted to flight lieutenant and transferred to newly-reformed No 266 Sqn at Sutton Bridge as a flight commander. The unit was equipped with Spitfire Is, and during a test flight by Gleed on 18 February 1940, one of these broke up in the air. Knocked out when the fighter came apart, he regained consciousness in time to open his parachute. Gleed had been badly injured, and he spent more than two months in hospital recuperating. After finally regaining his full flying status on 14 May, he was posted to No 87 Sqn in France as a replacement flight commander.

The Hurricane-equipped unit had suffered heavy attrition in men and aircraft since the launching of the *Blitzkrieg* in the West on 10 May, and Gleed immediately set about taking the fight to the Luftwaffe, as future ace and test pilot Plt Off Roland Beamont recalled:

Gleed was one of our replacement pilots and he came out from the UK to tell us exactly how to run the war – all 5ft 6in of him! He was immediately as good as his word and tore into the enemy on every conceivable occasion with apparent delight and an entire lack of concern. His spirit was exactly what was needed to bolster the somewhat stunned survivors of the week following 10 May. That was not to say that 87 Sqn's morale wasn't extremely high, but 'The Widge' somehow managed to raise it further.

By the time his unit was pulled back to England on 22 May, Gleed had claimed seven victories and one probable in the space of just 72 hectic hours. He would continue to add to his tally during the Battle of Britain, with No 87 Sqn flying from Exeter (with detachments at Bibury, in Gloucestershire, and Hullavington, in Wiltshire) as part of No 10 Group throughout the campaign. Gleed was awarded a DFC on 13 September 1940, having made an additional seven claims (including four victories) by the end of that month.

Given command of No 87 Sqn in late November, he led the unit to Charmy Down, Somerset, shortly thereafter. In the spring of 1941, Gleed took a flight of Hurricanes to St Mary's in the Scilly Isles in order to intercept German bombers that were attacking convoys in the Western Approaches. The flight enjoyed some success, and Gleed was credited with two destroyed and one probable between 17 and 28 May.

In November 1941, he was promoted to wing commander and made wing leader of the Middle Wallop Wing – he also subsequently led the nearby Ibsley Wing, with both outfits flying Spitfire VBs. On 12 February 1942, Gleed led the Ibsley Wing into action during the RAF's hastily organised response to the Channel Dash by the German capital ships *Scharnhorst*, *Gneisenau* and *Prinz Eugen* as they sailed from the French port of Brest to Norway. Tasked with providing direct fighter cover for an attack on the vessels by Beaufort torpedo-bombers, Gleed recorded in his logbook:

Descended through cloud. After five minutes' search found two large ships escorted by destroyers and small ships. Weather was low cloud with poor visibility and very low rain squalls. A 109

Flt Lt Ian Gleed sat for a studio portrait after receiving a DFC on 13 September 1940. Having flown with No 87 Sqn since mid-May, he had made 15 claims (11 of them credited as victories) by early October.

No 87 Sqn's A Flight night-flyers gather in front of a Hurricane I fitted with an exhaust glare shield at Exeter in October 1940. Gleed, standing third from right, was the commander of A Flight from May 1940 until he was promoted to lead the squadron in late December. As with most RAF Fighter Command Hurricane and Spitfire units of this period, No 87 Sqn enjoyed little in the way of success on nocturnal operations in 1940.

Promoted to wing leader of the Ibsley Wing in November 1941, Wg Cdr Gleed usually flew Spitfire VB AA742/IR-G during this period. The fighter was also marked with his Figaro the cat mascot, which adorned all of his assigned fighters. Finally, the Spitfire has his rank pennant beneath the windscreen. Gleed made five claims (including two destroyed) in this aircraft between 13 March and 25 April 1942.

joined formation but dived for cloud before it could be shot at. Lost this convoy in heavy rain squall but found another ship with large quantities of black smoke pouring from it, surrounded by escort ships. Nine 109s sighted; just sliding into attack when discovered nine more 109s on our tails. Luckily, they must have thought us friendly as we slid off without being chased. Petrol getting low so set course for home. Tried to escort several friendly bombers; they shot at us, then hid in clouds. Landed West Malling 1600 hrs.

One of Gleed's squadron commanders at Ibsley at the time was Sqn Ldr C F 'Bunny' Currant who, like Gleed, was a decorated Battle of Britain ace. CO of No 501 'County of Gloucester' Sqn, Currant would assume command of the wing upon Gleed's departure. He thought very highly of the diminutive ace:

He was, I would unhesitatingly say, one of the most courageous men I've ever had the privilege to know. He may have been tiny in stature but, by God, he had a big heart and seemed not to have any fear. He was unmoveable and unflappable, with a modest, unassuming manner, and always thought for his pilots and for the groundcrews and staff. A caring man, I remember him warmly with gratitude. A pocket-size man with care for others and courage beyond compare.

RAF Fighter Command suffered heavy losses to Bf 109s and the recently introduced Fw 190s – which Gleed described as 'bloody fast aircraft' – during his time as a wing leader in No 10 Group, and the two missions he led on 25 April were typical for the period.

Left: A smiling Wg Cdr Gleed leans on the fuselage of AA742, his IR-G codes clearly visible behind him. This aircraft had been delivered new to No 118 Sqn at Ibsley in early October, and it was 'appropriated' by Gleed upon his arrival at the Hampshire airfield the following month.

Below: Figaro was also applied to the last Spitfire flown by Wg Cdr Gleed, Mk VB AB502. Marked with his IR-G code letters, the fighter was used by him to make three claims in March–April 1943 prior to it being shot down on 16 April over Cape Bon. Both Gleed and his wingman, Sgt J K Rostant, were killed when they were bounced from above by a superior number of German fighters. This Air Ministry photograph of Gleed was released for publication just 24 hours prior to his death.

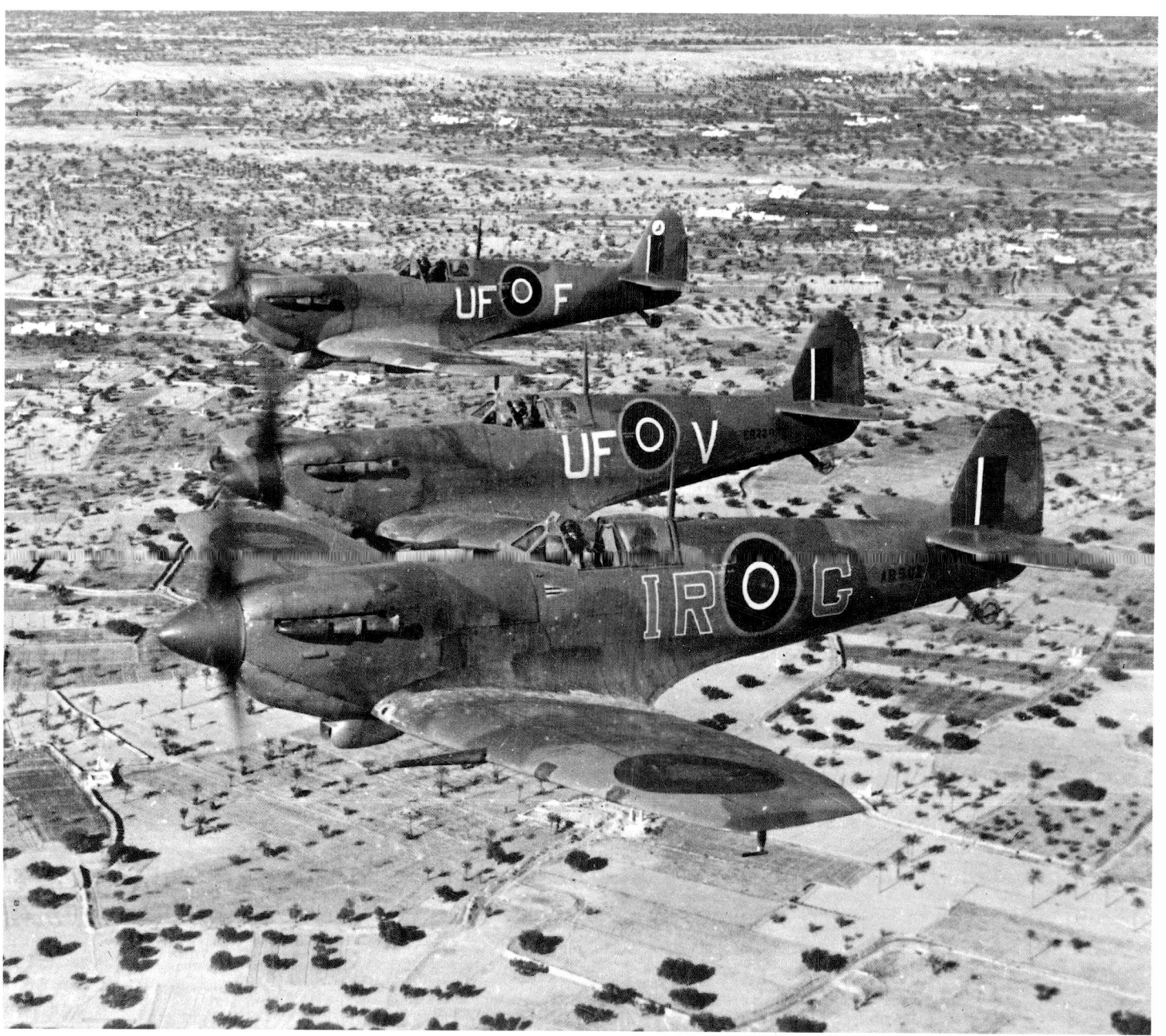

Wg Cdr Gleed, in AB502, leads two Spitfire VBs from No 601 Sqn on a patrol over northern Tunisia during his brief spell as wing leader of No 244 Wing at Goubrine South. All three aircraft are fitted with Aboukir filters and clipped wooden wing tips. Gleed flew at least 35 missions in this aircraft, and high-scoring American ace Sqn Ldr Lance Wade (who was then CO of No 145 Sqn) also damaged a German fighter in AB502.

The first operation was a Circus, Gleed noting in his logbook:

Set course 0904. Reached Cherbourg and bombed from east to west; intense flak, the first hitting a Boston, which force landed in France. Twelve 109Fs attempted to attack bombers and escort in flak area. I attacked one of these and damaged it, last seen by Boston gunners diving vertically with smoke pouring from it. The high cover Polish Wing was attacked over the target but enemy aircraft ran away. We lost two fighters and one Boston.

The second mission was a wing offensive sweep over the Normandy coast:

Led 501 Sqn on sweep of Cherbourg Peninsula. Attempted to attack eight enemy aircraft and was jumped by six more. Was attacked all the way back across the Channel by 109Fs. These enemy aircraft continually carried out diving attacks on the formation. Five of our aircraft were shot down; we probably downed one in return. About six Fw 190s attacked the formation south of Swanage. Bad show.

On 22 May 1942, Gleed received a DSO for his performance as a wing leader, the citation accompanying the award reading, 'This officer has led his Wing on 26 sorties over enemy territory. He has always displayed a fine fighting spirit which, combined with his masterly leadership and keenness, has set an inspiring example. Wg Cdr Gleed has destroyed at least 12 enemy aircraft, two of which he shot down at night.'

In July 1942, Gleed was taken off operations and posted to HQ, Fighter Command, as Wing Commander Tactics. Made Wing Commander, Operations, at year-end, he was posted to HQ, Middle East, in January 1943 and briefly attached to No 145 Sqn to gain experience of combat in North Africa. Gleed then became wing leader of Spitfire-equipped No 244 Wing, and he claimed his 16th, and final, victory on 17 March when he downed a Bf 109G over southern Tunisia.

The following month No 244 Wing flew a series of fighter sweeps over Cape Bon as part of Operation *Flax*. Its aim was to cut the air supply lines between Italy and the Axis armies fighting for their survival in North Africa. On 16 April, Gleed and his wingman had just intercepted a formation of Italian SM.82 transport aircraft flying low over the sea when they were in turn bounced by escorting Bf 109s and Fw 190s. Both pilots were shot down, with Gleed almost certainly falling to 174-victory ace Leutnant Ernst-Wilhelm Reinert of JG 77. His Spitfire VB crashed in sand dunes on the Tunisian coast, and he was initially buried by the Germans at Tazoghrane. His remains were later re-interred in an Allied cemetery at Enfidaville, Tunisia.

Flt Lt Neville Duke, who was also involved in this engagement and considered himself lucky to have escaped with his life after being chased by a 'persistent Fw 190', was fulsome in his praise of his late wing leader:

Ian Gleed was a highly respected and admired Wing Leader during his time with 244 Wing. He was a most aggressive fighter pilot who inspired the utmost devotion with his leadership. He had a somewhat boyish enthusiasm, but with authority – an ideal leader in the Desert Air Force [DAF], where respect for one's leaders was judged by their operational ability. With all, he was an officer and a gentleman in the true sense. He was a great loss.

Spitfire VB AB502/IR-G of Wg Cdr Ian Gleed, OC No 244 Wing, Goubrine South, Tunisia, April 1943

This aircraft was delivered to the RAF in January 1943 and shipped to Takoradi, Ghana, in what was then known as the Gold Coast. Once there, it was fitted with an Aboukir tropical filter and issued to No 244 Wing. AB502 became Wg Cdr Gleed's personal aircraft in early March 1943, featuring his Figaro the cat mascot beneath the cockpit on its starboard side and a rank pennant on its port side. He flew at least 35 missions in the fighter prior to his death, during which time he made three claims. Gleed was shot down and killed in AB502 on 16 April 1943.

COLIN GRAY

The highest scoring New Zealand fighter ace of World War Two, Colin Gray flew various marks of Spitfire in combat.

Colin Falkland Gray was one of twin boys born in Christchurch, New Zealand, on 9 November 1914. Upon the completion of his education at Christ's College, he found employment as a junior stock clerk until he and his brother Ken applied for short service commissions in the RAF in April 1937. Ken was accepted, but Colin was rejected on medical grounds, and a second attempt a year later also resulted in failure. Refusing to admit defeat, Gray took up sheep mustering at a remote farm in order to improve his fitness. This worked, and he was accepted into the RAF in September 1938.

Gray commenced his training in January 1939 at the de Havilland Flying School at Hatfield, Hertfordshire, and quickly progressed to No 11 FTS. He received his wings upon the completion of his course at the latter unit in October 1939, and with the rank of pilot officer, he was briefly sent to No 11 Group Fighter Pool before being posted to No 54 Sqn at Hornchurch in November. According to fellow Battle of Britain pilot Christopher Foxley-Norris, who wrote Colin Gray's obituary for *The Independent* in September 1995:

> He was a man of strong character, brusque manner and powerful personality. These together brought him into early conflict with his superiors, but

Plt Off Colin Gray patrols over Essex in one of 22 Spitfire Is delivered to No 54 Sqn at Hornchurch in November 1939. These aircraft were fitted with constant-speed Rotol metal propellers and improved TR 1133 VHF radios that did not need an aerial wire between the mast and the tail. Although the serial of this aircraft is unknown, Gray enjoyed great success in KL-T R6893 from 13 July through to 3 September, making 24 claims (12 of which were for aircraft destroyed).

his emerging operational performance soon erased any initial doubts. He was heavily involved in the fighting over Dunkirk [in May 1940], sustaining near fatal damage in combat with Bf 109s.

Thereafter, he was continuously in action for the whole of 1940, finishing the year with a confirmed total of at least 15 aircraft destroyed. These included an unusually large number of enemy fighters of approximately equal performance to his own. This was mainly attributable to the fact that, apart from his skill as a pilot, he was a superb natural shot. Many fine pilots produced disappointing results because they lacked this special ability. Among those who combined both and reaped the results were 'Sailor' Malan, 'Johnnie' Johnson and German ace Adolf Galland. Colin Gray was their acknowledged equal.

Awarded a DFC on 15 August 1940, Gray had been credited with 16 and one shared destroyed, five and two shared probables and nine damaged by the time No 54 Sqn was withdrawn from No 11 Group and sent north to Catterick on 3 September for an extended period of rest and re-equipping. The citation for the decoration stated:

Since May 1940, Pilot Officer Gray has flown continuously with his squadron on offensive patrols. He took part in numerous engagements against the enemy throughout the Dunkirk operations, and subsequently throughout intensive air operations over the Kentish coast and in protection of shipping in the Channel. He has shot down four Messerschmitt 109s and, it is believed, destroyed a further four. He also assisted in destroying one Messerschmitt 109 and one Dornier 215. His example, courage and determination in action have contributed materially in maintaining the high morale of his squadron.

Having seen so much aerial combat during the spring and summer of 1940, Colin Gray was well qualified to judge the merits of the three key fighter types involved in the Battles of France and Britain. He made the following observations in his autobiography *Spitfire Patrol*:

The official figures give the top speed of the Spitfire I as 355mph at 19,000ft, and the Hurricane as 325mph. By contrast, the Messerschmitt 109E had a top speed of 354mph at

No 54 Sqn's pilot cadre, and a pair of intelligence officers, pose in front of Plt Off Gray's KL-T at Hornchurch in June 1940. Eight of these aviators had been posted in as attrition replacements following the losses suffered by the unit over France during the evacuation of Dunkirk. Gray is standing far right at the back, while fellow Kiwi Plt Off Al Deere is seated second from left. Aside from Deere and Gray, four other pilots in this group would attain ace status flying Spitfires with No 54 Sqn.

12,300ft. For speed alone, the Spitfire and the 109E were more or less identical, and both were about 30mph faster than the Hurricane. The Messerschmitt 109 took 6.2 minutes to reach 16,550ft, and the Spitfire 6.2 minutes to 15,000ft, with the Hurricane being a little slower. To all intents and purposes, the three aircraft were on a par, with the Hurricane lagging slightly behind. However, in the combat situations in which we found ourselves, the questions of speed and rate of climb were not necessarily decisive factors.

The problem of manoeuvrability was of prime importance in enabling one to turn inside the enemy, certainly in fighter-versus-fighter-combats, and thus to get a shot in when attacking, or avoid being shot down when on the defensive – and here the British aircraft had a decided advantage, in my experience. The 109s did have one plus in that their Daimler-Benz 601 engines were fitted with a fuel injection device that eliminated the effects of negative 'G' and enabled pilots to shove the stick forward and go straight into a dive when attacked, whereas we lost quite a bit of 'ground' by having to half-roll and follow suit. The German fighters also had a heavier armament in that they had some cannon, whereas we had only .303 machine guns.

Having briefly flown Hurricanes with No 11 Group Fighter Pool, he got the chance to fly the Hawker fighter operationally when he was posted to No 43 Sqn as a flight commander in December 1940, although he returned to No 54 Sqn in the same capacity just a month later. Gray then transferred to No 1 Sqn (equipped with Hurricane IIBs) in June 1941, and undertook sweeps of France and night fighter missions with the unit.

He received a Bar to his DFC in September 1941, its citation stating, 'This officer has destroyed a further eight enemy aircraft, bringing his total victories to 17. In addition, he has probably destroyed a further nine enemy aircraft. Flight Lieutenant Gray has always shown the greatest keenness and enthusiasm and has been of great assistance to his squadron commander.' His leadership qualities saw him made CO of Canadian-manned No 403 Sqn that same month, only to be posted to No 616 'South Yorkshire' Sqn two days later. By the time Gray was transferred to HQ No 9 Group as Squadron Leader Tactics in February 1942, he had claimed 19 aircraft destroyed and logged more than 300 hours of operational flying since September 1939.

Returning to operations in September 1942, Gray took charge of No 64 Sqn at Fairlop, in Essex, this unit having received the then new Spitfire IX just two months earlier. In January 1943, he was posted to Algeria to take command of No 81 Sqn, which was the first unit in-theatre to be equipped with the Spitfire IX. Gray would enjoy great success over Tunisia with the aircraft, making nine claims (five of which were for the destruction of Axis fighters) and receiving a DSO as a result. He achieved one of his victories on 3 April in a dogfight near Tunis:

Sqn Ldrs Al Deere and Colin Gray (who would claim 47 victories between them) commanded Spitfire units in RAF Fighter Command during the autumn of 1941. Deere was CO of No 602 Sqn at Kenley and Gray was in charge of No 616 Sqn at Kirton-in-Lindsey. Seen here at a formal function in London, both men wear DFC and Bar ribbons on their service dress tunics. Gray also has *NEW ZEALAND* shoulder patches on his uniform.

I saw an aircraft coming towards me at high speed, and as he flashed past I recognised a 109G2. He also obviously recognised me as hostile because he immediately pulled into a screaming left-hand turn and attempted to dogfight. This was a big mistake because there was no way a 109 could turn inside a Spitfire. It took only a few minutes to get on his tail, and a short burst with cannon and machine guns produced much smoke, glycol and large chunks falling off. Jerry baled out and flashed by me going down, although his parachute appeared to stream and it did not open before the poor beggar hit the ground.

Promoted to lead No 322 Wing from Malta, Gray scored his final five victories while flying sweeps over Sicily from the island. Although he had shot down 25 Axis fighters during his frontline tours, his last successes took the form of two Ju 52/3m transports attempting to keep German and Italian troops resupplied in their beleaguered defence of Sicily. Gray's combat report noted, 'I saw three Junkers in formation just ahead of me, and a shot at the leader caused him to burst into flames and dive into the sea. I then turned to his number two, and the same thing happened. From the spectacular results it looked as if they must have been carrying petrol. It was all over in a few seconds.'

Awarded a second Bar to his DFC in November 1943, Gray had by then been posted to Rednal as CO of No 61 OTU. He eventually went back on operations as wing leader of the Spitfire XIV-equipped Detling and Lympne Wings from July 1944. 'Unusually, but by no means uniquely', noted Christopher Foxley-Norris, 'Colin Gray was on full operational flying duties for nearly the whole five-and-a-half years of the war, apparently without any impairment of his performance or enthusiasm. For him there was no suggestion of combat stress or trauma.'

In January 1943, Sqn Ldr Gray was posted to Algeria to take command of No 81 Sqn, just as the unit received Spitfire IXs. He would see considerable action over Tunisia through to the end of April, making nine claims (five of which were credited as victories) over Axis fighters. With the strain of combat etched on his furrowed brow, Gray is sitting on the wing root of his Spitfire IX – note the rank pennant – to check paperwork at No 81 Sqn's 'Paddington' (Souk el Khemis) home between operations in April 1943.

Surrounded by pilots from No 81 Sqn, a smoking Sqn Ldr Gray (centre, with **NEW ZEALAND** shoulder patches on his battledress tunic) makes a point during a debriefing at 'Paddington' following a recently completed sweep over Tunisia in the spring of 1943.

Wg Cdr Gray joined the Spitfire XIV-equipped Lympne Wing as its new wing leader on 11 August 1944, and he was allocated RM787 as his personal mount the following month upon its delivery to No 41 Sqn. In keeping with the privilege of his position, the fighter was marked with his initials and rank pennant. After participating in the latter stages of the V1 campaign, during which, to Gray's frustration, he was unable to engage any flying bombs, he started to lead the Lympne Wing on long-range bomber escort missions to targets in western Germany. With little sign of the Luftwaffe during these often tedious operations, Gray failed to add to his tally of aerial victories. RM787 was later transferred to No 130 Sqn and, after the war, it was sold to the Belgian Air Force.

Gray was granted a Permanent Commission in the RAF post-war, and he served in various staff and command postings through to his retirement with the rank of group captain in March 1961. Returning with his family to New Zealand, he worked for British multi-national consumer goods company Unilever as personnel director until he retired in 1979. In September 1990, Gray returned to Britain to participate in the ceremonies marking the 50th anniversary of the Battle of Britain, and he was one of the eight escorting officers to the Roll of Honour in Westminster Abbey. According to Christopher Foxley-Norris, 'No one more fully deserved that position.' Colin Gray passed away on 1 August 1995.

Spitfire IX MA408/CG of Wg Cdr Colin Gray, OC No 322 Wing, Lentini East, Sicily, August 1943

Wg Cdr Colin Gray led No 322 Wing throughout the Sicily campaign, and he flew his personally marked Spitfire IX EN350 during this period. However, that aircraft was replaced by MA408 in late July, Gray subsequently using it for the remainder of his tour, which concluded in early September. Wearing standard desert camouflage, the aircraft was adorned with Gray's initials in non-standard colours as used by some of the squadrons under his command. After Gray returned to England, MA408 served with Nos 74, 73 and 253 Sqns of the Balkan Air Force prior to it being scrapped in 1948.

PETER PROSSER HANKS

Yorkshireman Peter Prosser Hanks achieved ace status during the Battle of France, and subsequently served as a wing leader in the defence of Malta in 1942.

Peter Prosser Hanks was born in York on 29 July 1917 and educated at Worksop College in Nottinghamshire. He joined the RAF in late 1935, and undertook his flying training with No 6 FTS at Netheravon, Wiltshire. Having 'cut his teeth' on Tutors, Hanks progressed to Hart and Fury biplanes and was awarded his wings in the summer of 1936. He was then posted to Fury I-equipped No 1 Sqn, at Tangmere, in September of that year, where he showed sufficient promise at aerobatics to join a three-man team with Flg Offs Caesar Hull and Peter Townsend. Their flying was highly praised during a competition at the Zurich International Air Meeting in July 1937.

No 1 Sqn re-equipped with Hurricane Is in October 1938, and following the outbreak of war with Germany 11 months later, Hanks flew to France with the rest of the unit as part of the RAF's Advanced Air Striking Force (comprising 25 squadrons of fighters, bombers and reconnaissance aircraft). By now a flight commander, Flt Lt Hanks claimed his first victory on 1 April 1940 when he downed a Bf 110 near Longuyon in north-eastern France. He was also credited with the destruction of an He 111 on the 20th of the same month.

When 19-year-old Plt Off Hanks was posted to No 1 Sqn at Tangmere, which was part of the newly formed RAF Fighter Command, in the summer of 1936, awaiting him was the elegant but obsolete Fury I. He soon mastered the Hawker biplane fighter to the extent that he joined the unit's three-man aerobatics team the following year and competed internationally at the Zurich International Air Meeting in July 1937.

When German forces launched their *Blitzkrieg* offensive in the West on 10 May, Hanks and his squadronmates were all but overwhelmed. Claiming five victories in five days, his run of success came to an end on the 14th when his Hurricane was one of three No 1 Sqn fighters shot down by Bf 110s from ZG 26. The squadron had scrambled six Hurricanes from Berry-au-Bac, in northern France, after a large formation of Bf 110s had passed directly over the airfield at 0745hrs, the Messerschmitts escorting bombers targeting Laon. Hanks led the chase after the enemy fighters, but the Hurricane pilots failed to close on them until the Bf 110s changed direction. Here, he recalls what happened next:

We then got above them and I dived vertically on the leader and fired a burst, allowing deflection, and he just blew up. Nothing left of him but a few small pieces. Then I pulled up in a climbing turn to the left and saw a bugger coming up at right angles towards me from the left and firing at me. He wasn't allowing enough deflection and all his shots were going behind me. I then got on to his tail and managed to hit him, causing the enemy aircraft to burst into flames.

I was just turning over him when my aeroplane was hit by some other bugger behind me and I was suddenly drenched in hot glycol. I didn't have my goggles down and the bloody stuff completely blinded me. I didn't know where I was and somehow got into a spin. I could see damn all and the cockpit was getting bloody hot, so I undid the straps and opened the hood

Flt Lt Hanks (fourth from left) poses with the officer cadre from No 1 Sqn outside their hotel (the 'Marie') at Neuville in early 1940. The unit, led by Sqn Ldr P J 'Bull' Halahan (seen here wearing an Irvin jacket), had been in France since 9 September 1939, and by the time Hanks returned to England on 30 May 1940 he had been credited with seven victories.

to get out, but I couldn't. Every time I tried, I was pressed back. I started to scream then, but stopped screaming and then somehow or other I got out.

Having survived this fiercely fought engagement, which had cost No 1 Sqn the lives of two of its pilots, Hanks was sent home on 30 May and posted to Spitfire-equipped No 5 OTU at Aston Down as an instructor. Although no longer in a frontline unit, he still managed to down a Ju 88 from 5./KG 51 that was targeting the nearby Gloster factory at Hucclecote, in Gloucestershire, on 25 July 1940. His combat report noted:

I was flying over Cirencester at 3,000ft with two pupils when I looked up and saw what I thought was a Heinkel 111 at about 15,000ft. As I climbed up to intercept the bomber, a Hurricane dived out of the clouds above the enemy and engaged it. I watched

Dashing over the muddy expanses of Vassincourt towards their aircraft, pilots perform a mock scramble – note the smile on Flg Off 'Lorry' Lorimer's face – for the benefit of the visiting press corps. This scene would be repeated three or four times a day following the launch of Operation *Yellow* by the Germans in the early hours of 10 May 1940. The pilots in this photograph are, from left to right, Plt Off Billy Drake, Flg Offs Lorry Lorimer and 'Pussy' Palmer (in his pre-war 'prestige suit'), Flt Lt Hanks and Australian Flg Off Les Clisby.

the whole encounter, and eventually the Hurricane fell away in a spin. I carried on with my attack and gave one fairly long burst. The enemy immediately went down in a flat spin and several parachutes came out.

The engagement took place at approximately 1500 hrs at 17,000ft, and the enemy crashed one mile northeast of the aerodrome. I am convinced that the Hurricane did not collide with the enemy aircraft, as I saw the whole thing, and the Hurricane was some 150 yards behind the bomber when he went into a spin. The enemy aircraft flew on for several minutes after the Hurricane came down.

Awarded a DFC that same month for his victories in France, Hanks joined Hurricane-equipped No 257 Sqn at Coltishall in December. He would claim one destroyed and a probable while serving as a flight commander with the unit. In June 1941 Hanks was made CO of No 56 Sqn, and three months later the Hurricane II-equipped unit began receiving Typhoons at Duxford. Promoted to wing leader at the airfield in December, he was transferred to Coltishall in this capacity in February 1942.

Six months later, on 7 August, Hanks arrived on Malta to take command of the Spitfire V-equipped Luqa Wing. Heavily involved in the defence of the island during the final Axis attempts to bomb it into submission, he would claim four victories (taking his final tally to 13) and five damaged through to the end of the 'October Blitz'. Hanks' second success came during one of five raids mounted by Axis bombers, and their fighter escort, on Malta on 12 October. Leading four Spitfires from No 126 Sqn, his combat reported stated:

I saw 18 enemy aircraft (mostly Me 109s) in three vics of six aircraft in formation at 23,000ft. I dived to attack the right-hand section and immediately saw four to six Me 109s on our

Wg Cdr Hanks led the Luqa Wing from August through to December 1942, after which he switched airfields on Malta in order to take over the Hal Far Wing. He would make nine aerial and two strafing claims while flying Spitfire VCs from the island, the majority of his successes coming during the 'October Blitz' that marked the end of the Axis offensive against Malta. Hanks received a DSO for his exploits during this phase of the campaign.

Spitfire VC BR498 was assigned to Wg Cdr Hanks upon his arrival at Luqa, the fighter having reached Malta just four days before he had. Adorned with Hanks' initials and his rank pennant, BR498 repeatedly engaged Axis bombers and their escorts during the 'October Blitz'. Hanks made nine claims (including four victories) in the fighter during the course of just one week, while fellow ace Flt Lt Bill Rolls of No 126 Sqn was credited with five kills in BR498 during the same period.

Pilots from No 126 Sqn have jumped up on the wing roots of BR498 to gather around the fighter's open cockpit at Luqa in October 1942. The fair-haired individual sat in the fighter is probably Wg Cdr Hanks, as he flew the aircraft multiple times per day during this period.

tails. I gave the order to break right, and as I broke, went into a violent spin and recovered at 20,000ft. I weaved around preparatory to climbing up and saw one Me 109 at 15,000ft going towards Sicily. I dived to attack, opening fire from 250 yards and closing to point blank range, giving the enemy aircraft an approximately four-second burst (port cannon unserviceable) and observed strikes on the fuselage and cockpit, followed by thick smoke and flames. The enemy aircraft went through cloud, shedding pieces and burning fiercely.

On 3 November, Hanks was awarded a DSO following his actions of the previous month. The citation that accompanied the medal detailed his actions against the first of three raids mounted on 17 October:

This officer led 126 Sqn in an engagement against a force of seven enemy bombers, escorted by 25 fighters, which attempted to attack Malta. The enemy were intercepted before reaching the island and, in a head-on attack, three of their aircraft were destroyed; one of them, a Junkers 88, was shot down by Wg Cdr Hanks. This officer is a fearless fighter whose example and leadership have instilled great confidence in his fellow pilots. While flying from Malta, Wg Cdr Hanks has destroyed four enemy aircraft.

In December 1942, Hanks switched airfields on Malta in order to take charge of the Hal Far Wing. He remained on the island until February 1944, when, following promotion to group captain, he was sent to Grottaglie, in southern Italy, as OC of No 286 Wing. Flying Spitfire fighter-bombers, Hanks led missions in Italy and over the Balkans, where his units provided Yugoslav Partisans with aerial support. Returning to Britain in October 1944, he was station commander of Aston Down when the war in Europe ended in May 1945.

Remaining in the RAF post-war, Hanks served as Wing Commander Flying at Wunstorf, in West Germany, in 1948, before assuming command of the Day Fighter Leader's School at West Raynham, Norfolk, later that same year. He was station commander of Coltishall in the 1950s and was later Senior Air Staff Officer at Air Headquarters Levant, Cyprus, prior to its disbandment in April 1958. Retiring from the RAF in June 1964, Hanks found employment with Hawker Siddeley until he moved to South Africa, where he passed away in Natal on 31 January 1986.

Spitfire VC BR498/PP-H of Wg Cdr Peter Prosser Hanks, OC Luqa Wing, Luqa, Malta, October 1942

First flown on 15 June 1942, this aircraft reached Malta on 3 August – just four days before Wg Cdr Hanks arrived at Luqa. Marked up with Hanks' initials and his rank pennant, BR498 saw much action in the 'October Blitz'. Hanks made nine claims (including four victories) in the fighter in just a week, while fellow ace Flt Lt Bill Rolls was credited with five kills in BR498 during the same period. Like many Spitfire VCs sent to Malta from August 1942, this aircraft had no tropical air filter fitted in an attempt to improve the fighter's performance. With nine victories to its credit, BR498 tied with Mk VC BR301 for the title of the highest scoring Spitfire in the defence of Malta.

RAYMOND HARRIES

Ray Harries was the leading Griffon-powered Spitfire ace, being credited with 11 victories during Channel Front operations in 1943.

Raymond Hiley Harries was born in Llandilo Fawr, South Wales, in 1916. He had studied as a dental student at Guy's Hospital in London prior to securing employment with Prudential Assurance as a District Agent in Canterbury, Kent. On the outbreak of war in September 1939, he joined the RAFVR and completed his flying training in early 1941. Posted to Hurricane-equipped No 43 Sqn at Drem, Harries' only encounter with the enemy during his first operational tour took the form of an inconclusive night engagement with a German bomber. He was subsequently posted to No 52 OTU at Debden as an instructor in July 1941, the unit moving to Aston Down the following month.

In February 1942, Harries returned to operations when he joined Spitfire VB-equipped No 131 Sqn at Llanbedr, Wales, as a flight commander. He was credited with a half-share in a Ju 88 downed over North Wales on 12 March, and subsequently added a further six claims to his tally after the unit moved to Merston two months later. Harries received a DFC in August, the citation accompanying the award stating, 'This officer, who has completed numerous sorties, is an excellent flight commander. He has spared no effort in the training of his pilots, among whom he has fostered a fine team.'

Sqn Ldr Ray Harries (centre front row) and his pilots from No 91 Sqn have gathered in front of a Spitfire VB at Hawkinge for a group photograph in April 1943. The following month the unit transitioned to the Spitfire XII, having flown the Mk VB in the demanding anti-*Jabo* role off the Kent coast since March 1941. Harries made six claims (three of which were victories) in Spitfire VBs with No 91 Sqn between 20 January and 24 March 1943.

Promoted to squadron leader in December 1942, Harries was given command of No 91 Sqn, which flew Spitfire VBs from Lympne and nearby Hawkinge on the Kent coast. The unit was specifically tasked with flying anti-*Jabo* (fighter-bomber) and Jim Crow coastal shipping patrols in search of enemy aircraft over the English Channel. Harries had notable success with the squadron, achieving ace status with the destruction of an Fw 190 mid-Channel on 24 March.

The following month, No 91 Sqn was withdrawn to Honiley, Warwickshire, to convert from the Spitfire VB to the new Griffon-engined Spitfire XII. The latter was seen as the ideal fighter to defeat the Luftwaffe's 'tip and run' fighter-bomber campaign against targets on the Channel coast. Leading his unit back to Hawkinge on 21 May, Harries went into action with the Mk XII four days later when he downed two Fw 190 *Jabo* from SKG 10. The No 91 Sqn diarist described the engagement in colourful terms:

> We got the Huns tonight – five of them, all in the drink. It was a grand occasion for 91 Squadron, and this entry ought to be typed in red. We had been flying all day, but the weather closed in towards evening with heavy clouds. In fact, F/O Hoornaert and F/Sgt McPhie had to land at Lympne because of heavy rain when returning from patrol at 1930 hrs. However, the CO [Harries], with F/O Johnny Round as his No 2 and F/O Maridor and P/O Davy as Nos 3 and 4, went on a low patrol of the Dungeness area at 2125 hrs. They were not out long, and came in to land at 2150 hrs.

This was when the fun started, for about 12 Fw 190s came in with the intention of dealing a shrewd blow at Folkestone at about this time. The CO and Johnny had landed and just taxied to dispersal when the greens [flares] were fired, so they whipped off again smartly. Meanwhile, Maridor and Davy, who were circling to land, went 'through the gate' [the throttle lever had a wired gate, which restricted the level of boost to prevent the engine being damaged – in emergencies the gate could be broken to permit maximum boost, after which the engine had to be inspected upon the fighter's return to base] to Folkestone.

There were guttural cries of 'Alarm, Alarm' from the surprised Huns, who broke away and ran for home, dropping their bombs in the sea, except for one, which fell in a bathing pool and injured one person. The XIIs had the legs of the 190s, and having flown through a lively AA barrage, smacked down five of them, two falling to the CO and one to each of the others. Matt and Kyn, who had been scrambled, saw some of this, but didn't get a chance to have a crack at anything themselves, while F/O Bond, who made a smart getaway on a second scramble a minute or so later, saw a 190 go straight in near Gris Nez. It turned out that this must have been the one that Davy had engaged, which was disappointing for Bond, who thought he had scared the bandit in the drink himself. After this, the CO was in the chair and behind the bar, and rather more of the odd beers were drunk rather later than usual.

In June, No 91 Sqn moved to Westhampnett to join No 41 Sqn in forming a Spitfire XII wing. Harries received a Bar to his DFC at this time, and he would enjoy more success with the aircraft flying from the Sussex airfield, including claiming three Bf 109s destroyed on 18 July during a wing-strength Ramrod sweep of Luftwaffe airfields in northern France. His combat report noted:

> I was leading Blue Section of 91 Squadron on Ramrod 143. Between Abbeville and Poix I sighted several enemy aircraft in front and above. I picked out three Me 109s, which were

EN625 was one of the first Spitfire XIIs delivered to No 91 Sqn on 13 May 1943, and Sqn Ldr Harries was at its controls 12 days later when he downed two Fw 190 *Jabo* off Folkestone as the fighter-bombers attempted to flee back to France at low level. EN625 was subsequently used by Flg Off Ray Nash to destroy an Fw 190 and a Bf 109G later in the year prior to the fighter being written off following a forced landing on 11 December that saw the Spitfire lose its starboard wing.

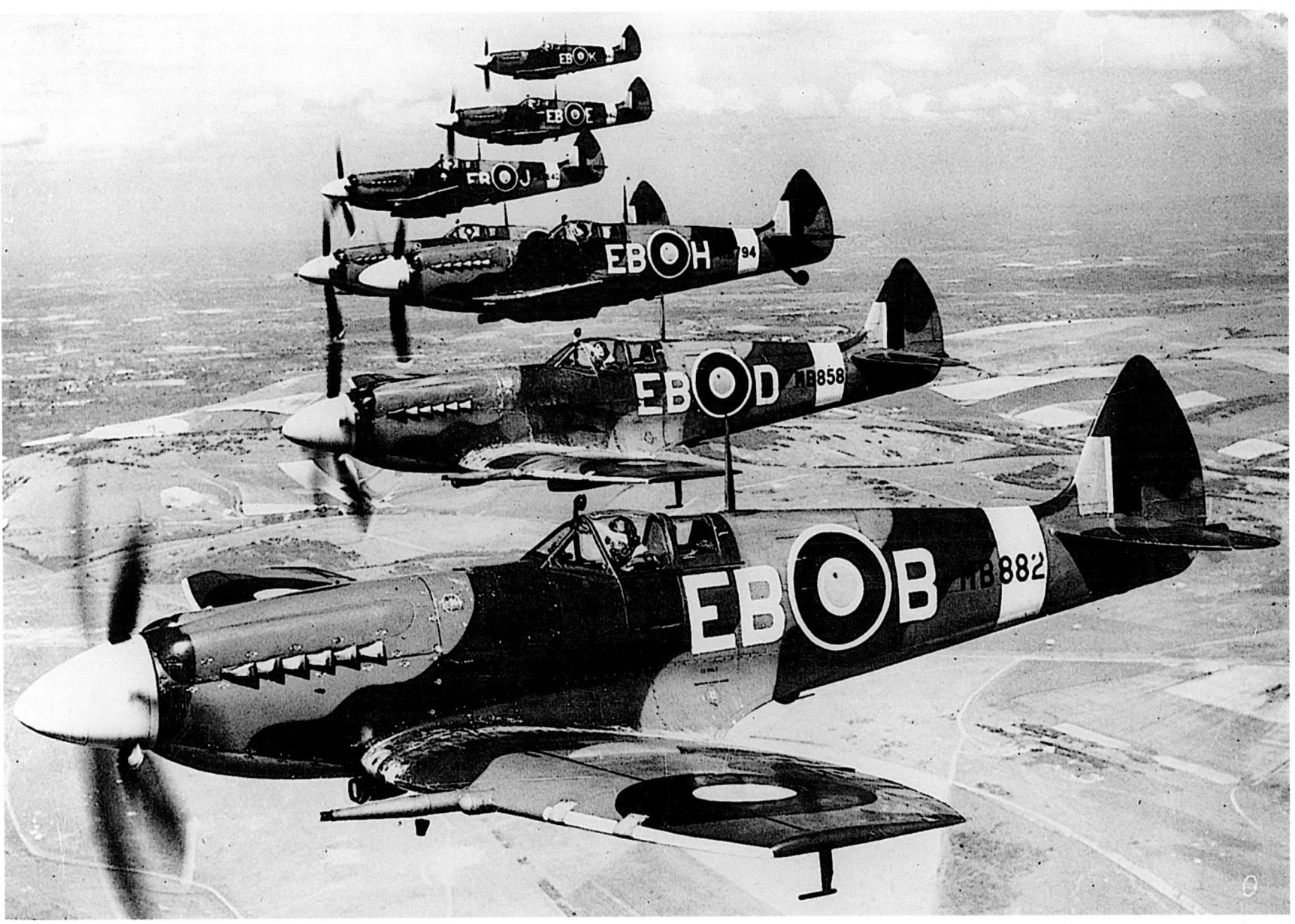

Promoted to wing leader of the Westhampnett Wing in August 1943, Wg Cdr Harries led the RAF's only Spitfire XII-equipped units – Nos 41 and 91 Sqns – in sweeps over northern France. Flying fighters from each unit, he would claim ten victories in the Mk XII by year-end. These aircraft are from No 41 Sqn, which was equipped with Spitfire XIIs from February 1943 through to September 1944.

in fairly close formation 700ft above and to port. I immediately climbed up and engaged the port aircraft of the section, opening fire from approximately 250 yards and seeing strikes on the wings and fuselage. This was confirmed by Sgt Watterson (Blue 2).

As the middle enemy aircraft was now closer to my line of fire, I turned my aircraft slightly to starboard and, allowing approximately 1½ rings deflection, shot his tail clean away with my first burst. The enemy aircraft spun towards the ground. The third enemy aircraft half-rolled and dived away, white streamers showing from his wing tips. I half-rolled after him and closed rapidly in the dive. I opened fire at approximately 200 yards, my strikes hitting the port wing and fuselage and starboard wing root. The enemy aircraft gave off white smoke and burst into flames. This was seen by a pilot from 197 Squadron.

Promoted to wing leader of the Westhampnett Wing in August 1943, Harries was also awarded a second Bar to his DFC at this time, followed by a DSO three months later. The citation for the latter described him as being 'an exceptionally skilled, courageous and determined fighter', noting that 'within the past weeks he has led his fighter force on various sorties during which 27 enemy aircraft have been shot down, three of them by his own guns. These successes pay an excellent tribute to this officer's inspiring leadership and great tactical ability.'

Harries' final victories with the Spitfire XII had come on 20 October, and as with his first successes in the Griffon-engined aircraft, he claimed a brace of German fighters:

I was leading the Tangmere Wing on Rodeo 263 and was flying with No 41 Squadron. We swept Bernay, Beaumont and Evreux area at 8,000ft. After turning approximately ten miles north of Evreux, I sighted between 25 and 30 109s and 190s 5,000ft above and coming round the sun. I increased speed as the enemy came down to attack. I put the Wing into a steep climbing turn to port. The enemy aircraft opened fire at extreme range without success; they then dived away steeply.

I spotted one Me 109G flying at 7,000 ft and approximately 1,000 ft below me, diving towards the ground. I immediately gave chase and opened fire with a five-second burst on this aircraft from approximately 400 yards. When the enemy aircraft was about 500ft from the ground it flipped over on its back and immediately went into the ground with a violent explosion. This was confirmed by my No 2, Group Captain Crisham.

The Spitfire XII airframe was based closely on the Mk V, which meant it had no extra fuel capacity. This proved problematic as the fighter's Griffon engine was appreciably thirstier than its Merlin predecessor. The Mk XII's range was, therefore, even worse than the notoriously short-legged Merlin Spitfire. In an effort to improve their fighters' combat radius, Nos 41 and 91 Sqns routinely flew Spitfire XIIs fitted with 30-gallon underbelly slipper tanks on operations from Westhampnett. Just such a store is seen here affixed to MB882 – the last Mk XII delivered to the RAF.

Wg Cdr Harries sits in a Spitfire IX from No 349 'Belgian' Sqn at Tangmere in July 1944. This unit was part of No 135 Wing, which Harries commanded from just before D-Day through to January 1945. He made two claims with the wing, one of which was his 18th, and final, victory.

Wg Cdr Harries poses with his recently awarded *Croix de Guerre*, which he received from the Belgian government on 15 June 1945. He had also been presented with a *Croix de Guerre* by the Free French government in March 1944. The ribbons on Harries' service dress tunic show that he had previously received a DFC and two Bars and a DSO and Bar.

I was now at deck level and headed out for the coast. When I was near Rouen, four 109s came down from starboard to attack me. I broke between them and a dogfight ensued, which lasted about 2½ minutes. I managed to get around, and allowing approximately 2½ rings deflection gave the enemy aircraft a short burst. The enemy aircraft whipped on its side and exploded on hitting the ground. I managed to climb up and make use of slight cloud cover, thereby evading the other three enemy aircraft, and I did not see them again. One of the enemy aircraft hit my aircraft behind the cockpit with light ammunition, but did not cause much damage. I re-crossed the French Coast near Fécamp and did not experience any flak.

Given a break from operations at year-end and sent on a lecture tour to the USA in early 1944, Harries returned to take command of Spitfire IX-equipped No 135 Wing – part of the 2nd TAF – in the spring. Leading the unit to France shortly after D-Day, he claimed his final victory in July 1944 to take his tally to 15 and three shared destroyed. Harries was posted to No 84 Group as Wing Commander Training in early 1945, and he remained in this position through to war's end – by which point he had received a Bar to his DSO.

Harries continued to serve in the RAF post-war, and he was given command of Meteor F 4-equipped No 92 Sqn at Linton-on-Ouse, North Yorkshire, in late 1949. On 14 May 1950, he became lost in bad weather over Liverpool Bay and was killed while trying to bale out of his fuel-starved Meteor.

Spitfire XII EN625/DL-K of Sqn Ldr Ray Harries, OC No 91 Sqn, Hawkinge, Kent, May 1943

This aircraft was delivered new to No 91 Sqn on 13 May 1943. Twelve days later, it was being flown by unit CO Sqn Ldr Ray Harries when the Griffon-engined Spitfire had its first significant encounter with the Luftwaffe. Harries was credited with two Fw 190s destroyed, and went on to claim a further nine victories with Mk XIIs, making him the most successful pilot in Griffon-engined Spitfires. EN625 was subsequently used by Flg Off Ray Nash to destroy an Fw 190 and a Bf 109G later in the year prior to it being destroyed in a forced landing on 11 December that saw the fighter lose its starboard wing.

SVEIN HEGLUND

Svein Heglund was the highest-scoring Norwegian ace of World War Two, and he claimed most of his 15 victories in Spitfires.

Born in Kristiania (now Oslo) on 10 December 1918, Svein Heglund tried unsuccessfully to enlist in the Norwegian Army Air Service in the autumn of 1939. Having subsequently travelled to Zurich in Switzerland to study engineering, he was on a cycling trip in Italy when Norway was invaded by Germany in April 1940.

Returning to Switzerland, Heglund managed to flee to the United States via Bordeaux and Portsmouth. Once in North America, he headed north to Toronto, Canada, upon hearing of the establishment of a Royal Norwegian Air Force (RNoAF) training camp – soon christened 'Little Norway' – in southern Ontario.

From July 1940, Heglund spent a full year learning to fly, progressing from the Cornell primary trainer to the Harvard, before graduating to RNoAF Curtiss Mohawks and Douglas 8A-5s. Posted to Britain in July 1941, he undertook conversion training on to the

No 331 Sqn flew south from Skeabrae to North Weald on 4 May 1942, and this photograph was taken at the Essex airfield shortly after the unit had arrived en masse. One of these Spitfire VBs was flown south from the Orkney Islands by Sgt Svein Heglund.

Hurricane II with No 59 OTU at Crosby-on-Eden, Cumberland, and was then posted to recently formed No 331 'Norwegian' Sqn at Skeabrae as a sergeant pilot in October. The unit received Spitfire IIAs in place of its Hurricane IIBs shortly thereafter.

Following months of tedious convoy escort missions and patrols over the naval base at Scapa Flow, No 331 Sqn was issued with Spitfire VBs in April 1942. Just a matter of weeks later, the unit was sent south to No 11 Group to join the North Weald Wing. Heglund quickly hit his stride, making six claims (all of them against Fw 190s or Bf 109s) between June 1942 and February 1943. With more than 200 hours of operational flying in his logbook, and having attained the rank of second lieutenant, he was sent to Spitfire-equipped No 57 OTU at Eshott, Northumberland, as an instructor in February 1943. Returning to No 331 Sqn three months later, he had been promoted to captain and made a flight commander by June.

Flying a Spitfire IX, Heglund would enjoy considerable success through to November 1943, when he concluded his second tour with No 331 Sqn. The Norwegian made no fewer than 18 claims during this period, all of them against German fighters. His first success in the Mk IX came on 2 February over Saint-Omer, France. Heglund's combat report stated:

I was flying Yellow 1 when the squadron, after having climbed through clouds, was flying level at 25,000ft on a southerly course. About ten minutes after having crossed the French coast at Dunkerque, we met a single aircraft flying an opposite course 2,000ft below. I reported the aircraft over the R/T, half-rolled and dived down behind it. Yellow 2 and 3 followed, and we quickly caught up with it. At about 100 yards, and still unobserved by the aircraft, I recognised it as an Me 109F. I opened fire with about ten degrees deflection, and after a short burst I saw an explosion in the cockpit and heavy black smoke and fire coming out. The Me 109 rolled over to the left into a dive. I believe the pilot was killed before he knew what happened, and when I pulled up I saw Yellow 3 fire at the aircraft, resulting in two explosions and pieces falling off the Me 109. The squadron reformed afterwards and returned to base.

Heglund 'made ace' with the destruction of an Fw 190 off Dunkirk on 9 August:

I was flying as Yellow 1 when, about five miles inland from the French Coast on the way out, I reported seeing an enemy aircraft diving on 331 Sqn from behind. I broke to the right and saw some enemy aircraft firing at some of ours. I picked out some FWs that were making a gentle climb after an attack and came in on a port turn above and

Pilots from No 331 Sqn enjoy the sunshine at North Weald in February 1943. Lt Heglund, standing at far right, had by then made six claims (two of which were for victories), and he was posted to No 57 OTU as an instructor later that same month.

behind them. I tried to get close in behind the right-hand one but he made a barrel roll and I thought he was going to dive away, so I went after the other one. However, he dived away and I closed on the first one. He made a sharp turn to port and I opened fire from astern from about 300 yards, giving a burst of a couple of seconds, but missed him owing to too little deflection.

I closed in further to 100 yards, giving more deflection, and saw a large explosion in the cockpit. He went slowly into a dive, with a great deal of flames coming out from the front fuselage. I believe it was the petrol tank burning. Several of the pilots saw it going down in flames, including Lt Bache (Blue I), who first saw it hit in the wing roots and cockpit and then, finally, burning on the beach.

The Norwegian's seventh victory, on 16 August, almost resulted in the destruction of his own Spitfire, as Heglund recounted in his combat report:

I was leading Yellow Section when, over the second target [Abbeville], I saw approximately ten enemy aircraft attacking bombers from behind at the same height. 331 [Sqn] dived to break off the attack and most enemy aircraft flicked over and dived down. Two, however, turned sharply to port and went right below Yellow Section on an opposite course. I rolled over and got into position dead astern on the last of two enemy aircraft. Opening up at 300 yards with machine guns and cannon, I closed to 200 yards. Cannon strikes were observed all over the cockpit and fuselage and a big explosion, followed by large pieces falling off, one of which (part of the hood from the enemy aircraft) hit my spinner. The Fw 190 then turned on its back as if to dive away, and I also turned. From this position I gave the enemy aircraft another burst, resulting in a large explosion in the wing – probably ammunition. As other Fw 190s were in the vicinity, I pulled up. My No 4, 2/Lt Larsen, saw the enemy aircraft I attacked dive down vertically and finally crash into the ground in flames.

That same month Heglund was awarded a DFC, followed by a Bar for this decoration in October. His final claims in a Spitfire with No 331 Sqn came on 24 October ten miles east of Abbeville during a Ramrod by the North Weald Wing:

Capt Heglund came close to being lost during an action with an Fw 190 near Poix, in northern France, on 16 August 1943 after his Spitfire IX, MA568, was struck by part of the canopy hood as it was discarded by his opponent while abandoning his mortally damaged fighter. Despite MA568's spinner being severely dented, the Spitfire remained fully serviceable and Heglund returned to North Weald. This victory took his tally to eight. Note the Norwegian national colours applied to the cannon barrel.

Above: This rare photograph shows Capt Heglund's MA568 about to be refuelled at North Weald in September 1943, while two Spitfire IXs from No 331 Sqn prepare to break and land following an operation. MA568 was delivered new to the Norwegian-manned unit in late June 1943, and it was assigned to Heglund in mid-August. He duly made 12 claims in the fighter between 15 August and 24 October, with six of them being credited to him as victories. All of his victims were either Fw 190s or Bf 109Gs.

Right: Capt Heglund claimed his final successes in the Spitfire on 24 October 1943, taking his tally in the aircraft to 11 and one shared destroyed, five probables and six and one shared damaged. Seen here at North Weald shortly thereafter, he ended his tour with No 331 Sqn the following month. Aside from the three months he spent instructing with No 57 OTU, Heglund had completed two tours in two years on operations with the Norwegian-manned unit.

I was flying as Yellow 1. After enemy aircraft were reported and 332 Sqn tried to engage them, I followed four of them with Yellow Section on a northerly course. Two broke to starboard and started to climb, and I followed these two enemy aircraft. The other two turned in behind us, but they were quite far behind so we took no notice. I pushed everything forward but did not close much before I came through blower [supercharger] height.

The enemy aircraft were ME 109Gs, and I opened fire from a range of 400 yards, closing to 200 yards. The first bursts were misses, but at close range I noticed machine gun hits and later several cannon hits underneath the wing root and the fuselage. This was followed by a large explosion, and the enemy aircraft was hidden from sight by black and white smoke. The enemy aircraft flicked around and went down pouring smoke. This was seen by the rest of Yellow Section, and Yellow 3 (Sgt Dogger) saw this enemy aircraft crash in a field. After attacking this one, I followed the other enemy aircraft and opened fire from 400 yds. I noticed several strikes before I ran out of ammunition.

After almost 11 months off operations, Capt Heglund secured a posting to Mosquito night fighter-equipped No 85 Sqn at Swannington in October 1944. Showing his undoubted skill as a fighter pilot, Heglund was credited with downing three Bf 110s while defending RAF Bomber Command Lancasters and Halifaxes from Luftwaffe night fighters during the night offensive over Germany through to VE Day. These victories were achieved in Mosquito XXXs, four examples of which are seen here parked in the No 85 Sqn dispersal area in the spring of 1945.

In November, Heglund was posted to RAF Ferry Command for a rest from operations, undertaking a twin-engined conversion course at Spittlegate, Lincolnshire. He was posted to No 45 Atlantic Transport Group at Dorval, Montreal, in March 1944, and over the next six months he ferried three Canadian-built Mosquitos, two Bostons and a Mitchell across the Atlantic to Britain.

Thanks to the assistance of high-scoring night-fighter ace Wg Cdr John 'Cat's Eyes' Cunningham, Heglund managed to secure a posting to Mosquito XXX-equipped No 85 Sqn at Swannington, Norfolk, in October 1944. The unit, which had formerly been led by Cunningham, was assigned to No 100 Group and tasked with defending RAF Bomber Command aircraft from Luftwaffe night fighters during the night offensive over Germany. Heglund and his navigator, Flg Off Robert Symon, were credited with three Bf 110s destroyed during the eight months the Norwegian ace served with No 85 Sqn.

In October 1945, Heglund was awarded a DSO, having finished the war as Norway's ranking fighter ace with 14 and one shared destroyed, five probables and six and one shared damaged. Briefly serving as the Norwegian Air Attaché in Sweden post-war, Heglund left the RNoAF in late 1945 in order to complete his studies in Switzerland. Re-joining in 1948, he then served principally in logistics until 1982. Retiring with the rank of major general, Svein Heglund passed away on 18 June 1998.

Spitfire IX MA568/FN-L of Capt Svein Heglund, No 331 Sqn, North Weald, Essex, September 1943

Delivered new to No 331 Sqn at North Weald on 25 June 1943, this aircraft was allocated to high-scoring ace Capt Heglund in mid-August. He would make 12 claims in the fighter (which had its cannon barrels painted in Norwegian national colours) between 15 August and 24 October, with six of them being credited to him as victories. All of his successes with MA568 took the form of Fw 190s or Bf 109Gs. The aircraft later saw operational service with Nos 229 and 603 Sqns, and it was sold to the *Armée de l'Air* in June 1946. MA568 was written off in a crash in April 1950.

EUGENIUSZ HORBACZEWSKI

The leading Polish Spitfire ace, Eugeniusz Horbaczewski claimed 11 victories in the fighter during combat on the Channel Front, in North Africa and over Italy.

Although born in Kiev, the capital of Ukraine, on 28 September 1917, Eugeniusz Horbaczewski was raised in Brest-Litovsk, then part of the Second Polish Republic. He was taught to fly gliders while at school and entered the Polish Air Force (PAF) Academy at Dęblin in 1938, graduating the following year. Horbaczewski received his commission on 1 September 1939 – the day Poland was invaded by neighbouring Germany. Lacking any operational experience, he saw no combat during the brief aerial campaign that ensued.

Like many surviving PAF pilots, he fled to France via Romania, Yugoslavia and Greece. Once there, Horbaczewski was assigned to a Polish-manned flight within the *Armée de l'Air* at Bordeaux, but again he failed to engage the enemy. Escaping to Britain in June 1940, Horbaczewski eventually received training on the Spitfire and joined No 303 'Warsaw-Kosciuszko' Sqn at Northolt, Middlesex, in August 1941. Flying a Mk VB, Horbaczewski made his first claim on 6 November 1941 when No 303 Sqn performed the close escort role for eight Hurricanes attacking barges on canals between Bergues and Nieuport during Low Ramrod 5. His combat report for this mission read as follows:

> Flying as No 2 to Flg Off Bieńkowski, I shared with him the attack on the first factory, and also saw bright flames issuing from the target. Later, I gave a burst from machine guns and cannon into another factory, which was comprised of two tall containers that appeared to be connected by horizontal pipes. Later, I saw an iron bridge over a canal blow up, apparently as a result of a bomb, and some pieces of the bridge hit and damaged my wings. Near Nieuport I fired at a large water tank and registered hits on it with my cannon.

Plt Off Horbaczewski (standing, with cigarette, fifth from right) and other pilots from No 303 Sqn pose in front of, and on, a Spitfire VB from the unit at Northolt in the spring of 1942. A number of them are wearing red scarves, synonymous with aircrew from the squadron. Horbaczewski made four claims (three destroyed) with No 303 Sqn between 6 November 1941 and 19 August 1942.

After leaving the French coast I covered two Hurricanes, and was later warned of some enemy aircraft on my starboard side. Noticing two other Hurricanes in that direction, I flew towards them and gave them cover. One of the Hurricanes appeared to have been hit by AA (anti-aircraft) fire or an enemy aircraft, as it was developing plenty of smoke and eventually dived into the sea. I was intending to circle the spot when I noticed an aircraft coming towards me. Its red nose showed me that it was enemy, and I turned sharply to port and met it head-on. Although it fired at me, its bullets went below me.

I was then warned of further enemy aircraft, and saw three approaching head-on. I recognised the light blue nose of a Spitfire at the front, being pursued by two Me 109s. When I turned towards them, the two enemy aircraft broke off and turned away. The Spitfire turned out to be that of Sgt Czeżowski of No 315 Sqn. I told him over the R/T that my compass was u/s and asked him to lead the way home. Then I lost him in the clouds, and when I came out I saw about eight Me 109s at approximately 600ft, and I again found myself over France, where much flak was coming around me. I took cloud cover, and in a gap I saw an Me 109E ahead of me, turning to starboard. Firing with cannon and machine guns with deflection, as I was approaching him I had to break off when I saw tracer bullets passing my aircraft. A short time later, however, I saw the same Me 109 again, and it was surrounded by a thick cloud of black smoke. I was then lucky enough to join up with Sgt Czeżowski again, who led the way to England, and we both landed at West Malling. I only had two to three gallons of petrol left in my tanks.

Following this combat Horbaczewski was credited with the only 'probable' of his career as a fighter pilot. His first confirmed

With his POLAND shoulder patch clearly visible on his battledress tunic, Plt Off Horbaczewski stares down the lens from the cockpit of a well-weathered Spitfire VB at North Weald in 1942. Although he enjoyed success in the air, the future ace earned a reputation for being 'hard to handle' when not in action, and he was eventually posted away from No 303 Sqn in September 1942.

victory came on 4 April 1942 in the form of an Fw 190. A Bf 109 followed 12 days later, and he was credited with shooting down a second Fw 190 during the disastrous Dieppe raid on 19 August. Despite these successes, Horbaczewski was deemed to be 'hard to handle' when not in action, and he was eventually posted away to No 302 'Poznan' Sqn at Kirton-in-Lindsey in September 1942 by his commanding officer, Sqn Ldr Jan Zumbach, following a series of minor infractions that culminated in him destroying a Spitfire.

Faced with little in the way of action if he remained with No 302 Sqn, Horbaczewski volunteered for service with the Polish Fighting Team (PFT) in March 1943. Attached to

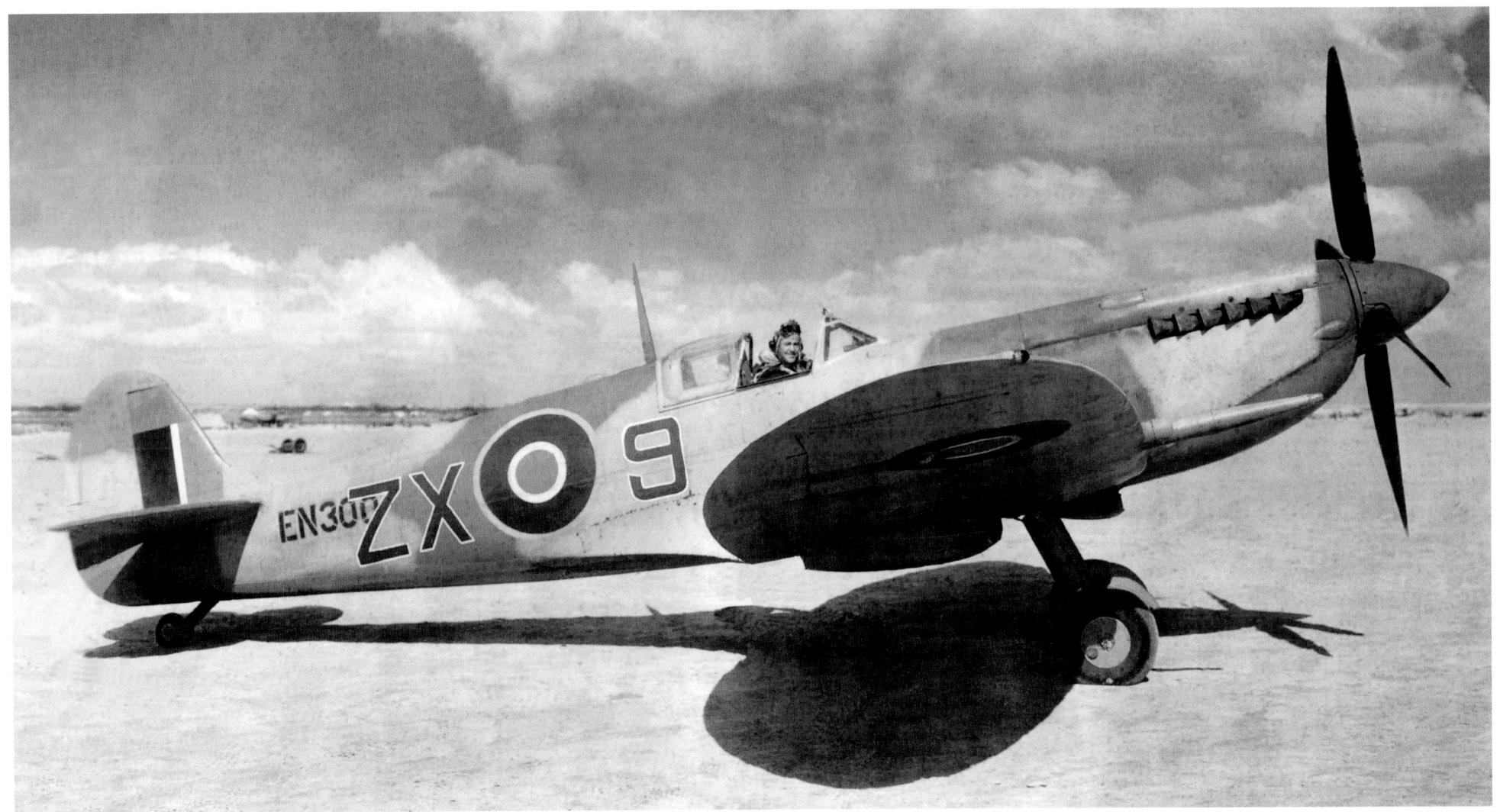

From March to mid-May 1943 Flt Lt Horbaczewski flew Spitfire IXs as part of the PFT within No 145 Sqn, claiming five victories in just 25 days. EN300 served with the unit throughout this period, and PFT members WOs Bronislaw Malinowski and Władysław Majchrzyk used the fighter to claim a victory each on 7 and 20 April, respectively. Transferred to No 1 Sqn SAAF, EN300 was eventually shot down in error by USAAF P-38 Lightnings off Catania on 14 July 1943.

Above left: Delivered to the PFT on 15 April 1943, EN355/ZX-O was flown in combat by aces WO Mieczyslaw Popek and Flt Lt Horbaczewski during the next two days. However, on 18 April, Flg Off Mieczysław Wyszkowski was shot down in it and taken prisoner.

Above right: Marked with full D-Day stripes and Sqn Ldr Horbaczewski's burgeoning mission and victory tallies, Mustang III FB382/PK-G of No 315 Sqn is seen at Coolham, in West Sussex, with its groundcrew after being armed with two 500lb bombs. This photograph was taken in mid-June 1944.

Right: Sqn Ldr Horbaczewski poses with Mustang III FB387 at Brenzett, in Kent, in July 1944. The fighter is marked with a detailed scoreboard that shows how many bombing missions he had flown in it, his overall victory tally and the number of V1s he had shot down. The Mustang III also has a PAF checkerboard beneath the exhaust stubs and the distinctive No 315 Sqn insignia forward of the cockpit.

the DAF, the PFT was heavily involved in the fighting over Tunisia through to the Axis defeat in North Africa on 13 May, operating as a third flight within No 145 Sqn. Although Horbaczewski got his all-important fifth victory on 2 April, the mission he flew four days later was more thrilling for him. The PFT's official account of the action read as follows:

> When flying north at 10,000ft, approximately ten miles south of Cekhira, Flt Lt Horbaczewski saw five Me 109s at the same height approaching from the east into the sun. He reported the enemy aircraft, but apparently his message was not received and he left his section to engage the Me 109s. He turned in behind the enemy aircraft, flying on the starboard side of a loose vic. A deflection shot from 200 yards was followed by a stern attack, closing in to 50 yards. There was an explosion in the Me 109 and the pilot baled out – the parachute did not open.

At this point Flt Lt Horbaczewski's aircraft was hit by fire from another Me 109. He turned on to his back to bale out as the engine was on fire, but this manoeuvre appeared to put out the fire, so he righted the aircraft and glided to Gabes L/G [landing ground].

Following the defeat of Axis forces in North Africa, the pilots of the PFT were given the option to join RAF units of the DAF in-theatre, rather than return to Britain as originally planned. Three of them accepted the offer, with Horbaczewski being posted to No 43 Sqn as a flight commander in July 1943 – he was made CO the following month. Horbaczewski would prove to be one of the RAF's best fighter leaders, earning both admiration and respect among his subordinates. This was primarily because he was an outstanding pilot and a courageous commander, leading his men into action. Having previously been something of a 'rogue pilot' in Britain, Horbaczewski also knew which disciplinary measures were desirable and effective.

Flg Off Jack Torrance of No 43 Sqn recalled many years later:

He came as 'A' Flight commander at a time when many experienced pilots had become time-expired and been posted away. Morale was not particularly high, and 'Horby' immediately injected a new spirit of aggression and confidence firstly into 'A' Flight and soon into the whole squadron. There was a great feeling of a new spirit in 43 Sqn. His first act, when appointed CO, was to lead a gaggle of 12 Spitfires on a training flight, put us all into line astern and, without warning, lead us into a formation loop. He also took individual pilots up for mock combats, and I consider him to have been the most accurate pilot of a Spitfire in my experience – he could perform aerobatics at a slower speed than any other pilot I knew.

Credited with eight victories (including three with No 43 Sqn) in six months in the Mediterranean, Horbaczewski was posted back to England in October 1943 and given command of Mustang III-equipped No 315 'City of Deblin' Sqn four months later. This unit was part of the 2nd TAF's No 133 Wing, and Horbaczewski claimed two-and-a-half victories and four V1s destroyed during operations in the early summer of 1944. On 18 August, during a Rodeo sweep of France, No 315 Sqn bounced 60 Fw 190s of JGs 2 and 26 over an airfield at Beauvais, in northern France. Although Horbaczewski was seen to down three Focke-Wulfs (and his unit was credited with destroying 16 in total), he was posted missing in action. His remains were eventually found in the wreck of his Mustang III near Valennes in 1947.

Spitfire VC JK539/FT-C of Flt Lt Eugeniusz Horbaczewski, No 43 Sqn, Pachino, Sicily, August 1943

Delivered to the RAF in March 1943, JK539 was shipped to the Mediterranean in April and arrived on Malta at the end of May. Supplied to No 43 Sqn, it was flown from Pachino airfield, southern Sicily, by Flt Lt Horbaczewski (among others) in early August 1943. Following operational service, JK539 was delivered to the Air Gunnery and Bombing School (Middle East) at El Ballah, Egypt, where it was written off in an accident on 4 July 1945.

PETRUS 'PIET' HUGO

Hailing from South Africa, 'Piet' Hugo had flown Hurricanes during the Battles of France and Britain before scoring many victories in Spitfires from 1942.

Born to farming parents in the Victoria West district of Cape Province, South Africa, on 20 December 1917, Pietrus 'Piet' Hendrik Hugo subsequently studied at the Witwatersrand College of Aeronautical Engineering. Following graduation, he travelled to England and joined the RAF on a short service commission in February 1939. His *ab initio* training was undertaken with No 6 E&RFTS at Sywell, after which Hugo completed his advanced course at No 13 FTS at Drem. Rated as an 'exceptional' pilot, he received his wings in October and was then posted to No 2 Ferry Pool at Filton, South Gloucestershire. From there, Hugo joined B Flight of No 615 Sqn at Vitry-en-Artois, France, on 17 December. At that point the unit was still equipped with Gladiator IIs, although these were replaced with Hurricane Is in April 1940.

Nicknamed 'Dutch' by the groundcrew of No 615 Sqn because they struggled to understand his Afrikaans accent, Hugo was credited with downing an He 111 on 20 May just 48 hours prior to his unit being pulled back to Kenley. He would make seven claims (including three and one shared destroyed) during the first month of the Battle of Britain. Two of these were for unconfirmed victories over the Channel during the early evening of 20 July when No 615 Sqn intercepted Ju 87s and their Bf 109 escorts near the Goodwin Sands. Hugo's combat report stated:

Plt Off Hugo (fourth from left) points something out on a map held by his flight commander, Flt Lt James Sanders, much to the amusement of his fellow No 615 Sqn pilots. In this staged shot, taken by a visiting press photographer at Vitry-en-Artois in April 1940, the unit's obsolete Gladiator IIs form an impressive backdrop. Fortunately for these pilots, the Gloster biplanes had been replaced by Hurricane Is prior to the launching of the *Blitzkrieg* in the West on 10 May.

At 1820 hrs, I was No 2 in Red Section of 615 Squadron, sent to intercept enemy aircraft off Dover. Sighted a large number of Me 109s which attacked us. After firing about four or five short bursts at 109s, I had a very good deflection shot at one 109, the attack developing into line astern. Length of burst – five seconds. Distance – 150 yards. Enemy aircraft poured forth grey smoke, turned over and spun down. Later I saw a parachute nearby, but do not know whether it was the pilot of the machine. A few seconds later I spotted a 109 gliding down with the engine apparently stopped. I attacked from above, and after firing about three–four seconds at a range of 300 yards down to 50 yards, enemy aircraft emitted black smoke and turned on its back. I later engaged two more 109s and expended all my ammunition.

On 18 August, however, it was Hugo's turn to be shot down after his Hurricane was bounced by a Bf 109 from JG 3 'out of the sun'. Having tried, unsuccessfully, to bale out, he crash-landed near Orpington, Kent, and was admitted to hospital with wounds to his head and left leg. He was awarded a DFC while convalescing, the citation to the decoration stating, 'Pilot Officer Hugo has displayed great keenness to engage the enemy on every possible

A pair of Hurricanes from No 615 Sqn return to Kenley following a patrol during the Battle of Britain in August 1940. Plt Off Hugo primarily flew P2963 during the campaign, making five of his claims in the aircraft. It was damaged in an engagement with Bf 110s on the afternoon of 16 August, with Hugo being slightly wounded.

occasion. During June and July 1940, he destroyed five enemy aircraft.' Hugo re-joined his unit on 22 September.

By then, No 615 Sqn had been posted north to Prestwick, Scotland, for a rest. Hugo would serve with the unit until November 1941, seeing considerable action in the cannon-armed Hurricane IICs issued to No 615 Sqn some four months earlier. Flying from Manston, Hugo was involved in the sinking of more than 20 ships, including three oil tankers, sailing just off the coast of France, Belgium and the Netherlands, as well as the destruction of four distilleries and a locomotive. Promoted to flight commander in September 1941 and then given command of Spitfire VB-equipped No 41 Sqn two months later, Hugo was awarded a Bar to his DFC on 25 November. The citation for the decoration stated:

Since early September 1941, this officer has participated in numerous attacks on enemy shipping, during which some 35 vessels have been either sunk, set on fire or damaged; also several E-boats were damaged in two further attacks. Other losses sustained by the enemy were a petrol storage tank, which was set on fire, and one of their aircraft destroyed. In the execution of operational tasks necessitating the greatest skill and determination, Flight Lieutenant Hugo has displayed high qualities of leadership and courage. Although he has been continuously engaged on operational flying since the war began, his enthusiasm remains unabated.

Having survived the disaster in France, where he was credited with downing an He 111 on 20 May, Plt Off Hugo made seven more claims during the early phase of the Battle of Britain. However, on 18 August, shortly before this photograph was taken, he was bounced by a Bf 109 and forced to crash-land his Hurricane near Orpington with wounds to his head and left leg.

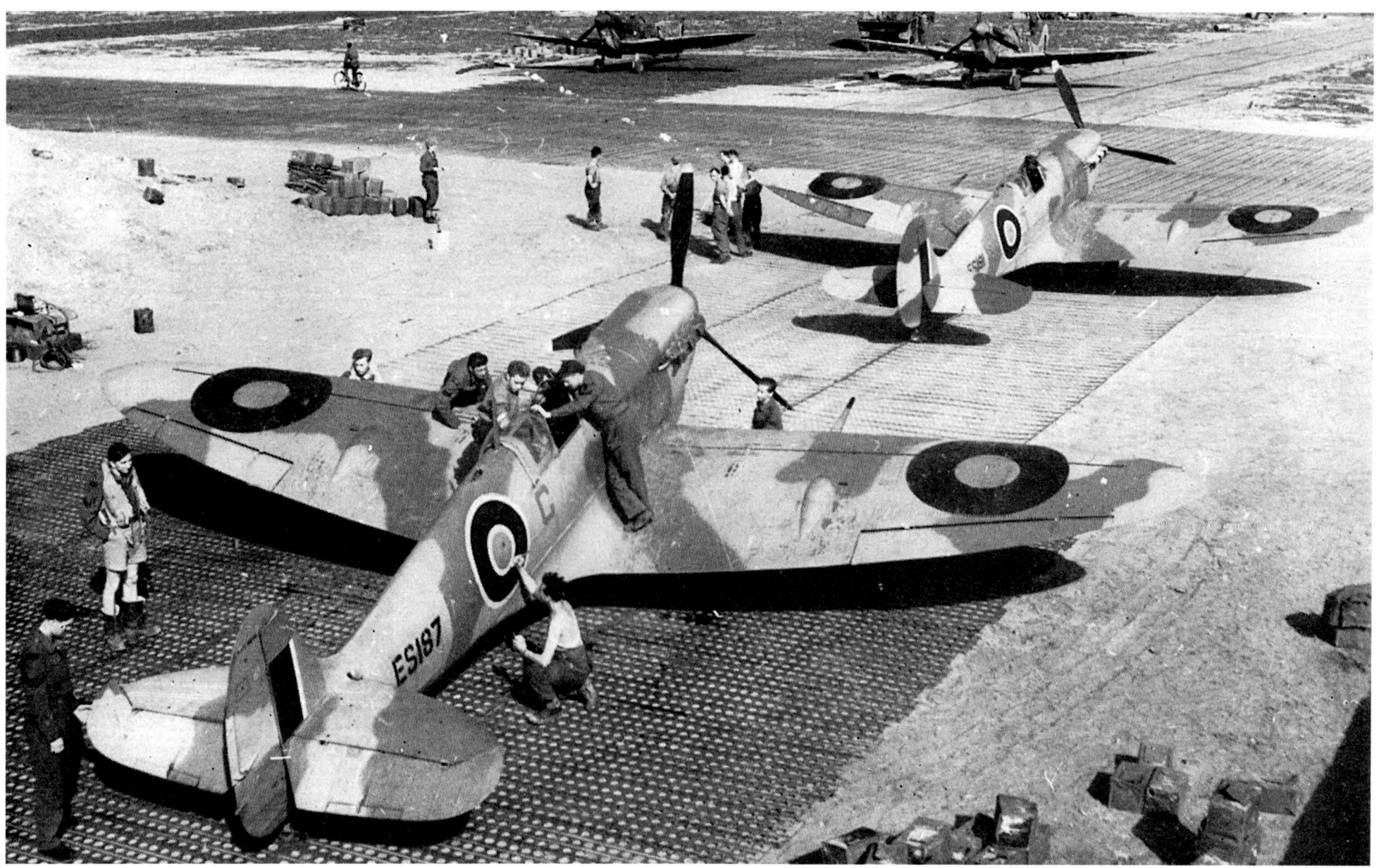
Spitfire VCs from No 154 Sqn are made ready for their next mission from the recently captured airfield at Djidjelli, in Algeria, in December 1942. This unit had been assigned to No 322 Wing upon its arrival in North Africa the previous month, and Wing Leader Gp Capt Hugo would frequently fly a No 154 Sqn aircraft on sweeps over enemy-held territory.

PETRUS 'PIET' HUGO

Flying from Westhampnett with No 41 Sqn as part of the Tangmere Wing, Hugo claimed three Bf 109s shot down in February–March 1942. Promoted to wing leader on 12 April, he was wounded for a second time just 15 days later when he was shot down into the Channel following a running battle with Fw 190s from II./JG 26. Hugo was awarded the DSO while recuperating, the medal citation reading as follows:

> This officer has completed over 500 hours operational flying, a large proportion of which has been on patrols over enemy territory. During the autumn of 1941, he performed outstanding work in attacks on enemy shipping. He is a fine leader and, during a period of five months from November 1941, his unit destroyed at least 12 and damaged several more enemy aircraft. Both as squadron commander and Wing Leader, this officer has displayed exceptional skill, sound judgement and fighting qualities, which have won the entire confidence of all pilots in his command. He has destroyed 13 hostile aircraft and damaged a further seven.

Posted to No 11 Group HQ following his spell in hospital, Hugo briefly led the Hornchurch Wing prior to assuming command of No 322 Wing in northwest Africa on the eve of Operation *Torch* in early November. By now a group captain, he would claim 11 victories at the controls of a Spitfire VC over Algeria and Tunisia during the next 12 months. Among Hugo's kills was a Ju 88 downed over the Algerian port city of Bone, as described by the CO of No 72 Sqn, Sqn Ldr Bobby Oxspring:

Piet led 81 Sqn and us in 72 on a sweep to the Tabarka area. As we climbed out of Bone we sighted a lone Ju 88 pushing his luck as he crossed our track. We poured on the coals in a race to get there first and Piet got the edge and bored in on a full quarter attack.

Gp Capt Hugo handed over control of No 322 Wing to high-scoring Spitfire ace Wg Cdr Ronald 'Ras' Berry in January 1943, after which he was posted to HQ, Northwest Africa Coastal Air Force. Hugo subsequently returned to command No 322 Wing for a further 18 months from June of that year.

His shooting was a sight to behold, as with one long burst his cannon shells raked the enemy from nose to tail. With a momentary fiery explosion, it disintegrated and fell in a shower of bits.

Piet was everywhere at this time, urging us to maximise our efforts. In spite of all his onerous command responsibilities, he found time to fly with us whenever he could.

After a short spell at HQ, Northwest Africa Coastal Air Force in the spring of 1943, during which time he received a second Bar to his DFC, Hugo returned to command No 322 Wing for a further 18 months from June of that year. His wing flew from airfields on Malta and Sicily, before moving to Italy in September 1943. Hugo also led the wing over Corsica, southern France and the Balkans. Indeed, it was while on a sweep along the Albanian coast

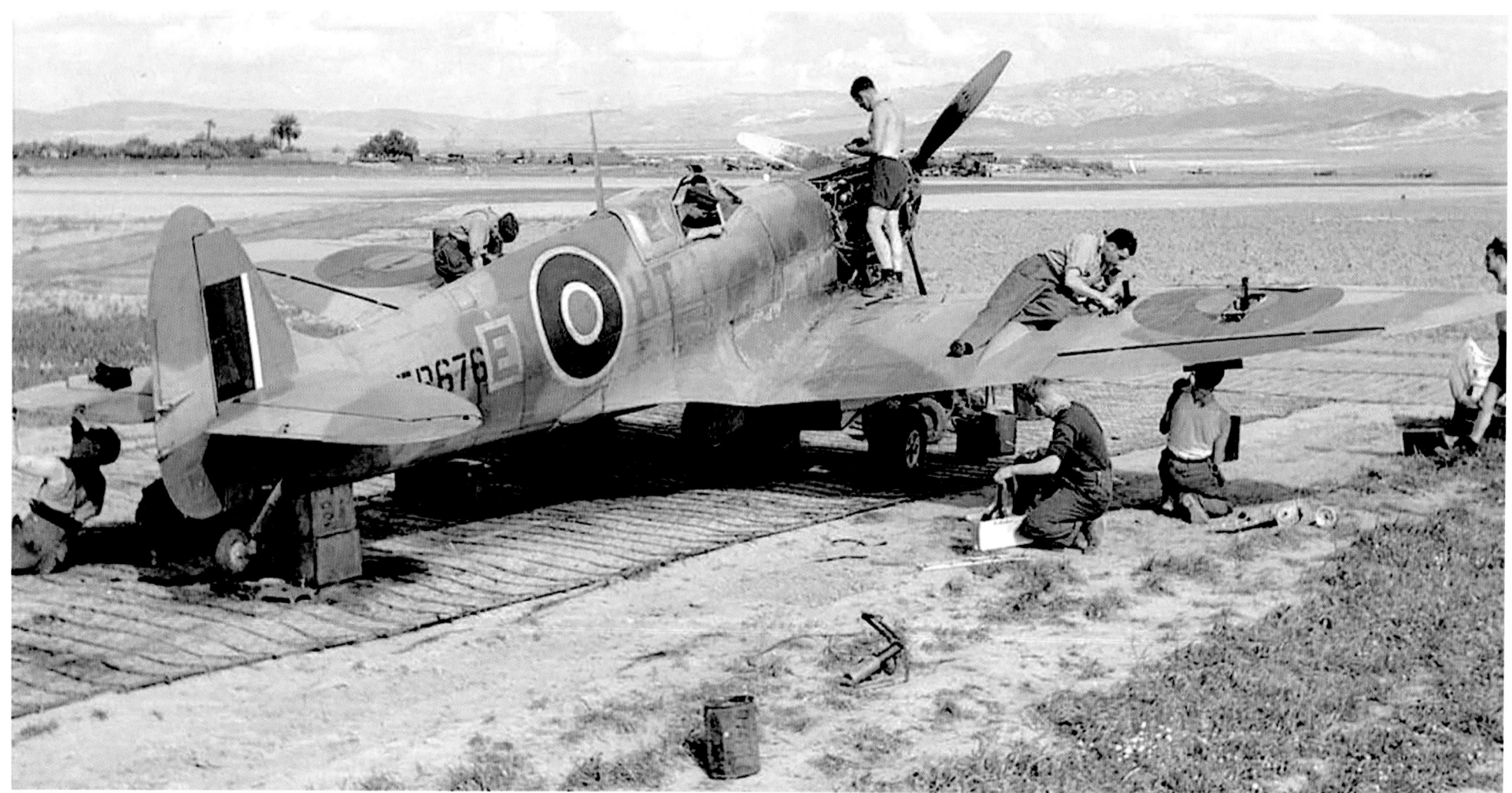

Spitfire VB ER676 of No 154 Sqn is serviced out in the open at 'Victoria' (Souk el Khemis). This aircraft, which had previously served with fellow No 322 Wing unit No 242 Sqn, was lost while escorting B-25s targeting Tunis on 25 April 1943. Hugo enjoyed notable success during his two spells in command of No 322 Wing, making 15 claims (11 of which were confirmed victories) between 12 November 1942 and 10 July 1944.

with Spitfire VC-equipped No 232 Sqn that Hugo achieved his final success when he spotted a lone Ar 196 floatplane flying low over Tivat Bay:

> I caught up with the aircraft at 100ft, about eight miles due south of Tivat and about 200 yards offshore. At 250 yards I opened fire with cannon and machine guns, almost immediately scoring hits on the port float, which caught fire, and the port wing and fuselage. The aircraft turned slightly left, the engine and whole fuselage caught fire, and just as I stopped firing and broke away, it blew up. After straightening up from the breakaway, I saw most of the aircraft on fire crash into the sea very close inshore, with other fragments falling around it and a few fragments on shore.

By the time No 322 Wing was disbanded in November 1944, Hugo had taken his final tally to 17 and three shared destroyed, two unconfirmed destroyed, three probables and seven damaged. Aside from his British decorations, he had also received an American DFC for his leadership of No 322 Wing in Italy. The award citation noted:

> For extraordinary achievement while participating in aerial flights from Corsica under American command from 23 April to 23 June 1944. During this period, his command was in tactical support of the Allied ground forces in Italy, and flew more than 536 missions, destroying 20 enemy aircraft, 234 motor transport and miscellaneous enemy shipping. Group Captain Hugo was personally responsible for great destruction and damage to materiel and communications so vital to the enemy. His inspiring aerial leadership, steadfast devotion to duty and personal example reflect great credit to himself and the Allied Air Forces.

A series of staff postings followed, and Hugo remained in the RAF until taking retirement in February 1950. With help from the British government, he acquired a farm on the slopes of Mount Kilimanjaro in Tanganyika (now Tanzania), where he grew wheat and ran cattle. His land was expropriated by order of the Tanzanian government in 1971 and Hugo was deported to South Africa, where he started farming once again near where he was born in the Victoria West district of Cape Province. 'Piet' Hugo died of a heart attack on 6 June 1986.

Spitfire VIII MT678/P-H of Gp Capt 'Piet' Hugo, OC No 322 Wing, Calenzana, Corsica, August 1944

Like most wing leaders, Gp Capt Hugo had his initials applied to his aircraft – in this case, Spitfire VIII MT678. No 322 Wing consisted of four units from the spring of 1944, with Nos 154 and 451 flying Mk VIIIs and Nos 232 and 242 Sqn equipped with Mk IXs. Hugo made no claims in this aircraft, which was issued to him as a brand new airframe upon its arrival in-theatre in late May 1944. MT678 was later passed on to No 92 Sqn.

'JOHNNIE' JOHNSON

'Johnnie' Johnson was not only the leading Spitfire ace of World War Two, but he was also a highly effective wing leader.

James Edgar 'Johnnie' Johnson was born in Barrow upon Soar, near Melton Mowbray in Leicestershire, on 9 March 1915. Graduating from Nottingham University with a degree in civil engineering in 1937, he found employment as a surveyor and then as an assistant engineer. It was during this period he started to take flying lessons while trying – unsuccessfully – to join the Royal Auxiliary Air Force. Accepted into the Leicestershire Yeomanry instead, Johnson was called up for service with the RAFVR in August 1939 and commenced flying training shortly thereafter.

Mobilised the following month upon the outbreak of war, he completed some flying on Tiger Moths with No 21 E&RFTS at Stapleford Abbots, Essex, and was then sent to No 22 Elementary Flying Training School (EFTS) in Cambridge in December 1939. He flew solo on 29 February 1940 and eventually completed the course in early May. Johnson then moved to No 5 FTS at Sealand, Wales, before concluding his training with Master-equipped No 7 OTU at Hawarden on 7 August. Flying a Spitfire for the first time shortly thereafter, Johnson was briefly posted to No 19 Sqn, before moving to No 616 Sqn at Coltishall on 6 September.

Having made it on to operations, he was quickly troubled by an old rugby injury from 1938 in which he had broken a collarbone. The bone had been incorrectly reset, leaving him with trapped nerves that caused numbness in his right hand when dogfighting in the Spitfire. Johnson was forced to have an operation, removing him from flying duties until late December 1940. Making up for lost time, and the disappointment of having missed the Battle of Britain, he played an active part in the cross-Channel offensive undertaken by No 616 Sqn from Tangmere in 1941. By the end of September, Johnson had made 13 claims (including five Bf 109s destroyed and one shared destroyed), resulting in him being awarded the DFC and promotion to flight leader.

A fighter pilot through and through, Johnson was no fan of the missions being flown over Occupied Europe by the Spitfire-equipped wings in Nos 10 and 11 Groups. He was particularly critical of ground-attack oriented Rhubarbs:

By the time this photograph of Wg Cdr Johnnie Johnson was taken at Kenley in the autumn of 1943, he had already made 45 claims (including 28 victories) during almost three years of uninterrupted combat. Leading the Canadian Wing from March 1943, Johnson enjoyed great success through to September, when he was finally posted out of the front line.

The 'leaning out' doctrine of the offensive included low-level flights over France known as Rhubarbs. The idea was to take full advantage of low cloud and poor visibility to slip sections of Spitfires across the coast, then let-down below the cloud to search for targets of opportunity – rolling stock, locomotives, aircraft on the ground, staff cars, enemy troops and the like. These flights were usually arranged on a voluntary basis, and a few pilots seemed to prefer this type of individual, low-level work to the clean, exhilarating teamwork of the dogfight. But the great majority of fighter pilots thought privately that the dividends yielded by the numerous Rhubarb operations fell far short of the cost in valuable aircraft and trained pilots.

I loathed those Rhubarbs with a deep, dark hatred. Apart from the flak, the hazards of making a let-down over unknown territory with no accurate knowledge of the cloud base seemed too great a risk for the damage we inflicted. During 1941, hundreds of pilots were lost on either small or mass Rhubarbs, and when I later held an appointment of some authority at No 11 Group, my strong views on this subject were given a sympathetic hearing and Rhubarbs were discontinued over France, except on very special occasions.

Away from the action, and southeast England, for extended periods in 1942, Johnson nevertheless received a Bar to his DFC in June and was given command of No 610 Sqn the following month. His victories during this period were an Fw 190 and a Bf 109 downed off Dieppe on 19 August during Operation *Jubilee*. Following the hectic action on this day, Johnson stated, 'Our Spitfire Vs were completely outclassed by the Fw 190s, and on this occasion I was certainly lucky to get back.'

Spitfire IX EN398 and Wg Cdr Johnson proved to be a deadly combination for German fighters in 1943, when the pair were credited with the destruction of 17 Bf 109s and Fw 190s over occupied Europe during operations by the Kenley Wing and, from August, No 127 Wing after the Kenley units were assigned to the newly formed 2nd TAF. This aircraft had been delivered new to No 402 Sqn in February 1943, and it was subsequently flown by Canadian-manned Nos 416 and 421 Sqns at Kenley through to the autumn of that year. EN398 wore Wg Cdr Johnson's JE-J codes for much of that time.

In March 1943, Johnson was promoted to wing leader of the Canadian Wing at Kenley. Its units were equipped with Spitfire IXs, which he used to make many claims during the spring and summer. On 15 June, for example, he was credited with two Fw 190s destroyed. His combat report for this mission stated:

I was leading the Kenley Wing (403 and 421 RCAF Squadrons) on Ramrod 95. We met other Spitfire wings off Fécamp at 27,000ft, and almost immediately afterwards Operations called up and said that the bombers were returning, but that we could carry out a shallow penetration at my discretion. There was a lot of high cumulus cloud, but as there was little in the Rouen area I decided to fly in that direction. Operations then told me that bandits were climbing over Rouen and flying west. I set a course to intercept these bandits and flew at 24,000ft in order to avoid making smoke trails.

Shortly afterwards, we saw 15 Fw 190s flying towards the coast in line abreast. I ordered 421 to remain top guard and led 403 to attack. I myself attacked the starboard 190 with cannon and machine gun, closing to 200 yards. I registered several cannon strikes on this enemy aircraft, which pulled violently upwards almost to the stall. The hood was jettisoned and I saw the pilot drop out, but I did not see his parachute open; this enemy aircraft is claimed as destroyed.

I then saw a further 15 Fw 190s on my port side, and they had gone into line astern – all turning to port very slowly and covering about two miles. I closed in on the last enemy aircraft and attacked him with cannon and machine guns from five–ten degrees port astern, closing to good range. I registered several cannon strikes and pieces flew off this enemy aircraft. As he went into a slow spin his magazine in the starboard wing appeared to explode and

Wg Cdr Johnson, Wing Leader of No 144 Wing, and his dog 'Sally' are seen sat on the wing of Spitfire IX MK392 at Bazenville (B2) on 31 July 1944. By then, the fighter's D-Day stripes had been heavily weathered due to the high tempo of operations in the wake of the Normandy landings almost two months earlier. Johnson claimed 12 fighters destroyed in this Spitfire (including his final success on 27 September 1944), which served exclusively with Canadian squadrons.

Wg Cdr Johnson is surrounded by the No 127 Wing leadership cadre at Evere (B56), in Belgium, in January 1945. They are, from left to right, Sqn Ldr Danny Browne (OC No 421 Sqn), Gp Capt W R 'Iron Bill' McBrien (CO of No 127 Wing), Wg Cdr 'Johnnie' Johnson (Wing Leader, No 127 Wing), Sqn Ldr Jim Collier (OC No 403 Sqn) and Sqn Ldr E P 'Eep' Wood (formerly OC No 403 Sqn).

huge pieces of fuselage and wing were blown off. He was soon completely enveloped in black smoke, and this enemy aircraft is claimed as destroyed. Cine gun fitted and used.

In August, the Kenley Wing became No 127 Wing in the new 2nd TAF. Leading sweeps and bomber escort missions over France, Belgium and the Netherlands, Johnson was credited with 14 and five shared victories (all fighters) between April and September 1943. He was awarded a DSO in June and a Bar to this decoration three months later.

Rested from operations in September 1943, Johnson became part of the Planning Staff at HQ No 11 Group until he was posted as wing leader to newly formed, Spitfire IX-equipped, No 144 Wing of the RCAF in March 1944. He would claim ten more victories with the wing through to early July 1944, by which time Johnson had led it to Normandy following the D-Day invasion – a second Bar to his DSO was gazetted that same month.

Left: 'Johnnie' Johnson continued to serve in the RAF post-war, completing an exchange tour with the USAF that involved more combat in the Korean War, commanding fighter and bomber bases in Britain and West Germany and eventually rising to the rank of air vice-marshal.

Below: On 11 July 1957, Gp Capt 'Johnnie' Johnson made his final flight in a Spitfire when he ferried this aircraft, PR 19 PS853, from Duxford to Biggin Hill, where it joined the newly formed Historic Aircraft Flight – the precursor to the Battle of Britain Memorial Flight. Delivered to the RAF in January 1945, it had been flown along with other PR 19s by the Meteorological Research Flight Temperature and Humidity Flight at Woodvale, in Merseyside, from July 1950 until its retirement. The aircraft has been owned and operated by Rolls-Royce since 1996.

When No 144 Wing was disbanded in early August, Johnson returned to the command of No 127 Wing. The last of his 34 and seven shared victories (officially making him the RAF's top-scoring fighter pilot of World War Two) were claimed with this unit, Johnson downing two Fw 190s on 23 August during a sweep of the Paris area at the head of Nos 421 and 443 'Hornet' Sqns. Despite his success, Johnson was impressed by the performance of his opponents during the engagement. 'I was attacked by six short-nosed '190s, which possessed an exceptional rate of climb. By turning into each attack, I managed to evade most of their fire, only receiving one hit in the starboard wing root.' This was the first, and only, time his Spitfire was hit by fire from an enemy fighter. Johnson's final victory came on 27 September while leading No 443 Sqn on patrol over the town of Rees, Germany. He described the action in his combat report:

> I saw nine Me 109s flying at ground level immediately below us. I led the squadron down to attack but enemy aircraft saw us and broke upwards into the attack, and a general melee ensued. I closed to 250 yards on an Me 109 turning to port, firing short bursts of cannon and machine gun. Strikes were seen on the port wing of the enemy aircraft. He peeled away and crashed into the ground.

On 6 April 1945, and now a group captain with more than 500 operational sorties to his name, Johnson took command of Spitfire XIV-equipped No 125 Wing and subsequently led it to Denmark shortly after VE Day.

Remaining in the post-war RAF, Johnson completed an exchange tour with the USAF in 1950–51 that saw him undertake combat missions in F-80 Shooting Stars and F-86 Sabres during the Korean War. Subsequent postings included station commander of RAF Wildenrath, West Germany, and V-bomber base RAF Cottesmore, Rutland. Eventually promoted to air vice-marshal, Johnson served as air officer commanding-in-chief, Air Forces Middle East, until he retired in March 1966. Highly active in civilian life, Johnson wrote several books on his wartime exploits. He also established a housing association (which currently provides homes for more than 5,000 residents) and a foundation supporting disabled charities. 'Johnnie' Johnson succumbed to cancer on 30 January 2001.

Spitfire XIV MV268/JEJ of Gp Capt 'Johnnie' Johnson, OC No 125 Wing, Reinsehlen (B154), Germany, April 1945

When Gp Capt Johnson took command of No 125 Wing in early April 1945, he chose MV268 as his personal Spitfire. It had only been with the wing a matter of days, having been issued to No 130 Sqn on 29 March. Struggling to find any enemy aircraft to engage during the final weeks of the conflict in Europe, Johnson failed to add to his tally in MV268. The fighter was assigned to No 401 'Ram' Sqn shortly after VE Day and then No 411 Sqn in late June. It was written off in a forced landing at Celle (B118), Germany, on 4 March 1946 while still serving with No 411 Sqn.

JAMES 'GINGER' LACEY

Having achieved great success flying Hurricanes in 1940, James 'Ginger' Lacey subsequently added to his victory tally in Spitfires on the Channel Front and in Burma.

Born in Wetherby, West Yorkshire, on 1 February 1917, James Harry 'Ginger' Lacey attended King James Grammar School in Knaresborough and then studied at Leeds Technical College from 1933. Lacey subsequently found employment as an apprentice pharmacist, although he never qualified. Having joined the RAFVR in January 1937, he was taught to fly in Perth, Scotland, on the first course run by No 11 E&RFTS. Indeed, he was also the first student to fly solo with the unit. The following year, Lacey qualified as an instructor with the Yorkshire Aeroplane Club, and he spent six weeks on attachment with No 1 Sqn at Tangmere in January 1939.

By the time he was called up in September 1939, Lacey had logged more than 1,000 flying hours. Posted to Hurricane-equipped No 501 Sqn at Tangmere as a sergeant pilot, he moved to France with the unit on 10 May 1940. Surviving being bombed on the ground and almost drowning following an emergency landing in a swamp, Lacey had been credited with five victories by the time No 501 Sqn was withdrawn to England on 19 June. He had also been Mentioned in Dispatches and awarded the French *Croix de Guerre*.

Although Lacey was forced to take to his parachute three times during the Battle of Britain, he also claimed 18 victories, five probables and six damaged between 20 July and 30 October. His first success of the campaign came during a convoy patrol from Warmwell, Dorset, when 12 Hurricanes from No 501 Sqn engaged Bf 109s escorting bombers that were attacking a Royal Navy destroyer south of the Isle of Wight. The unit's intelligence report noted in part:

Yellow Section, when approaching the destroyer, saw three Me 109s at 5,000ft turning to port, and Yellow 2 (Sgt Lacey) reported this to Red 1 over the R/T. F/Lt Cox (Yellow 1) led the section round in pursuit and dived at the enemy 2,000ft below

No 501 Sqn pilots enjoy a brief moment of respite between operations from Béthenville, France, several days after the start of the *Blitzkrieg* on 10 May 1940. Four of these men would become aces – Flg Off 'Gus' Holden (far left) and Sgts Don McKay (second from left), 'Ginger' Lacey (third from left) and Paul Farnes (far right).

him. He made a first attack on one of them at 600 yards, and it dived and turned away. He then climbed and attacked another at 250 yards, closing to 50ft. The Me 109 dived into the sea. Yellow 2 attacked and shot down the third Me 109 from a range of 150 yards.

Lacey would engage numerous Bf 109s during the course of the Battle of Britain, making 17 claims (including 13 destroyed) against the Luftwaffe's primary fighter. One of these came on the morning of 2 September, when No 501 Sqn sent 13 Hurricanes aloft from Gravesend, Kent, to patrol between Maidstone and Ashford. The unit soon spotted a large formation of Do 17s, escorted by more than 50 Bf 109s, approaching from Folkestone. As No 501 Sqn circled round to attack from the beam, it was bounced by the escorts. Lacey's combat report for the ensuing action read as follows:

I was leading Yellow Section when 501 Squadron attacked the Me 109s escorting Do 215s [actually Do 17s of III./KG 3]. Three Me 109s had climbed above the flight, and to prevent them diving on the squadron from behind, I also climbed and attacked them.

I was able to get in a good burst of about five seconds at a red-cowled Me 109, but the enemy aircraft immediately turned and I observed no damage. As I followed it round in the turn, I was unable to bring my guns to bear, but after about 30 seconds of circling, the Me 109 pilot jumped out and did a delayed drop of about 5,000ft before opening his parachute.

Most of the other Me 109s were engaged, so I dived out of the dogfight and attacked No 5 in the last formation of Do 215s. Almost as soon as I opened fire, the Do 215 broke out of formation and turned southeast with smoke issuing from its starboard engine. I continued to fire until my ammunition was exhausted, when I broke away to observe results. The enemy aircraft lost

Commissioned as a pilot officer in January 1941, 'Ginger' Lacey made the conversion to the Spitfire I with the rest of No 501 Sqn at Colerne, Wiltshire, in April of that year. The unit would switch to the Spitfire IIA two months later and move to Chilbolton, from where Lacey claimed four victories in two weeks.

height rapidly until it reached 5,000ft, which seemed to be its absolute ceiling on one engine, and then proceeded out to sea towards France, losing height very slowly. I then returned to base and landed.

Lacey had been awarded a DFM on 23 August, followed by a Bar to this decoration on 26 November. The citation to the latter read, 'Sgt Lacey has shown consistent efficiency and great courage. He has led his section on many occasions, and his splendid qualities as a fighter pilot have enabled him to destroy at least 19 enemy aircraft.'

On 16 July 1941, recently promoted Flt Lt Lacey was presented with a silk scarf and the first parachute manufactured in Australia for use by the RAF. The scarf was autographed by the workers employed by Dominion in its parachute factory in Sydney. Wearing both the scarf and the parachute, and watched by other pilots from No 501 Sqn, Lacey prepares to climb into his Spitfire II, P7990, at Chilbolton. He had shot down a Bf 109 in this aircraft just six days earlier, and Lacey would claim an He 59 floatplane destroyed ten miles south of Portland (in P7448) 24 hours after this photograph was taken.

Having survived being shot down or forced to crash-land as a result of enemy action on no fewer than nine occasions during the Battles of France and Britain, Lacey was commissioned as a pilot officer in January 1941 and promoted to flight commander with No 501 Sqn six months later. During July of that year, while flying a Spitfire II from Chilbolton, Hampshire, he added four more victories to his tally.

After more than a year on operations, Lacey was posted to No 57 OTU at Hawarden in August to serve as an instructor. Eventually returning to operations with Spitfire VB-equipped No 602 Sqn at Kenley seven months later, Lacey claimed two Fw 190s damaged prior to his tour being cut short when he was posted to HQ, No 81 Group as Tactics Officer. Following two more staff postings, Lacey was sent to India in March 1943 to join No 20 Sqn as it transitioned from Lysanders to Hurricanes. A move to No 1572 Gunnery Flight ensued in July 1943, when he helped Blenheim IV squadrons convert to Hurricane IIs and, later, Hurricane II squadrons switch to Thunderbolts.

Finally, in November 1944, Lacey returned to operations with No 155 Sqn, equipped with Spitfire VIIIs. He then took command of similarly equipped No 17 Sqn shortly thereafter. Upon his arrival at his new unit he noted, 'Morale on the squadron is excellent, although it appears to have spent too much time in Ceylon and has become a

Built by Westland Aircraft at its Yeovil factory in the spring of 1941, Spitfire IA AR213 was delivered to No 57 OTU at Hawarden on 31 July that year. Just days later, Flt Lt Lacey joined the unit as E Flight commander after being posted out of the frontline for a rest from operations. He chose AR213 as his personal aircraft, and it had horizontal 'bouncer' stripes applied to the nose during Lacey's seven-month spell with the unit. Remarkably, this aircraft remains airworthy in Britain, having been owned by Comanche Fighters and based at Duxford since 2011.

little stale. This staleness disappeared almost immediately, and we are now expectantly awaiting the appearance of the first Jap aircraft of No 17 Sqn's second Far East operational tour.'

Flying from a series of airfields in Burma, Lacey and his unit clashed with IJAAF Ki-43 'Oscar' fighters during the final months of World War Two. This allowed him to claim his 28th, and last, victory on 19 February 1945 south of Mandalay, reporting afterwards:

The enemy aircraft started a gentle turn to starboard and took no evasive action. Allowing just over one ring deflection, and from an angle off of about ten degrees, I fired a one-second burst [totalling just nine rounds] at a range of about 150 yards. Three cannon strikes were seen on the cockpit, which disintegrated the hood. The enemy aircraft turned slowly on its back and dived vertically towards the ground. We followed it down to 12,000ft but broke off when jumped by another 'Oscar' from above. This aircraft was evaded by a vertical climb to 18,000ft. On looking down, I then observed a large cloud of dust and smoke rising from the ground directly below the combat.

In early June, No 17 Sqn moved back to India to convert to the Spitfire XIV in preparation for the invasion of Malaya, codenamed Operation *Zipper*. Among its pilot cadre was Flt Lt Don Healey, who recalled the arrival of the new aircraft. 'We didn't get off to a great start with the Spitfire XIVE as the first one that arrived at Madura had the latest cutback fuselage, which drew the retort "that isn't a bloody Spitfire" from our somewhat maverick CO, "Ginger" Lacey, who promptly had it passed on to 11 Sqn! He refused to budge, and eventually high back aircraft arrived for 17.'

No 17 Sqn CO Sqn Ldr Lacey is flanked by two of his pilots, Plt Off F Irvine (right) and Flg Off Bob Connell (left). The latter was credited with scoring the last RAF victory over Burma on 29 April 1945 when he shot down an IJAAF fighter. Lacey had claimed his only aerial success in-theatre two months earlier on 19 February, taking his final tally to 28 destroyed, five probables and nine damaged.

Leading by example, Lacey became the first pilot in his unit to convert to the Spitfire XIV. Having made the switch, he confidently told his pilots 'there is no marked difference between it and the early marks [of Spitfire], although one is always comfortably aware of the enormous extra power'.

The Japanese surrender – announced by Emperor Hirohito on 15 August – meant that *Zipper* was not needed, although No 17 Sqn still flew its aircraft off the carrier HMS *Trumpeter* and landed at Kuala Lumpur, then in Malaya. On 30 April 1946, Lacey became the first pilot to fly a Spitfire over Japan when his unit was transferred to Miho as part of the British Air Forces of Occupation (BAFO). Returning to Britain the following month, Lacey was granted a Permanent Commission in the RAF, and he served as a fighter controller at various stations both at home and abroad until he retired with the rank of squadron leader in March 1967. He subsequently ran an air freight business and also instructed at a flying school near Bridlington on the East Riding of Yorkshire coast. 'Ginger' Lacey died from cancer on 30 May 1989.

When Spitfire XIVs of No 17 Sqn first moved to Japan from Singapore as part of BAFO, the unit was commanded by Sqn Ldr Lacey. His assigned fighter, RN135, marked with a squadron leader's pennant that features RAF wings and the number 17, heads this line-up of Mk XIVs seen at a damp Miho shortly after the unit arrived in Japan on 30 April 1946.

Spitfire XIV RN135/YB-A of Sqn Ldr James 'Ginger' Lacey, OC No 17 Sqn, Seletar, Singapore, September–December 1945

Marked with Lacey's full victory tally, his command pennant and No 17 Sqn's gauntlet insignia, inspired by the unit's operation of Gauntlet biplane fighters in the 1930s, RN135 had been shipped to India from England in February–April 1945. Issued new to the squadron in June of that year, it was immediately assigned to Lacey. When the squadron was transferred from Seletar to Miho in April–May 1946 as part of BAFO, the fighter remained Lacey's mount, although its markings were changed. RN135 was scrapped in Japan following the RAF's withdrawal in February 1948.

DON LAUBMAN

Don Laubman was one of the most successful pilots to fly a Spitfire with the 2nd TAF following the D-Day landings.

Donald Currie Laubman, born on 16 October 1921, in Provost, Alberta, was the eldest of seven siblings. His family moved to Edmonton shortly thereafter, where, as a child, he spent countless hours watching aircraft movements at the city's municipal airport. After graduating from high school, Laubman secured employment in a grocery store in downtown Edmonton situated directly across the street from an RCAF recruiting office.

Following his enlistment in September 1940, Laubman completed his flying training with No 3 SFTS in Calgary, Alberta, in May 1941. Rated an above average pilot, he was sent as an instructor to No 31 EFTS at De Winton, also in Alberta. Commissioned in July 1942, Laubman was posted to Kittyhawk-equipped No 133 Sqn at Boundary Bay, British Columbia, two months later.

No 412 Sqn Spitfire IX MJ485/VZ-Z, parked alongside a Typhoon on a Normandy ALG in late June 1944, was flown by Flg Off Don Laubman following the unit's move to Bény-sur-Mer (B4) 12 days after the commencement of Operation *Overlord*. He would claim three Fw 190s destroyed while in the aircraft in early July, but it was lost on operations on 8 August, resulting in the death of Flg Off G T Schwalm.

DON LAUBMAN

In August 1943, he was sent to Britain, where he joined Spitfire VB-equipped No 412 Sqn at Redhill. This unit was assigned to Canadian-manned No 126 Wing, which was in turn part of the newly formed 2nd TAF. Laubman would serve with No 412 Sqn until early November 1944, during which time he claimed 14 and two shared aircraft destroyed and three damaged. From D-Day through to VE Day, 13 RCAF pilots assigned to 2nd TAF were credited with more than 120 victories between them, and Don Laubman was the top scorer.

Eight of his victories were over Fw 190s, and he claimed his first two on 2 July 1944 during a dive-bombing mission southeast of Caen. 'There was an explosion and the Focke-Wulf was enveloped in flames', Laubman noted in his combat report. 'The pilot baled out.' A short while later he and two squadronmates spotted 15 more Fw 190s and gave chase. Singling out an enemy fighter and opening fire, he saw strikes on its engine and a wing. 'White smoke poured from him and his engine stopped', Laubman noted. 'I made a new attack and blew his port tailplane and rudder off with machine gun fire. The aircraft blew up.'

Laubman, who had now been promoted to flight commander, 'made ace' on 10 August. His greatest success came in late September, when the Canadian's growing tally of victories prompted coverage by news agency Reuters:

> With the Tactical Air Force in Belgium, September 27, 1944 – F/L Don Laubman, 23, of Edmonton, today destroyed four German planes and damaged two more to set a record for eight kills in three days. Laubman got two this morning, two more during the afternoon and damaged two more during the same patrol. All except one of his 'kills' were either Messerschmitts or Focke-Wulfs. Laubman's total of confirmed victories, all gained since D-Day, is now 13. His wing today destroyed 22 and damaged ten more.

Laubman claimed his final successes on 28 October when he downed two Fw 190s near Hohenbudberg during a day of intensive operations. The multi-volume official history *The RCAF Overseas – The Sixth Year* described Laubman's brace as follows:

> On the seventh operation undertaken by the Falcons [No 412 Sqn] on the 28th, Don Laubman, after attacking a train at Dorsten, sighted an aircraft below. Diving, he lost the enemy behind cloud but, continuing to ground level, he saw two FW190s which he chased across the Ruhr. As one of them was about to land near Krefeld, he closed in and

With 16 victories and three damaged between 30 December 1943 and 28 October 1944, 22-year-old Flt Lt Don Laubman of No 412 Sqn became the most successful Spitfire pilot in the 2nd TAF. He is seen here relaxing between operations at Evere (B56) in early September.

forced him to crash-land, the nose of the FW gouging into the ground and much smoke coming away from the wreckage. He then attacked the other, which went into the ground and exploded. Laubman, who had just been awarded a DFC, was now the leading scorer among Canadian pilots on operations at that time, his score amounting to 16 destroyed and three damaged. Ten of these victories were obtained in a period of five weeks.

As previously noted, Laubman had been awarded a much deserved DFC on 24 October. The medal's citation stated, 'This officer has consistently displayed outstanding courage and determination to engage the enemy and has destroyed at least five enemy aircraft. He has invariably pressed home his attacks with great success.' A Bar to the DFC followed on 24 November, with its citation reading:

Since being awarded the DFC, Flt Lt Laubman has completed many sorties against the enemy. He continues to show tenacity of spirit and outstanding courage in the face of overwhelming odds. Flt Lt Laubman had led his flight with such ability that it has accounted for 16 out of 26 enemy aircraft destroyed by his squadron, and he was responsible for the destruction of eight and the damaging of two in three days. This officer's squadron was outnumbered by the enemy on all three occasions, but with undaunted courage and determination it successfully broke up repeated attacks to destroy bridges vital to our ground forces in the Arnhem and Nijmegen areas.

Rested from operations, Laubman enjoyed leave in December, including spending time at home. This prompted the writing of the following story by the Canadian Press:

Holding his helmet, goggles and oxygen mask in his right hand, and with his parachute slung over his left shoulder, Flt Lt Laubman stares off into the middle distance for the benefit of a press photographer at Le Culot (B68) in late September 1944. He would make ten claims (eight of which were credited as victories) in just three days while flying from here in the defence of the recently captured bridges at Nijmegen, in the Netherlands. The Spitfire IX behind Laubman is almost certainly MJ393, which he used to make nine of his claims.

VZ-H of No 412 Sqn taxis out loaded with 1,000lbs of bombs at Volkel (B80) on 19 October – the first time Spitfire IXs of No 126 Wing carried one 500lb and two 250lb bombs as a full load. It was a heavy burden for the Spitfire, and the structural stress resulted in many 'wrinkled' wings. Replacement wings were easily obtained, however. Flt Lt Laubman participated in a handful of dive-bomber operations prior to being rested in late November.

Dutch workmen dig drainage ditches at Heesch (B88), while MJ275 VZ-J and MJ452 VZ-L stand ready with single 500lb bombs on their underbelly shackles in October 1944. Flt Lt Laubman's final aerial successes were claimed on 28 October when, during No 412 Sqn's seventh dive-bombing mission of the day, he downed two Fw 190s from II./JG 26 near their airfield at Hohenbudburg.

When recently promoted Sqn Ldr Don Laubman re-joined No 126 Wing in early April 1945, he was made CO of Spitfire XIV-equipped No 402 Sqn at Heesch (B88). Among the aircraft under his command was RN119, which later served with Laubman's old unit, No 412 Sqn, prior to being transferred to the Belgian Air Force in 1948.

Canada's highest scoring fighter pilot since D-Day, June 6, F/L Don Laubman, 23, DFC and Bar, with a score of 16 enemy aircraft to his credit, came home to Edmonton yesterday. He arrived here during the weekend with a large group of airmen repatriates, and after going through documentation formalities at nearby Rockcliffe Air Station, he boarded a train for home. The former Edmonton grocer was enthusiastic about being home, but he hoped to back in England again shortly. 'That's where I belong', he said.

The dawning of D-Day started his high-scoring effort. Up to that time his score against the Germans was a share in a downed aircraft. On June 16, the Canadian Spitfire Wing, of which Laubman was a member, landed in France. On July 2 he destroyed two

Focke-Wulf 190s – his first two kills. September 27 was the red-letter day in the life of the young Edmontonian. Just shortly after the airborne landings in the vicinity of Arnhem, the Canadian Spitfire Wing was working from early morning until late at night, and Laubman finished the day's work – three sorties – with four enemy aircraft destroyed and two damaged.

Once back from leave, Laubman undertook staff duties through to 6 April 1945, when he was given command of Spitfire XIV-equipped No 402 Sqn at Heesch (B88). His spell as CO lasted just a week, however. On 14 April, he strafed two half-tracks near Rethem, on the German side of the Rhine. After shooting up the first one, Laubman lined up the second just as his previous target exploded. 'I attacked them when I was no more than 20ft off the ground,' he recalled. 'They exploded in a ball of fire and I was right in the middle of it.' The conflagration engulfed his brand new Spitfire XIV, literally cooking its Griffon powerplant. Climbing to 7,000ft with his engine temperature rapidly rising, Laubman headed for Allied territory. Unfortunately, his damaged Spitfire burst into flames and he was forced to bale out into captivity. Laubman subsequently re-joined his unit on 5 May.

Post-war, he remained in the RCAF, commanding, successively, No 416 'City of Oshawa' Sqn, No 3 Wing, No 1 Air Division and, finally, Canadian Forces Europe. While based in West Germany, Laubman met a number of his former Luftwaffe opponents. 'They acted, and thought, exactly the same as we did,' he recalled. 'They were good guys – I liked them. I think in their eyes, as in ours, it was just a game to us fighter pilots.' Retiring from military service with the rank of lieutenant general in October 1972, Laubman then managed a series of stores for Canadian Tire until fully retiring in 1986. A committed servant to his community in the Alberta city of Red Deer, Don Laubman passed away on 20 June 2018, aged 96.

Spitfire XIV NH744/AE-Z of Sqn Ldr Don Laubman, OC No 402 Sqn, Rheine (B108), Germany, April 1945

When ace Sqn Ldr Don Laubman re-joined No 126 Wing as the new CO of No 402 Sqn on 7 April 1945, he was assigned Spitfire NH744, which had reached the unit just ten days earlier. On 14 April, Laubman spotted a pair of German half-tracks in the Rethem area of Lower Saxony, and after strafing one, he was in the process of lining up the second when his first target exploded. The subsequent fireball engulfed NH744, fatally damaging its Griffon powerplant. Climbing to 7,000ft with his engine temperature rapidly rising, Laubman headed for Allied territory. His damaged Spitfire soon burst into flames, however, and he was forced to bale out into captivity. Laubman was subsequently reunited with his unit on 5 May.

ERIC LOCK

Eric Lock was the RAF's leading Spitfire ace of the Battle of Britain with 20 confirmed victories, although he was gravely wounded shortly thereafter.

Unlike many of his high-scoring contemporaries from the bloody summer of 1940, Eric Lock, who was born in Shrewsbury, Shropshire, on 19 April 1919, had not served in a frontline RAF fighter unit pre-war. He had, however, briefly experienced flying in April 1933 when his father treated him to a 15-minute flight with Sir Alan Cobham's Flying Circus as a 14th birthday present. Five years later, Lock joined the RAFVR, and in February 1939 he was sent to No 28 E&RFTS at Meir, Staffordshire, to undertake a six-month *ab initio* training course. The flying element of the training was provided by civilian company Reid & Sigrist Ltd, with a variety of biplane types being used to teach would-be pilots.

Having completed the course by early August, Sgt Lock was posted to No 4 ITW at Bexhill-on-Sea, East Sussex, at the end of October, and then on to No 6 Service Flying Training School (SFTS) at Little Rissington, Gloucestershire, in December. Flying time in the Harvard I advanced trainer featured heavily in his logbook through to March 1940, when Lock received his wings. Having been promoted to pilot officer shortly thereafter, Lock was posted to Spitfire I-equipped No 41 Sqn at Catterick on 18 June.

During the first five weeks of the Battle of Britain, he and his squadronmates flew largely uneventful coastal patrols off the north coast of England. This all changed on 15 August when Norway-based *Luftflotte* 5 launched a raid on targets in northern England. No 41 Sqn was one of several Spitfire and Hurricane units from No 13 Group scrambled to intercept the approaching He 111 and Ju 88 bombers and their escorting Bf 110s. Spotting the enemy aircraft off Newcastle, the 13 Spitfires from No 41 Sqn manoeuvred into a line-astern formation and attacked from an altitude of 20,000ft. Lock went after a Bf 110 in the unit's second pass at the aircraft, as he described in his combat report:

> I fired two short bursts into the starboard engine of an Me110. This started to smoke, [and] it went down in a steep dive to port. I followed it down to 10,000ft, firing at the

Following six months recovering from severe wounds suffered in combat with a Bf 109 on 17 November 1940, Flt Lt Eric Lock returned to operations on 1 July 1941 as a flight commander with No 611 Sqn. Being one of the RAF's top four aces at this time, his arrival at Hornchurch was covered by the national press. This photograph was taken at the airfield in late June.

fuselage. The machine gunner stopped firing, then, continuing my dive, I fired at the port engine, which was then on fire. I left it at 5,000ft still in a vertical dive and with both engines on fire.

Despite participating in only his third operational mission, Lock had claimed his first victory. Eighteen days later, No 41 Sqn was posted south to Hornchurch, and between 5 September and 17 November Lock would be credited with 22 aircraft destroyed and eight probably destroyed – a record unmatched by any other RAF pilot during this period of intense action. Lock's first success flying from Hornchurch (on 5 September) saw him claim two He 111s and a Bf 109 destroyed in what proved to be No 41 Sqn's most successful day in aerial combat of the entire war. Its pilots were credited with nine victories, five probables and five damaged at a cost of two killed and three wounded during two missions patrolling between Thames Haven and Gravesend. Lock participated in the first of these operations, and his combat report read as follows:

I was Red 2, flying in formation with the rest of the squadron, when we intercepted a formation of enemy aircraft. We attacked the bombers first. After we engaged, we broke away to port, then I saw Red 1 shoot down an Me 109, which exploded in mid-air. It then developed into a dogfight. I engaged an He 111, and I followed this down until it crashed into the river. I climbed back to 8,000ft and saw an He 111, which had left the main formation. I engaged the bomber, and his starboard engine was set on fire. I closed in to about 75 yards and fired two long bursts and smoke came from the fuselage. The enemy aircraft then put his wheels down and started to glide. I stopped firing and followed him down.

I was then attacked by an Me 109, who fired at me from below and wounded me in the leg. As he banked away, he stall-turned. I fired at him and he exploded in mid-air. I then followed the bomber down that I had previously attacked, and he landed on the sea about ten miles from the first one in the mouth of the river. I circled round a boat, which was at hand. I also flashed my downward light – I saw the boat go to the enemy aircraft. I was then joined by Red 3. On our return we saw the first bomber, which was still floating.

With its pilots flying multiple times a day at this point in the campaign, RAF Fighter Command's resolve was being put to its greatest test. On 11 September, No 41 Sqn engaged a large formation of bombers (estimated at between 70 and 80 in number) and their Bf 110 escorts as they approached the Maidstone patrol line during mid-afternoon. Lock's combat report details the ensuing action:

I was patrolling with 41 Squadron as Yellow 2, when we sighted enemy aircraft. We went into echelon starboard – peeled off to port and dived on the enemy bombers, which broke up. I attacked a Ju88 [actually an He 111 from I./KG 26] from astern, giving it several bursts. This had little effect, so I then did a ¼ attack on same. Having carried out this attack, it dived. I did not see any effect from this ¼ attack, so I then attacked from below. This attack must have killed the pilot because it crashed in a field about 17 miles south of Maidstone. I circled it for a few minutes and noticed it was on fire. After about five minutes I saw it explode. I noticed that the Ju88 had white and black stripes painted on the tail fin.

I had climbed back to about 6,000ft when I was attacked by an Me 110. After a dogfight, which lasted for 20 minutes, he crashed with his starboard engine on fire about ten miles southeast of the Ju88. I received heavy fire from the rear gunner.

On 7 July 1941, an Air Ministry photographer visited Hornchurch and took a series of shots featuring No 611 Sqn aircraft and pilots. This staged image shows Flt Lt Eric Lock, Plt Off Wilfred Duncan Smith, Flg Off Peter Dexter and Sgt William 'Mac' Gilmour striding towards the camera. All four aviators would achieve ace status flying the Spitfire, with Duncan Smith claiming his fifth success the day after this photograph was taken. Dexter, who had actually 'made ace' on 7 July, was killed exactly one week later in a mid-collision with a No 54 Sqn Spitfire over Boulogne-sur-Mer.

I force landed at West Malling as I had run out of ammunition and petrol. Port wing damaged.

Nicknamed 'Sawn Off Lockie' by his squadronmates due his diminutive stature (he was 5ft 6in tall), Lock was awarded a DFC in late September. The citation for the decoration noted, 'This officer has destroyed nine enemy aircraft, eight of these within a period of one week [from 5 to 11 September]. He has displayed great vigour and determination in pressing home his attacks.' A Bar to this decoration would follow on 22 October, the citation accompanying it stating:

> In September 1940, while engaged on a patrol over the Dover area [on 20 October], Pilot Officer Lock engaged three Heinkel 113s [Bf 109s], one of which he shot down into the sea. Immediately afterwards he engaged an Henschel Hs 126 and destroyed it.

> He has displayed great courage in the face of heavy odds, and his skill and coolness in combat have enabled him to destroy 15 enemy aircraft within a period of 19 days.

On 17 November, No 41 Sqn intercepted an estimated 70 Bf 109s that were covering a raid targeting a convoy in the Thames Estuary. The unit had sortied 12 Spitfires, with Lock flying in the rear vic of three. Vectored on to at least 40 fighters at 20,000–25,000ft between Clacton and Herne Bay, No 41 Sqn 'was fortunate enough to be able to dive on them out of the sun in line astern', according to the Hornchurch Operations Record Book entry for that date. Lock's combat report stated:

> Being at the rear of the Squadron, I picked out an enemy aircraft and gave him two two-second bursts from below and behind, the enemy aircraft emitting smoke and flame. It went into a steep dive and I followed and watched him hit the sea. I climbed back to 20,000ft and did another astern attack on another Me 109, firing two two-second bursts, which set the enemy aircraft on fire and he dived into the sea.
>
> I was then about 20 miles off the coast, and the next thing I remember was diving towards the sea. I tried to open the hood but could not do so and crash-landed near Martlesham Heath.

Flt Lt Lock was assigned Spitfire VB W3257 upon joining No 611 Sqn, this aircraft having been issued to the unit new just 12 days after he had arrived. The fighter was marked with his burgeoning tally and Churchill's V for Victory, and Lock claimed three victories (all Bf 109Fs) with it on 6, 8 and 14 July 1941.

A flight of six Spitfire VBs fly in tight near-line abreast formation above cloud while on patrol off the Channel coast during 1941. No 611 Sqn was in the process of swapping its Spitfire IIAs and VAs for Mk VBs when Flt Lt Lock was posted in as flight commander of A Flight. His first operational sortie with the unit took place on 1 July.

On 31 July, Flt Lt Lock was photographed with his dog 'Scruffy' sat astride the open cockpit door of W3257 – the hatch covering the fighter's radio set is also open. Lock failed to return from a Rhubarb in this aircraft just three days later.

The blazing wreckage of a No 611 Sqn Spitfire VB, believed to be W3257 flown by Flt Lt Eric Lock. The fighter was almost certainly shot down while strafing German troops and vehicles on a road near Boulogne-sur-Mer on 3 August 1941.

Lock's Spitfire had been struck by a volley of cannon shells from another, unseen, Bf 109, severely injuring his left arm and both legs. Unable to bale out due to his wounds, Lock managed to glide his fighter in over the Suffolk coast and force-land at Buckenay Farm, near Alderton. He was found in the cockpit of his fighter by two soldiers and rushed unconscious to hospital. Lock would undergo 15 operations and take six months to recover, during which time he was awarded a DSO.

Cleared to return to operations in June 1941, he briefly re-joined No 41 Sqn before being posted to Spitfire V-equipped No 611 Sqn as a flight commander in July of that same year. Having claimed three victories with his new unit, taking his tally to 26 destroyed, Lock was killed during a Rhubarb over France on 3 August. It is believed he was shot down by ground fire while strafing German troops and vehicles on a road near Boulogne-sur-Mer.

Spitfire VB W3257/FY-E of Flt Lt Eric Lock, No 611 Sqn, Hornchurch, July 1941

Having made its first flight on 27 May 1941, this aircraft was issued to No 611 Sqn at Hornchurch on 9 July as part of the unit's re-equipment with Spitfire VBs. Its delivery coincided with the arrival of high-scoring Battle of Britain ace Flt Lt Eric Lock, who was returning to operations some eight months after he had been seriously wounded by a Bf 109E from JG 54. This aircraft was marked with his burgeoning tally and Churchill's V for Victory, and Lock posed with it while holding his dog 'Scruffy' for a series of Air Ministry photographs on 31 July 1941. He and W3257 were almost certainly lost to German flak near Boulogne-sur-Mer just three days later.

EVAN MACKIE

The leading ace of the RNZAF in World War Two, Evan 'Rosie' Mackie scored the majority of his victories flying Spitfires in the Mediterranean theatre.

Evan Dall Mackie was born in Waihi, New Zealand, on 31 October 1917. Following the completion of his schooling, he studied at the Waihi School of Mines and then undertook an electrical apprenticeship with the Martha Gold Mining Company. Mackie joined the RNZAF in January 1941, and learned to fly on Tiger Moths at Whenuapai before progressing to Harvards in Canada.

Having earned his wings, Mackie was posted to Spitfire VB-equipped and New Zealand-manned No 485 Sqn at Kenley in January 1942. Once here, he acquired the nickname 'Rosie' due to his ruddy complexion – reputedly caused by his years of working in the mines in his native New Zealand. He even had his aircraft adorned with a red rose beneath the cockpit. Mackie was credited with a half-share in the destruction of a Bf 109 destroyed on 26 March, followed by an Fw 190 probably destroyed on 26 April.

Posted to No 243 Sqn at Souk el Khemis, Tunisia, in March 1943, Mackie enjoyed his most productive period as a fighter pilot in the final weeks of the North African campaign while serving with this unit. Between 7 April and 8 May, he was credited with eight and one shared destroyed and five damaged. His first successes in-theatre took the form of a brace of Ju 87s from 15 spotted northeast of Oued Zarga, Tunisia. The aircraft, from II./StG 3, were badly mauled in the subsequent action despite having a Bf 109 escort. Mackie noted in his combat report:

As I went in to attack, I noticed two Me 109s with white spinners above the Squadron and flying across it. The Ju 87s were flying in vics of three, four vics fairly close together with the rear vic lagging. Coming up from below, I attacked the starboard 87 of this vic, opening fire at approximately 50 yards with cannons and machine guns. I saw strikes on the wings and fuselage of the aircraft. Large pieces broke away, passing on both sides of my aircraft. The 87 went into a dive and was seen to crash by Sgt McKay, who was my No 3.

After completing my first attack, I climbed into cloud and was flying approximately eastwards when I saw and attacked a second 87 from the starboard quarter, opening fire from 50 yards range with cannon and machine gun and closing rapidly to dead astern. I saw strikes all over the fuselage and around the cockpit and engine. Volumes of black smoke issued from the engine, which became enveloped in flames. I last saw the aircraft in a steep dive flying eastwards.

Mackie, who had been promoted to flight commander shortly after joining the Spitfire VB/C-equipped unit, was himself shot down near Pont du Fahs, Tunisia, on 24 April by a Bf 109 from I./JG 53 while trying to attack Ju 88s that the Messerschmitts were escorting. He returned to No 243 Sqn the next day on foot carrying a set of Spitfire IX stub exhausts that he had fitted to his replacement Spitfire VC. Mackie received a DFC in May for his successes in the final weeks of the campaign in North Africa.

In June, No 243 Sqn moved to Hal Far in preparation for operations leading up to the invasion of Sicily – codenamed Operation *Husky* – the following month. Mackie became

Plt Off Evan Mackie, who joined No 485 Sqn in early 1942, claimed the first of his 23 victories over France on 26 March. His personal marking reflected his nickname, 'Rosie', which had been bestowed upon him because of his ruddy complexion – reputedly caused by his years of working in the mines in his native New Zealand. This photograph of Mackie in his Spitfire was taken at Kenley in April 1942.

CO of the unit at this time, and he led by example by claiming six victories in just nine days. His first success from Hal Far came on 4 July while on an escort mission for USAAF B-17s attacking the Sicilian port city of Catania:

> I saw approximately six Me 109s at 26,000ft, which attacked myself and my No 2. After evasive action, I found myself in a suitable position to attack a 109, which was approaching from starboard. I fired three deflection bursts, the last from approximately 70 yards' range. I saw cannon and machine gun strikes all over the cockpit and fuselage. The enemy aircraft immediately burst into flames. I last saw it at 25,000ft going down vertically in flames with black smoke pouring from it.

Mackie was back over Sicily with No 243 Sqn the following day, again escorting Flying Fortresses. Succeeding in getting on to the tail of a Bf 109, he claimed his tenth victory. 'I saw an Me 109, line astern, and fired cannon from 100 yards' range, breaking off to avoid a collision. Just before I broke away, I saw cannon strikes on the fuselage and wings. The enemy aircraft rolled on its back and went down streaming glycol. I saw it crash and burst into flames just north of Palazzolo.'

His run of success continued on 13 July as Allied forces advanced across Sicily, following the launch of *Husky* four days earlier. Leading 12 Spitfires on patrol over the invasion beach codenamed 'Acid', Mackie spotted an equal number of unescorted Italian Ju 87s south of Gerbini. Five of them were quickly shot down, two by the Kiwi ace. 'We attacked from astern, having come out of the sun. I made attacks on three enemy aircraft. I attacked one Ju 87 from astern, firing from a range of 100 yards, and giving it another short burst from 60 yards. Its bomb was jettisoned. The 87 disintegrated in mid-air. I attacked another from astern at a range of 50 yards. This aircraft burst into flames.'

No 243 Sqn moved to Sicily shortly after its occupation, and the unit was then committed to operations over southern Italy in preparation for the Salerno landings on 9 September. Mackie claimed his final victory with the squadron 48 hours after Allied troops had come ashore on the Italian mainland,

Between April and October 1943, Sqn Ldr Mackie, CO of No 243 Sqn, flew 180 hours in Spitfire VC JK715/SN-A and was credited with eight enemy aircraft destroyed, one probably destroyed and four damaged all while flying this machine over Tunisia and Sicily. These claims made the fighter one of the most successful Spitfire VCs to serve with the RAF.

Spitfire VC JK715/SN-A, seen here at Hal Far in June 1943, was fitted with exhaust stubs from a Spitfire IX. These had been 'discovered' by Mackie while returning to No 243 Sqn on foot after he had been shot down over Tunisia on 24 April 1943 by a Bf 109 from I./JG 53 while trying to attack Ju 88s.

the invasion prompting a fierce response from the Luftwaffe as it made a concerted attempt to destroy the beachhead. Leading a mixed formation of No 243 Sqn Spitfire Vs and IXs between Salerno and Naples, Mackie received reports that hostile aircraft were in the area. Although bomb bursts were seen, they could not catch the culprits – probably Fw 190 *Jabo* from SKG 10. Another aircraft was then spotted by Mackie:

When flying southwards resuming our patrol, I noticed another bomb burst towards the southern end of the beach, and observed a Do 217 at 16,000ft – 3,000ft above us – turning to port, and making off north-northwest. I climbed after the enemy aircraft, which then dived. I fired two bursts but saw no results and broke as enemy fighters were reported behind us. The enemy aircraft went into cloud and I followed. During the chase in and out of cloud I fired several bursts, experiencing return fire from the enemy aircraft. After seeing strikes along the fuselage, I saw pieces break away. The enemy aircraft went down in a spiral dive and crashed, whereupon it burst into flames.

Mackie's success while leading No 243 Sqn earned him a Bar to his DFC later that same month. In November, he was given command of Spitfire VIII-equipped No 92 Sqn at Triolo, Italy, Mackie later recalled:

My appointment as commanding officer of 92 Squadron, then based on the east coast of Italy, came on 5 November. As this was then the top-scoring fighter squadron in the RAF, I regarded it as something of an honour. The unit was flying Spitfire VIIIs, which were definitely superior to any enemy aircraft we encountered in Italy, especially above 15,000ft. Operations in this area were mainly patrols over the Sangro River area, and there was considerable enemy aircraft activity.

Making the most of his new mount, and notable Axis opposition, Mackie claimed three victories and two damaged prior to being declared tour-expired and returning to Britain on 20 February 1944. His final success in a Spitfire had been achieved 18 days earlier over Anzio, where Allied forces had come ashore on 22 January. Flying off the coast from the beachhead, he had spotted an Fw 190 as it levelled out over land, then closed in. 'I fired

Sqn Ldr Mackie poses for the camera among Spitfire VIIIs of No 92 Sqn at Canne, in Italy, in late 1943. He had assumed command of the unit in November of that year, and he would make five claims (three of them confirmed victories) while CO.

When Sqn Ldr Mackie took command of No 80 Sqn at Volkel (B80) in early January 1945, fellow New Zealanders dominated the command structure of No 122 Wing, to which the Tempest V-equipped unit was assigned. Photographed at this time, from left to right, are Mackie, Sqn Ldr K F Thiele (CO of No 3 Sqn), unknown Army officer, Spitfire ace Gp Capt P G Jameson (OC No 122 Wing) and Sqn Ldr A E Umbers (CO of No 486 'New Zealand' Sqn). Typhoon/Tempest V ace 'Spike' Umbers was killed in action on 14 February 1945.

many short bursts and saw strikes on the fuselage just in front of the cockpit and starboard wing roots. Streams of white smoke trailed from the engine and there was a burst of flame. The 190 half-rolled and, diving through some cloud, crashed in a cloud of dust.'

Following an extended spell out of the cockpit on a staff tour, Mackie converted on to the Tempest V and joined No 274 Sqn at Volkel (B80) as a supernumerary squadron leader in December 1944. Claiming his first victory with the Hawker fighter on Christmas Eve, he later took command of No 80 Sqn, also at Volkel, in early January 1945. Mackie would be credited with his final aerial victories while leading the unit, prior to being promoted to wing leader of the 2nd TAF's No 122 Wing in April. Credited with three and two shared aircraft destroyed on the ground in the final week of the war in Europe, Mackie received a DSO and an American DFC shortly after VE Day.

Remaining with No 122 Wing until September 1945, Mackie chose to leave the RNZAF upon returning to New Zealand shortly thereafter in order to pursue his career as an electrician. Eventually promoted to Chief Inspector of the Tauranga Power Board, Mackie died on 28 April 1986.

Tempest V SN228 was assigned to Wg Cdr Evan Mackie when he became wing leader of No 122 Wing at Fassberg (B152), in Germany, in April 1945. Seen here immediately post-war, the fighter features his initials, rank pennant and victory tally, as well as the No 122 Wing crest on the fin.

Spitfire VC JK715/SN-A of Sqn Ldr Evan Mackie, OC No 243 Sqn, Hal Far, Malta, June 1943

Delivered to the RAF in February 1943, this aircraft was shipped to the Middle East the following month and issued to No 243 Sqn in April, where it became Sqn Ldr Mackie's personal mount. Between then and mid-September, Mackie – who clocked up more than 180 flying hours in the fighter – was credited with eight enemy aircraft destroyed, one probably destroyed and four damaged all while flying this machine. This record makes JK715 one of the most successful Mk VCs to see service with the RAF. It was fitted with non-standard Spitfire IX-type exhaust stubs, which Mackie obtained specifically for JK715. The aircraft later flew with the USAAF in North Africa and then No 208 Sqn in the tactical reconnaissance role, before being struck off charge in April 1945.

ADOLF 'SAILOR' MALAN

Adolf 'Sailor' Malan was one of RAF Fighter Command's leading air fighting tacticians of the early war period, claiming more than 30 victories in the Spitfire in 1940–41.

Born on 3 October 1910 to an Afrikaner family in Wellington, South Africa, Adolf Gysbert Malan had served as a naval cadet from the age of 14 on board the training ship *General Botha* prior to finding employment as an officer with the shipping company Union-Castle Line in January 1928. In late 1935, he joined the RAF on a short service commission, gaining his first flying experience in Tiger Moths at No 10 EFTS at Filton in January 1936. Christened 'Sailor' by his fellow students, Plt Off Malan had received his wings by year-end and was rewarded with a posting to Demon-equipped No 74 Sqn at Hornchurch. By the time he had attained the rank of flying officer in May 1938, the unit had switched to Gauntlets.

Malan was promoted to flight lieutenant and made a flight commander in March 1939, just as No 74 Sqn received its first Spitfire Is. A veteran fighter pilot by the time Britain declared war on Germany on 3 September, Malan played a central role in a friendly fire incident three days later when No 74 Sqn downed two No 56 Sqn Hurricanes, resulting in the death of Plt Off Montague Hulton-Harrop.

After many months of inactivity, No 74 Sqn was committed to the defence of Dunkirk from 21 May 1940. Malan led a number of patrols over the evacuation beaches that resulted in him making ten claims,

Spitfire Is of No 74 Sqn take off from Hornchurch in flight strength during the summer of 1939. These aircraft are wearing the JH codes allocated to the unit until the outbreak of war, when No 74 Sqn switched to ZP. Flt Lt Malan had become a flight commander in the squadron in March 1939, just as it transitioned from Gauntlet IIs to Spitfire Is.

seven of them for aircraft destroyed. Two of these victories came on 24 May, as recounted in Malan's combat report:

I was leading four aircraft of Yellow Section on offensive patrol, Dunkirk–Calais–Boulogne. Spotted anti-aircraft fire at 12,000ft over Dunkirk when 500ft off the coast, west of Dunkirk. Climbed in line astern to investigate and saw three vics, approximately 9–12–9 [the bombers were flying in vee-shaped formations of nine, 12 and nine]. Intercepted second vic at 12,000ft and passed through very heavy and accurate anti-aircraft barrage. Attacked starboard flank in echelon port from astern as Me 109s and Me 110s were observed above and into the sun, turning on to our flank for attack. Observed about eight of these, although probably more were about. Delivered three one-second bursts at the engine and fuselage of He 111 from starboard flank, 250 yards to 150 yards. I was then hit in starboard mainplane and through fuselage by anti-aircraft fire, which severed electrical leads near my seat and extinguished reflector [gun]sight.

As I broke off I observed one Me 110 coming up on the starboard quarter and one Me 109 astern. I executed some very steep turns into the sun and lost sight of the two fighters. I changed bulb in reflector sight, but as it failed to function I concluded that the wiring had been cut. By this time the battle had gone out of sight and I hadn't enough petrol to give chase. While climbing into the sun I observed crew of He 111 I had shot take to parachute and aircraft gradually lose height on zigzag course. While climbing up to the attack I observed one bomber badly hit (presumably by AA) with port engine stopped and left wing well down and dropping out of formation.

Malan was awarded a DFC on 28 May for his achievements over Dunkirk and Calais, as the accompanying citation noted. 'During May 1940, this officer has led his flight, and

The RAF's first Spitfire aces (and a bugler) raise their side caps in salute to HM King George VI following their receipt of DFCs and a DSO at Hornchurch on 11 June 1940. These pilots are, from left to right, Plt Off Johnny Allen (No 54 Sqn), Flt Lts Bob Tuck (No 92 Sqn), Al Deere (No 54 Sqn) and 'Sailor' Malan (No 74 Sqn), all of whom were awarded DFCs, and Sqn Ldr James Leathart (No 54 Sqn), who received a DSO.

on certain occasions his squadron, on ten offensive patrols in Northern France. He has personally shot down two enemy aircraft and, probably, three others. Flt Lt Malan has displayed great skill, courage and relentless determination in his attacks upon the enemy.'

Malan received a Bar to this decoration after he succeeded in downing two He 111s during the Luftwaffe's first large-scale nocturnal raid on 18–19 June. His combat report gave a full account of this unusual action – few RAF Fighter Command pilots flying single-seat aircraft achieved night victories in 1940:

> During an air raid in the locality of Southend, various enemy aircraft were observed and held by searchlights for prolonged periods. On request from Squadron I was allowed to take off with one Spitfire. I climbed towards enemy aircraft, which was making for coast and held in searchlight beams at 8,000ft. I positioned myself astern and opened fire at 200 yards and closed to 50 yards with one burst. Observed bullets entering enemy aircraft and had my windscreen covered in oil. Broke off to the left and immediately below as enemy aircraft spiralled out of beam.
>
> Climbed to 12,000ft towards another enemy aircraft held by the searchlights on northerly course. Opened fire at 250 yards, taking good care not to overshoot this time. Gave five two-second bursts and observed bullets entering all over enemy aircraft with slight deflection as he was turning to port. Enemy aircraft emitted heavy smoke and I observed one parachute open very close. Enemy aircraft went down in spiral dive. Searchlights and I followed him right down until he crashed in flames near Chelmsford.
>
> As I approached target in each case, I flashed succession of dots on downward recognition light before moving into attack. I did not notice AA fire after I had done this. When following second enemy aircraft down, I switched on navigation lights for short time to help establish identity. Gave letter of period only once when returning at 3,000ft from Chelmsford, when one searchlight searched for me.

On 8 August, Malan was given command of No 74 Sqn, by which point he had already abandoned the RAF's rigid 'vic' formation for a looser 'finger-four' as employed by the Bf 109E *Schwarm* that the unit had been encountering with increasing frequency. When the squadron was withdrawn to Kirton-in-Lindsey shortly thereafter, Malan used the break from combat to write his *Ten Rules of Air Fighting*. With 12 victories to his name by then, he was more than qualified to develop a set of rules for successful aerial combat that were subsequently published and widely distributed throughout RAF Fighter Command.

On Christmas Eve Malan was awarded a DSO, the citation for which outlined his achievements as CO of No 74 Sqn. 'This officer has commanded his squadron with outstanding success over an intensive period of air operations and, by his brilliant leadership, skill and determination, has contributed to the success obtained. Since early August 1940, the squadron has destroyed at least 84 enemy aircraft and damaged many more. Sqn Ldr Malan has himself destroyed at least 18 hostile aircraft and possibly another six.'

Strapped into the cockpit of a Spitfire IX from No 611 Sqn, Gp Capt Malan prepares to undertake a local flight on 2 January 1943. He had taken over as Station Commander at Biggin Hill the previous day, with the national press reporting that Britain's 'number one fighter station' was now being run by the RAF's 'number one fighter pilot'.

Malan remained in command of No 74 Sqn until March 1941, when he was promoted to wing commander and became one of the RAF's first wing leaders tasked with taking RAF Fighter Command on the offensive over occupied Europe. Flying from Biggin Hill, Malan had increased his tally to 27 and seven shared destroyed, two and one shared unconfirmed destroyed, three probables and 16 damaged by the time he was posted away from No 11 Group in August 1941. He had received a Bar to his DSO late the previous month following his successful leadership of the Biggin Hill Wing, the award citation stating:

This officer has displayed the greatest courage and disdain of the enemy while leading his wing on numerous recent operations over Northern France. His cool judgement, exceptional determination and ability have enabled him to increase his confirmed victories over enemy aircraft from 19 to 28, in addition to a further 20 damaged

Left: Gp Capt Malan converses with Australian ace Sqn Ldr Hugo 'Sinker' Armstrong, who was CO of No 611 Sqn when the South African ace returned to Biggin Hill in January 1943. Armstrong was lost over the Channel on 5 February 1943 after his section of three fighters was bounced by eight Fw 190s from II./JG 26 off Boulogne.

Right: From March 1945 Gp Capt Malan commanded Spitfire IX-equipped No 145 'Free French' Wing of the 2nd TAF. Based at Merston, he led the wing until shortly after D-Day. Here, he is seen climbing into the cockpit of his Spitfire IX, which is marked with his personal codes, AGM, at Appledram, in West Sussex.

SPITFIRE ACES

This studio portrait of Gp Capt Malan was taken in mid-1945 while he was at RAF Staff College. Despite not scoring a single kill after 6 July 1941, his tally of 27 and seven shared victories in the Spitfire was only bettered by 'Johnnie' Johnson with 34 and seven shared victories.

and probably destroyed. His record and behaviour have earned for him the greatest admiration and devotion of his comrades in the wing. During the past fortnight the wing has scored heavily against the enemy with 42 hostile aircraft destroyed, a further 15 probably destroyed and 11 damaged.

A series of training and staff jobs then followed for Malan, including a spell as station commander of Biggin Hill. He returned to operations as OC of No 19 Fighter Wing within the 2nd TAF in October 1943, after which he led No 145 (Free French) Wing until July 1944. Malan was CO of the Advanced Gunnery School at Catfoss, East Riding of Yorkshire, when the war in Europe ended.

Despite attending RAF Staff College shortly after VE Day, Malan was released from service in April 1946 with the rank of group captain and he returned to South Africa, where he eventually took up farming. He also became active in politics with the Torch Commando organisation, which was opposed to the implementation of apartheid. Malan was diagnosed with Parkinson's Disease in the late 1950s, and he passed away on 17 September 1963 at the age of 53. Shortly after Malan's death, Air Chief Marshal Sir Hugh Dowding, who had led RAF Fighter Command during 1940, commented, 'I looked on Malan as one of the great assets of the Command – a fighter pilot who was not solely concerned with his own score, but as one whose first thoughts were for the efficiency of his squadron and the personal safety of his junior pilots who fought under his command.'

Spitfire I K9953/ZP-A of Flt Lt Adolf 'Sailor' Malan, No 74 Sqn, Hornchurch, Essex, May 1940

First flown on 28 April 1939, this aircraft was issued new to No 74 Sqn four days later. It had been assigned to Flt Lt Malan by the time he saw action over the Dunkirk evacuation beaches on 27 May 1940. He would use the fighter to make six claims, three of them for aircraft confirmed shot down. The Spitfire was passed on to No 7 OTU in November 1940 and then transferred to No 57 OTU in June 1942 after it was repaired in the wake of an accident. K9953 was lost in a mid-air collision with fellow No 57 OTU Spitfire I R6883 over Eshott on 7 October 1943.

ROBERT 'BUCK' McNAIR

Both a high-scoring ace and a successful squadron and Wing Leader, 'Buck' McNair flew Spitfires on the Channel Front and in the defence of Malta.

The son of a railway engineer, Robert Wendell McNair was born in Springfield, Nova Scotia, on 15 May 1919. Following his graduation from North Battleford High School in 1937, he worked with the Saskatchewan Ministry of Natural Resources as a ground wireless (radio) operator. Upon the outbreak of World War Two, McNair enlisted in the RCAF in June 1940 and was sent to No 7 EFTS at Windsor, Ontario, where he received instruction on Finch II trainers. He then progressed to Battles and Harvards at No 31 SFTS at Kingston, also in Ontario, in December, and received his wings three months later. McNair was posted to Britain shortly thereafter, where he converted on to Spitfires with No 58 OTU in May 1941.

Presentation Spitfire IIA P7923 *VENTURE I* (paid for by the Midland Bank Staff Association) had served with Nos 610 and 130 Sqns prior to it being sent to newly formed No 411 Sqn at Digby on 27 July 1941 shortly after Plt Off McNair had joined the unit. The fighter remained with the Canadian-manned squadron until 19 November, when it was left behind at Digby after the unit was posted south to Hornchurch to be re-equipped with the Spitfire VB.

He joined No 411 Sqn at Digby the following month, just days after the unit had formed – indeed, he arrived before the CO, Sqn Ldr P B Pitcher. After three months of work-ups on Spitfires, McNair and No 411 Sqn would finally see combat on the Channel Front from September. Having damaged a Bf 109 while escorting Blenheims over France on 27 September, he claimed his first victory on 13 October off the coast of Boulogne. McNair noted in his combat report:

I was on a sweep and saw a number of Messerschmitts below me. I dived on them and saw they were circling a pilot in the sea. I picked one out and gave him a three-second burst. I overshot him, and pulling away, I saw him go into the sea. This took place just off Boulogne. The pilot did not bale out. I climbed again and turned for home. Then a Jerry dived on me from out of the sun, his fire hitting my engine. My cockpit filled with smoke and the enemy overshot me. He came around directly in front of me.

It was my turn then, and I gave him a burst and saw hits registering. His hood came off. Only my starboard guns were firing now, and flames were coming out of the cockpit so I put my nose down. Finding my engine cutting, I baled out into the sea. I got rid of my parachute immediately upon touching the water and had no trouble inflating my dinghy. I was picked up 15 minutes later by a sea rescue motorboat.

McNair left No 411 Sqn in February 1942, and on 3 March he was flown to Malta on board a Sunderland flying boat. Here, he joined No 249 Sqn, which would soon exchange its Hurricane IIs for Spitfire VBs flown in from the aircraft carrier *Eagle*. McNair would become one of the unit's most successful pilots during the bitter fighting that ensued in defence of the beleaguered island, making 17 claims (including seven destroyed) between 18 March and 10 June. His first victory in-theatre came on 20 March when he downed a Bf 109 from 7./JG 53. The Canadian's combat report for this action read as follows:

The '109 went into a spiral dive, and looking around and seeing no other Huns about, I went down after it, having no trouble in following. I waited my chance to fire again, and got a good burst into it. I saw hits on the starboard wing, and pieces came off, but he still didn't take any evasive action – he just continued with the spiral dive down to 3,000ft. I started clobbering the '109 all over. I emptied my cannon and continued with the machine guns. Oil and glycol from its cooling system poured out. The white glycol looked beautiful streaming out into the clear air – it was a really lovely day.

McNair was awarded a DFC for his exploits in defending the island, the citation for the decoration, awarded on 11 May 1942, stating that, 'This officer is a skilful and courageous pilot. He invariably presses home his attacks with the greatest determination irrespective of the odds.' Returning to England in July, he re-joined No 411 Sqn as a flight commander. Posted home in September for a rest, and to participate in a war bond tour, McNair was attached to the RCAF's Hurricane-equipped No 133 Sqn, based at Boundary Bay, for several months. He eventually returned to RAF Fighter Command in April 1943.

Looking every inch the fighter pilot, 22-year-old Plt Off 'Buck' McNair rides around No 411 Sqn's dispersal area at Digby on his motorcycle in early November 1941. He had made three claims (including one victory) over the previous two months.

Among the spring blossom at Takali, AB264 was one of the first 15 Spitfires flown into Malta from *Eagle* on 7 March 1942. It was used by future Spitfire ace Plt Off Peter Nash to destroy a Ju 87 on 25 March and by Plt Off McNair to claim a share in the destruction of a Ju 88 from I./KG 54 the following day.

After briefly serving with No 403 Sqn, McNair was given command of No 416 Sqn the following month and was then posted to No 421 Sqn at Kenley as its CO in June. He would enjoy notable success flying Spitfire IXs with the unit in the summer and autumn of 1943, claiming eight German fighters destroyed and three damaged. The first of these victories came on 20 June during a Kenley Wing Circus to Abbeville in search of enemy fighters. This proved to be a productive operation, as McNair recounted in his combat report:

I was flying Black 1, leading 421 Squadron on Circus 313. The wing flew a course to Abbeville–Amiens and then towards Poix. Shortly after turning, the wing was given a vector 010, which course we flew to the Doullens area. I saw six FW 190s pass under 403 Squadron, who were flying about 1,000ft below at one o'clock to me. At the same time 12+ enemy aircraft were reported coming in behind us, and someone said they were Spitfires. They turned out to be FW 190s, who fired at us. I fired at one from head on in a starboard quarter attack without seeing any results. Another came around me, and I delivered a ½-second from starboard rear quarter burst with no results. Putting on more deflection, I fired a two-second burst at 350 yards, seeing strikes all over the cockpit and fuselage. His undercarriage came down and parts broke off and he started to burn and go down. I then gained height to reform the squadron.

The Canadian ace was awarded two Bars to his DFC during this period, with the citation for the second decoration noting that, 'Sqn Ldr McNair is a tenacious and confident fighter, whose outstanding ability has proved an inspiration to the squadron he commands. He has completed a large number of sorties and has destroyed 15 and damaged many other enemy aircraft. His keenness has been outstanding.'

McNair's penultimate victory came while leading No 421 Sqn on a Ramrod over France on 6 September:

Left: Flg Off McNair enjoys a beer at St Paul's Bay during a break from the action in May 1942. Although he had only been on Malta a little over two months when this photograph was taken, he had already made 14 claims (four of which were victories) with No 249 Sqn.

Right: Promoted to flight commander and awarded a DFC while flying in the defence of Malta, Flt Lt McNair returned to England in July 1942 with eight victories to his name. Re-joining No 411 Sqn at Digby, he made a further four claims with the unit before being sent home to Canada to rest, and to participate in a war bond tour.

No 421 Sqn CO Sqn Ldr McNair (sitting fifth from left) poses with his pilots and Wg Cdr 'Johnnie' Johnson (sat to the right of McNair), Wing Leader of No 127 Wing, at Headcorn in August 1943. McNair would make 11 claims (eight of which were victories) while leading the squadron.

I was flying Black 3 on Ramrod S26 when in the Evreux area I saw two Me 109s shadowing Fortresses. We chased these unsuccessfully. Section reformed at 12,000ft when FO Love (Black 2) spotted another Me 109 below. He gave chase, opening fire at about 400 yards, and when at 200 yards the enemy aircraft disintegrated. Love continued to fire, closing to about 50 yards. Pieces of enemy aircraft struck his aircraft in the radiator, causing a glycol leak and eventually forcing him to bale out.

Section reformed again when I spotted another Me 109 below and chased him. When I was at about 500 yards he made a sharp turn to port. I fired for about three seconds from 300 yards, with no apparent results. The Hun then turned to starboard, diving slightly. I closed to about 100 yards dead astern and fired for about five seconds. He blew up and I saw him crash just north of Evreux.

Promoted to wing commander, McNair was made wing leader of No 126 Airfield (later redesignated Wing) in mid-October shortly after it had moved to Biggin Hill. The wing consisted of Nos 401, 411 and 412 Sqns, and among the pilots under his command at that time was Flt Lt George Beurling. He had briefly flown with McNair in the defence of Malta in 1942, when they were assigned to No 249 Sqn. Both men were exceptional aviators, as fellow ace Don Laubman of No 412 Sqn recalled:

The following story will act as a testament to Buck's skill as a pilot. It happened during the winter of 1943–44 while the wing was at Biggin Hill and Buck was Wing Commander Flying.

Because of the weather, we were grounded. The cloud base was in the order of 300–400ft and we, the pilots, were all hanging around our dispersal huts. To our surprise two Spitfires started up and became airborne. We later learned that they were being flown by Buck and George Beurling, who then proceeded to put on the most amazing display of dogfighting I had ever seen. For about 15 minutes they performed for us, never leaving the perimeter of the airfield and never going above 200ft. It was a fantastic performance.

However, McNair's vision had been permanently damaged when he suffered facial burns following an engine fire during a mission on 28 July 1943, which had forced him to bale out over the Channel, and in April 1944 he relinquished his post. Decorated with a DSO later that month, he took up a staff post at RCAF Overseas HQ and remained there until VE Day.

Serving with the RCAF post-war, McNair was a senior staff officer prior to becoming Air Advisor and Attaché to the Canadian Military Mission in Tokyo, Japan. Promoted to group captain in 1956, he was made commander of No 4 Fighter Wing at Baden-Soellingen, West Germany. Subsequently serving in the Canadian Joint Staff office at the High Commission in London, McNair succumbed to leukaemia, which he had been diagnosed with in late 1965, on 15 January 1971.

Spitfire VB AB264/GN-H of Flt Lt Robert 'Buck' McNair, No 249 Sqn, Takali, Malta, March 1942

AB264 was one of the first 15 Spitfires flown into Malta from *Eagle* on 7 March 1942. Future Spitfire ace Plt Off Peter Nash destroyed a Ju 87 with the fighter on 25 March, and Plt Off McNair used it to claim a share in the destruction of a Ju 88 from I./KG 54 the following day. AB264 had quite a long career on Malta, eventually being passed on to No 1435 Sqn in October and then transferred to the USAAF in May 1943. It was returned to the RAF on 31 August 1944.

'DICKIE' MILNE

Having become an ace in Hurricanes in 1940, 'Dickie' Milne enjoyed success flying Spitfires from Biggin Hill until he was shot down and captured in March 1943.

Richard Maxwell 'Dickie' Milne was born in Edinburgh on 8 July 1919. He attended Cheltenham College from 1931 to 1935 and joined the RAF on a short-service commission in July 1937, after which he undertook his flying training with No 11 FTS at Wittering, Cambridgeshire. Having been awarded his wings, Milne was initially posted as a staff pilot to No 8 Armament Training Station at Evanton, Scotland, in May 1938, where he flew various obsolescent types.

Plt Off Milne joined No 151 Sqn at North Weald in January 1939, shortly after the unit had replaced its Gauntlet IIs with Hurricane Is. He first saw action on 17 May 1940, when his squadron was sent to France following the launching of the *Blitzkrieg* one week earlier. Flying from Abbeville, Milne was credited with the destruction of a Ju 87 east of Valenciennes. He followed this up with a Bf 110 unconfirmed on 18 January and a second Stuka on 22 January. No 151 Sqn continued to fly sweeps over France until the completion of the evacuation of Dunkirk on 4 June.

Although North Weald would be home to No 151 Sqn throughout the summer of 1940, Milne and his squadronmates routinely flew on detachment from satellite airfields at Manston and Rochford. He 'made ace' on 13 August when he intercepted Do 17 bombers (which he misidentified as Dornier 215s in the following combat report) off the East Kent coast:

At 0530 hrs the squadron [12 Hurricanes] took off [from North Weald] for our forward base [Manston] but we were ordered to intercept an enemy Dornier formation [totalling 40 aircraft] at 8,000ft above solid cloud. Only three sections [nine aircraft] managed to form up together. We were airborne over an hour before finding the enemy, and when we sighted them, they were flying north. They flew in three large formations, stepped up, all of them Dorniers. We climbed up and positioned ourselves in the sun, taking our time. When in the perfect position we attacked the last large formation. I led my section in an astern attack from below following a dive down.

I opened fire at 200 yards but was travelling too fast and only got in a two seconds' burst. While firing, I saw an enemy aircraft leave the formation and go down but

Mk VB R6923 of No 92 Sqn is put through its paces by Spitfire ace Flt Lt Allan Wright, who made four claims with the fighter between 13 March and 17 June 1941. Wright left the unit shortly before Flt Lt Milne joined No 92 Sqn as a flight commander in August 1941, while R6923 was shot down over the Channel on 21 June.

did not see it again. I zoomed to several thousand feet above them and decided on a head-on attack to beat their armour plate. I tried one attack but did not fire owing to the enemy aircraft formation commencing to turn. I again pulled up and turned to head them off. I got several miles ahead and then attacked the outside member of the formation from head-on. I held a steady bead and opened fire when quite close. I was flying slowly and held fire for about four seconds. I pulled up after the attack and saw the starboard side of the enemy aircraft in flames. He was a long way ahead now, but I followed up and after hearing over the RT 'Achtung, Achtung', three of the crew baled out. The aircraft dived down for the clouds in flames, and I followed but did not see it on emerging over the sea. I searched for some time but was short of petrol.

While returning from the air action, I encountered a lone Dornier 215 [from 7./KG 2] flying towards me and below. I was just about over Eastchurch [Kent]. I half-rolled on to him and continued my dive below, pulling up slightly and opening fire at 200 yards after a short run up. After about four seconds' fire, the right rudder crumpled and the Dornier commenced diving slightly. I held my fire and saw everything I fired simply pouring into the fuselage. His dive became steep now and I broke off the attack at 50 yards, passing to starboard then pulling up and out. I only encountered slight fire from the bottom rear gunner, which ceased early on. The Dornier was now well below me and dived through the clouds at about 60 degrees. I followed shortly after and saw, on emerging, a huge cloud of dust and debris over a field with the remains of a blue fuselage bottom and planes, hardly recognisable as an aeroplane. I circled and saw a Spitfire approach and look at the crash. I now returned to the forward base with only a couple of gallons left.

By month-end, Milne's tally stood at seven and one shared destroyed, one unconfirmed destroyed and one damaged, and these successes resulted in him being awarded a DFC on 30 August. The citation accompanying the decoration stated, 'Flg Off Milne has led his section throughout with skill and courage, and has set an example to other members of the squadron.'

Tankards in hand and scoreboard to the fore, No 92 Sqn pilots and their adjutant celebrate the success enjoyed by Sqn Ldr Milne (standing third from the right) at Gravesend on 13 October 1941. The Battle of Britain ace had just claimed three Bf 109s destroyed and one damaged during Circus 108B, these victories being the last credited to No 92 Sqn while part of the Biggin Hill Wing.

In late November, Milne was posted to the CFS at Upavon, where he received training as an 'A' Category instructor. Following six months of teaching future RAF and Army pilots at Woodley, and time as a staff instructor and flight commander at the CFS, he joined No 92 Sqn at Biggin Hill in August 1941. Initially serving as a flight commander, Milne became CO of the Spitfire VB-equipped unit the following month. On 13 October, he claimed three Bf 109Fs destroyed in a single mission while leading the unit as part of the high cover escort supplied by the Biggin Hill Wing for 18 Blenheim IVs targeting the power station at Mazingarbe, in the Pas-de-Calais, in Circus 108B. Milne's clash with enemy fighters was recorded by the No 92 Sqn diarist as follows:

S/Ldr Milne of 92 Squadron broke away from the wing owing to a bad oxygen leak and continued into France at a lower level. When southeast of St. Omer, S/Ldr Milne was attacked by a 109F, which made off when the S/Ldr got around on to the enemy aircraft's tail. Finding himself alone, he proceeded homeward and was able to attack two 109Es, shooting one down in flames and damaging the other. A little later, S/Ldr Milne spotted two 109Fs in time to evade their stern attack and swung round quickly. He was able to get in a burst from about 70 yards on one, which then emitted smoke and crashed into the other enemy aircraft. Pieces flew off and both aircraft went down together, the pilot of one baling out.

Milne received a Bar to his DFC shortly thereafter, with its citation noting 'since assuming command, this officer has led the squadron on 19 offensive operations over enemy territory. His leadership has been characterised by dash and good judgement.'

Following a short spell as a staff officer in the Western Desert, Milne took over Spitfire VB-equipped No 222 Sqn at North Weald in January 1942. Rested from operations from May of that year, he was given command of RAF Ipswich and then completed the CGS course at Sutton Bridge. In January 1943, Milne commenced his fourth operational tour when he became wing leader at Biggin Hill. Flying a Spitfire IX, he claimed four

Sqn Ldr Milne routinely flew Spitfire VB W3444 while CO of No 92 Sqn, this aircraft (which was marked up with his victory tally) having been paid for by the Linen Trade Association of New York. Assigned new to the unit on 10 July 1941, W3444 was not, however, used by Milne to claim any of his successes with No 92 Sqn – these came in W3817 *Wellingborough*. W3444 was written off on 15 November when it crashed on landing at the end of a night-training flight.

Spitfire VB AD233 was assigned to Sqn Ldr Milne (note the command pennant beneath the windscreen) when he became CO of No 222 Sqn at North Weald in January 1942. He failed to add to his tally during the four months that he led the unit. Milne was replaced by Sqn Ldr Jerzy Jankiewicz at No 222 Sqn, the latter being the first Pole to command a British-manned unit in the RAF. His time in charge was to be brief, however, for he was shot down into the Channel, west of Dunkirk, by German fighters while flying AD233 in Rodeo 51 on 25 May 1942.

Having joined his first fighter squadron in January 1939, Wg Cdr Milne was a veteran of four operational tours by the time he took control of the Biggin Hill Wing in January 1943. Following action with Nos 151, 92 and 222 Sqns, his score stood at 10 victories and one shared victory one unconfirmed destroyed, one probable and 11 damaged. Milne would quickly claim four more victories.

more victories, with the first two falling on 20 January following a daring *Jabo* attack on London. This raid caused a major 'flap', as the No 611 Sqn diarist noted:

All the Squadron pilots were at lunch when a tannoy announcement reported that more than 30 enemy aircraft were approaching Biggin Hill from the southeast, being just seven miles away. As the pilots hurried to dispersal, a number of Fw 190s crossed the northern end of the airfield almost at ground level. Within eight minutes of the announcement being made 12 Spitfires were in the air, led by Wg Cdr 'Dickie' Milne. By this time the 'bandits' were just north of Bromley, where they dropped their bombs, before making a dash for the Channel coast, still at a very low level.

Wg Cdr Milne took the Biggin Hill Spitfire IXs to a point over Beachy Head to try and catch the raiders on their way back to Abbeville. The ploy worked, and in the resulting 'bounce' Wg Cdr Milne [flying his personally marked Spitfire IX BS240/R-M] succeeded in downing an Fw 190 and an Me 109.

Milne's tenure at Biggin Hill was cut short on 14 March when his Spitfire was hit hard during an engagement with Fw 190s over Berck-Montreuil shortly after he had claimed his 15th victory. With no radio, and glycol streaming from a punctured coolant line, he was forced to bale out over the Channel. Picked up by a German patrol vessel, Milne would spend the rest of the conflict as a PoW. Upon returning to England in May 1945, he was

This is the only known photograph – albeit of average quality – of Wg Cdr Milne's assigned Spitfire IX, BS240, when he was wing leader of the Biggin Hill Wing for the first two months of 1943. Issued new to No 340 Sqn in October 1942, the fighter had been allocated to Biggin Hill's Station Flight by the end of November. Marked with Milne's initials and rank pennant, BS240 retained No 340 Sqn's Free French Cross of Lorraine insignia beneath the cockpit. He claimed his final four victories in the fighter, although shortly after downing an Fw 190 for his 15th kill on 14 March 1943, the Spitfire was mortally damaged by another German fighter and Milne was forced to bale out over the Channel.

posted to HQ, No 13 Group, after which he served as Wing Commander Air Staff and, finally, became Wing Commander Flying at North Weald under Gp Capt Douglas Bader.

Choosing to leave the RAF in 1946, Milne joined English Electric's Aircraft Division and oversaw military aircraft sales and liaison with the RAF. He also worked closely with the RAAF during the licence-building of the Canberra bomber in Australia. Milne subsequently negotiated sales of this pioneering jet to several South American countries and was involved in securing its production under-licence by Glenn Martin for the USAF as the B-57. When English Electric became part of the British Aircraft Corporation, he headed up the company's activities with NATO. 'Dickie' Milne eventually retired to Andorra, and passed away there in 2004.

Spitfire IX BS240/R-M of Wg Cdr 'Dickie' Milne, OC Biggin Hill Wing, Biggin Hill, January–March 1943

First flown on 6 October 1942, BS240 was issued to No 340 Sqn at Biggin Hill later that same month. By the end of November, the aircraft had been assigned to the airfield's Station Flight, and in January 1943 it was allocated to Wg Cdr Milne after he became wing leader. The Spitfire retained the Free French Cross of Lorraine insignia worn by all No 340 Sqn aircraft beneath the cockpit, to which was added Milne's rank pennant and initials. On 20 January, Milne was flying BS240 when he shot down an Fw 190 and a Bf 109 off the Kent coast after a large-scale *Jabo* raid on London. He regularly led his wing in BS240, and on 14 March, over France, he used it shoot down an Fw 190 for his 15th victory. However, Milne's Spitfire was also mortally hit, and he was forced to bale out into the Channel.

'JAMIE' RANKIN

Scotsman 'Jamie' Rankin enjoyed great success against Luftwaffe fighters while flying Spitfire VBs from Biggin Hill, both as a squadron commander and wing leader in 1941–42.

Born in Portobello, a coastal suburb of Edinburgh, on 7 May 1913, James 'Jamie' Rankin subsequently attended the city's Royal High School before moving with his family to Longridge, near Preston in Lancashire. He joined the RAF in 1935, receiving a commission upon the completion of his flying training with No 2 FTS at Digby and orders to join Fury II-equipped No 25 Sqn at Hawkinge. Rankin was transferred to 825 Naval Air Squadron (NAS) in 1939 when the expanding Fleet Air Arm struggled to field experienced pilots. He flew Swordfish torpedo-bombers with the unit from HMS *Glorious* before returning to the RAF in June 1940 and becoming an instructor with No 5 OTU at Aston Down.

Rankin, who continued to instruct throughout the Battle of Britain, was eventually attached as a supernumerary squadron leader to No 64 Sqn at Hornchurch in January 1941 in order to gain operational experience flying Spitfire IIAs. He was credited with a shared

Cannon-armed Spitfire IBs R6908 and X4272 and standard Mk IA X4561 accelerate over the snow-covered grass runway at Manston in early 1941 after being scrambled to intercept approaching German aircraft. Both of the Mk IBs were upgraded to Spitfire VBs shortly after this photograph was taken and then returned to No 92 Sqn at Biggin Hill, from where they were flown by recently arrived CO, Sqn Ldr Rankin.

victory and two probables during his short spell with the unit. In February, Rankin took command of No 92 Sqn just as it was re-equipping with the first Spitfire VBs to reach RAF Fighter Command. The unit had a formidable reputation following great success in the air during 1940, and its veteran pilots had hoped one of their flight commanders would replace outgoing CO, Johnny Kent, who had been promoted to wing commander. Battle of Britain ace Flg Off Allan Wright explains how Rankin eased himself into leadership of the squadron:

> We wondered if he would be up to the job before he arrived, but he was a very good CO. With Rankin's full approval, Brian [Kingcome, who was A Flight commander] led the squadron on operations and he would fly as No 2 to somebody – he wasn't too proud to do that. After a few operational flights Rankin got to know the hang of things and said he thought he was then ready to take the job on operationally, and so he led us from then on – it was the obvious way to do it.

Rankin's score mounted rapidly as he led the unit on fighter sweeps and bomber escort missions over northern France. His first victory came on 24 April, as noted by future ace Plt Off Neville Duke in his diary:

> Up at 0415 hrs for dawn readiness this morning! Nothing doing until about 0830 hrs, when heard CO [Rankin] and one of our Netherlands East Indies boys, F/L Bruinier, had shot down a 109 [from 2./JG 52] over Dungeness. It came down in flames, the pilot baled out and was taken prisoner. He evidently mistook out chaps for his friends as he made no attempt to duck into cloud and even waggled his wings at them! He was machine gunning some town – Rye, I think. Some people have all the luck.

In June, Rankin was awarded a DFC after he had claimed nine victories (all bar one of them Bf 109s), and he continued to add to his tally during near-daily sweeps in July and August. Rankin's combat report from Circus 67 on 9 August, which saw No 92 Sqn provide high cover for Blenheim IVs hitting targets in Lille, noted a proliferation of Bf 109s as the bombers neared the French coast:

> The squadron split up into fours and was continually engaged. Enemy aircraft were numerous above, below and at same height, and there was no difficulty in finding targets. Two formations of seven, which I chased with Red Section, were caught, and in both cases I hit Me 109Fs with cannon, high explosive strikes being visible. Later, at Griz Nez, when

On 14 June 1941, Spitfires from the Hornchurch and Tangmere Wings escorted 12 Blenheim IVs on a Circus to Saint-Omer, during which Sqn Ldr Rankin, flying R7161/QJ-J, shot down the Bf 109E-7 flown by 18-victory *experte* Leutnant Robert Menge of 3./JG 26. His demise took Rankin to acedom. Rankin made three claims (two of which were victories) in this aircraft, which is seen here at Biggin Hill on 22 April 1941.

dogfighting with three '109s, I saw 10–12 more coming up and ordered section to dive out and squadron to return to base.

One '109F followed us down at more than 450mph from 20,000ft to 1,000ft, where he opened fire. I swung hard right and he overshot. Turning back on to him, I fired with ten degrees deflection with my machine guns only (cannon finished) and this enemy aircraft, now at 500ft, tried to turn right while pulling out and crashed into the sea, sending up a splash about 100ft high. I then returned to base.

Me 109s were much more inclined to stay and fight, and the engagement in the area Boulogne–St. Omer was one large dogfight. We could out-turn the '109Fs easily, but had not enough speed to close range when in a good position.

In September, Rankin was promoted to wing commander and he became Biggin Hill wing leader. Sgt Walter 'Johnnie' Johnston of No 92 Sqn, who served under Rankin during 1941–42 recalled his leadership qualities in Peter Caygill's volume *Spitfire Mark V In Action*:

When 'Jamie' took over as wing leader things did change a little bit. Malan [Rankin's predecessor, and high-scoring ace, Wg Cdr Adolf 'Sailor' Malan] was a very hard taskmaster. He expected that everybody who he picked to put into a job could do it, and if they couldn't, he got rid of them. He was an excellent tactician, but he was quite ruthless and had a bit of a reputation for losing his No 2s [wingmen]. Quite often he would take evasive action without any warning and the No 2 was left high and dry, miles behind, which was why some of us used to find ourselves stuck on our own at times.

'Jamie' was different. He had been a good CO, but he freely admitted that he was learning, the same as everybody else, because 92 was his first operational trip after time as an instructor. As far as gunnery was concerned, he was damn good, but the thing that impressed me most was his flying, which was absolutely immaculate. If you were

Sqn Ldr Rankin was photographed in his Spitfire VB W3312 at Biggin Hill shortly after claiming his tenth victory while at the controls of this aircraft on 26 June 1941. He enjoyed great success in the fighter, making 22 claims (including 15 destroyed) with it between 21 June and 27 October. W3312 was retained by Rankin when he became wing leader of the Biggin Hill Wing in September 1941.

A cold drink on a warm day breaks up the monotony of manning aircraft on readiness at Biggin Hill in the summer sun. Sqn Ldr Rankin, map tucked into his right boot, and two of his pilots are chatting to the young lady who has brought them their refreshments. The unidentified sergeant pilot is doing his best to ensure that she does not slip off the wing root of the well weathered No 92 Sqn Spitfire VB.

supposed to be going into a turn of 110 degrees, you did 110, not 105 or 115, but 110 exactly, so personally, I found life easier with him as Wing Leader.

Shortly after completing his tour as wing leader in October 1941, and with his score at 13 and four shared destroyed, three probables and eight damaged, Rankin received a DSO. Between December of that year and April 1942, he held a staff post as Wing Commander Training at HQ, No 11 Group, before returning to Biggin Hill for a second tour as wing leader.

Struggling on with Spitfire VBs, the wings in No 11 Group in particular were suffering heavy losses at the hands of the Fw 190-equipped *Jagdgeschwader*. Nevertheless, sweeps continued, and on 5 June, for example, the Biggin Hill Wing headed for France. No 91 Sqn (which occasionally flew with the wing despite being based at Hawkinge), with CO Sqn Ldr Bobby Oxspring, who flew as wingman to Wg Cdr Rankin, led the way, with Sqn Ldr Brian Kingcome's No 72 Sqn above them and No 124 Sqn, led by Sqn Ldr Myles Duke-Woolley,

Left: Wg Cdr Rankin was CO of No 125 Wing at Ford when this photograph was taken in the summer of 1944, the veteran fighter ace leading its three Spitfire IX-equipped squadrons (Nos 132, 453 and 602) over the D-Day beaches on 6 June. By then he had received a DFC and Bar and a DSO and Bar, as well as a Belgian *Croix de Guerre*.

Below: On 11 July 1957, Gp Capt Rankin (centre, in the flying suit) and fellow aces Gp Capt 'Johnnie' Johnson (to the right of Rankin) and Wg Cdr Peter Thompson (to the left) ferried the final three Spitfires in RAF service from Duxford – where Rankin was station commander – to Biggin Hill. Here, they joined Hurricane II LF363 in the newly formed Historic Aircraft Flight, which was the precursor to the Battle of Britain Memorial Flight.

as top cover. In the following account, Oxspring described Rankin's 22nd, and final victory, scored during the course of this mission:

> Over Abbeville a gaggle of Me 109s fell on us out of the sun, but not before we saw them. 124 Squadron turned into them and engaged as 72 Squadron cut across to help. At the same time, Jamie winged over, calling a sighting beneath us. As I followed him down, I saw a string of Focke-Wulf 190s climbing up in ones and twos, and way below more pairs taking off from an airfield. Jamie snaked down behind a '190 and let fly from close range – a cluster of shells from his cannons flashed into the fuselage around the cockpit area. Flame and smoke shot back as his victim fell into its fatal dive. Without pause, Jamie moved over and belted another '190 as it struggled for altitude. Pieces of cowling and the canopy peeled off, followed by the pilot, who hastily departed on his parachute. Lost in admiration at this awesome display of shooting, I almost forgot my primary duty to guard our tails.

Awarded a Bar for his DSO following the completion of his second spell as wing leader at Biggin Hill in July 1942, Rankin spent six months commanding the CGS at Sutton Bridge prior to being put in charge of No 15 Fighter Wing in the newly formed 2nd TAF. When that unit was disbanded, he assumed command of No 125 Wing, which he led during the Normandy invasion – both wings flew Spitfire IXs from Ford. Having been promoted to air commodore by VE Day, Rankin reverted to group captain rank when he chose to remain in the RAF post-war.

Serving as Air Attaché in Dublin in 1948, he was made station commander of Duxford in 1954. The highlight of Rankin's tenure at the Cambridgeshire airfield came on 11 July 1957 when he joined fellow aces Gp Capt 'Johnnie' Johnson and Wg Cdr Peter Thompson at the controls of the final three Spitfires (all PR 19s) in RAF service as they ferried them to Biggin Hill. Here, the aeroplanes joined the newly formed Historic Aircraft Flight – the precursor to the Battle of Britain Memorial Flight. He left military service the following year. 'Jamie' Rankin passed away in Edinburgh in March 1975, aged 61.

Spitfire VB W3312/QJ-J of Sqn Ldr 'Jamie' Rankin, OC No 92 Sqn, Biggin Hill, August 1941

W3312 was delivered new to No 92 Sqn on 20 June 1941, and the fighter was immediately 'acquired' by the unit's CO, Sqn Ldr Rankin. It is believed he made 22 claims (including 15 destroyed – all of Rankin's claims in the fighter were for Bf 109E/Fs, bar a solitary Fw 190 victory) in the aircraft between 21 June and 27 October. His first two victories in W3312 came within 24 hours of the aeroplane arriving at Biggin Hill. Rankin continued to fly W3312 after he had been made wing leader of the Biggin Hill Wing in September 1941. He was replaced in that post three months later, after which W3312 was passed on to recently arrived No 124 Sqn. Lightly damaged on operations in April 1942, the aeroplane joined No 65 Sqn the following month after being repaired. W3312 was eventually written off on 3 September when the aircraft suffered engine failure west of Deal, on the Kent coast, during a fighter sweep. Its pilot, Plt Off N R Macqueen, baled out too low over the Goodwin Sands and was killed.

BILL ROLLS

William 'Bill' Rolls claimed 18 victories in Spitfires during combat in the Battle of Britain, on the Channel Front and in the defence of Malta.

Born in Lower Edmonton, North London, on 6 August 1914, William Thomas Edward 'Bill' Rolls won a scholarship to the Higher Latymer Secondary School in 1925 and subsequently joined his uncle's firm as a building engineer's apprentice. He enlisted in the RAFVR in March 1939 and was taught to fly at No 19 E&RFTS at Gatwick. Receiving his wings in June, Rolls was mobilised as a sergeant pilot upon the outbreak of war. He received further tuition at No 3 FTS at South Cerney, Gloucestershire, after which he was one of just five pilots from a course of 40 sent to a Spitfire unit.

When Rolls joined No 72 Sqn at Acklington on 19 June 1940, he had never previously flown a Spitfire. He quickly converted on to the fighter after completing check flights in a Magister and a Harvard. He described his first time aloft in a Spitfire (on 25 June) in his autobiography *Spitfire Attack*:

Having become an ace and been awarded a DFM as a sergeant pilot with No 72 Sqn during the Battle of Britain, Bill Rolls was finally commissioned in January 1942 while undertaking his second operational tour, this time with No 122 Sqn. He had this portrait photograph taken to mark the occasion.

I tried out the controls and was amazed how light they seemed and how responsive, almost immediate, they were to the slightest touch, either of rudder or elevator. Compared with the Hart, which up till then I had thought was the perfect machine, the Spitfire was like a greyhound, so sleek and fast. I climbed to 5,000ft in no time at all and did various turns. I played with the controls to get the feel of them and waggled my wings from side to side, using the rudder and trimmer to see their response. It was magic. I felt that I was an integral part of the aircraft, and that the wings were fixed to my arms and I could fly like a bird. The cockpit was so small that there was no room to move, and this made it feel as though you had it strapped on you. I now tried some mild turns, and the smoothness of them and the grace of the aircraft in performing the moves was unbelievable.

On 31 August, Rolls was posted south with the unit to Biggin Hill, and the following day he engaged the enemy for the first time. Things did not go to plan:

I was all keyed up and ready for action when we sighted the enemy formations about 2,000 yards away. We were being vectored towards the starboard side of the formations and I wondered why because we would have had the sun behind us; I am sure the CO felt the same way. Suddenly it happened. There was a call to break, and there right above and behind us were yellow-nosed Me 109s. It was a question of every man for himself. Before I realised what was happening, I was in a steep turn to get this yellow nose from out of my rear mirror; at the same time I could see other Spitfires and Hurricanes milling around firing at everything. I had no time to get my sights on an aircraft, although I saw enough crosses. I had lost the Me 109 that was on my tail and by now I was well underneath the formations, which had turned back. I saw Green One, formated on him and heard the order to pancake [land].

Most of us had not even fired our guns; it was all over so quickly. One minute you were in the thick of it, the next minute you had lost height and it was impossible to climb up quick enough to engage again.

Rolls rapidly adjusted to the breakneck pace of aerial combat in southeast England, however, and after claiming two victories on 2 September, he downed a brace of Bf 110s between Ashford and Tunbridge Wells, Kent, 48 hours later:

I took off from Croydon as Blue 3 in the leading section at 1250 hrs. We intercepted the enemy, who were approaching us from the northeast at right angles to our course. The leader gave the order 'Line astern' and turned to port to attack. I turned steeply to port and did a quarter attack on one of the end JU86s [actually Bf 110s from II./ZG 76]. The port engine started to fire and two of the crew baled out as I went beneath. I turned steeply again to port and came up from the quarter on another JU86, which was in a steep bank. I gave a ring-and-a-half deflection shot and my bullets hit the fuselage at about 200 yards' range, and I saw the port engine smoke and the machine fall in. I followed it down and it was burning before it hit a wood southeast of Tunbridge Wells. I then flew back to base as I had run out of ammunition.

Between 2 and 20 September, Rolls was credited with the destruction of seven aircraft, along with one probable and one damaged. His feat of arms in just three weeks of near-constant action resulted in his CO recommending him for the DFM, and this was awarded on 8 November. Its citation stated that 'This airman, after very short experience of operational flying, has taken his place with the best war pilots in the squadron. In each of his first two engagements he shot down two enemy aircraft and has, in all, destroyed at least six.'

Rested from operations in January 1941, Rolls was posted to newly formed No 58 OTU at Grangemouth as an

During the spring and summer months of 1942, Spitfire VB-equipped Nos 64 and 122 Sqns operated side-by-side as part of the Hornchurch Wing. Despite RAF Fighter Command suffering badly at the hands of the Jagdwaffe at this time, Plt Off Rolls made four claims (including one shared victory) against Fw 190s in May and June.

B Flight of No 122 Sqn takes off from Fairlop in June 1942, the aircraft participating in a sweep over northern France with the Hornchurch Wing. Plt Off Rolls leads the way in Spitfire VB MT-V. The Hornchurch Wing would routinely send one of its units to fly from nearby Fairlop for extended periods, as a squadron could get airborne from here at full strength (12 Spitfires) far quicker than at Hornchurch, where formation take-offs were difficult to perform safely.

instructor. He transferred to No 61 OTU at Heston, west of London, seven months later, before returning to operations with No 122 Sqn at Scorton, North Yorkshire, in October 1941. Commissioned in January 1942, Plt Off Rolls claimed his eighth victory on 17 May when he downed an Fw 190 and claimed a second as a probable near Saint-Omer. Following two more claims over Focke-Wulfs in June, he was posted to Debden to test the feasibility of flying a Spitfire VB off the deck of the aircraft carrier *Furious*.

Rolls duly sailed with the vessel, loaded with Spitfires and pilots, from Greenock, Scotland, for Gibraltar in late July. On 10 August, *Furious* set sail for Malta, and the following day Rolls led seven fighters aloft from the carrier and headed east in the direction of Luqa. Once there, he joined No 126 Sqn, where he was soon promoted to flight lieutenant and made a flight commander. Between 13 August and 26 October Rolls again proved his skill as a fighter pilot by claiming nine Axis aircraft destroyed and one

No 122 Sqn's pilot cadre come together for a photograph at Hornchurch in May 1942. Plt Off Rolls is standing seventh from the left, and to the left of him is newly arrived flight commander Flt Lt Paddy Barthropp. The latter was shot down just days after he had joined the squadron, spending the rest of the conflict as a PoW. Standing ninth from the left is the unit CO, Belgian Sqn Ldr Léon Prevot.

This Spitfire VC was one of 38 aircraft sent to Luqa from the carrier *Furious* in Operation *Bellows* on 11 August 1942. Flg Off Rolls flew one of these fighters to the island, whereupon he joined No 126 Sqn.

damaged. Four of his victims were Ju 88s, including one that he downed on 13 October. He noted in *Spitfire Attack*:

> We were to intercept some bombers with fighter escort that were approaching Valletta Harbour. We had time to get to the right height, and I had soon positioned the squadron to make a frontal attack slightly to starboard so that I could open up on the Ju 88s and then pull up to the port side where the fighter cover would be spread.

> We attacked from almost head-on and I told my No 2 to take the right hand Ju 88 and keep with me as I was going for the leading aircraft. The attack was very short; a couple of seconds' firing and I saw the two leading aircraft hit by cannon. I pulled up in a steep climb to the right. I looked in my mirror and saw that my No 2 was right behind me. Things then got really hectic as one of the other Spitfire squadrons was going into the fighters above us and then it became a free for all. It took all my time and skill to avoid crashing into other aircraft. The sky was now full of aircraft and it

Shortly after reaching Malta, Flg Off Rolls was made a flight commander in No 126 Sqn and subsequently claimed nine victories between 13 August and 26 October. His run of success came to an end when he accidentally broke his foot, leading to his repatriation to England for treatment.

was impossible to tell who was who in the melee that followed. I called over the R/T for my chaps to withdraw, as I knew they must be out of ammunition by now. We all made for base individually.

Having survived numerous engagements over Malta during the 'October Blitz', Rolls sustained a broken foot the following month when the wall of a bomb-damaged building fell on him. He was eventually repatriated to England for treatment, and during the return flight the Catalina on which he was a passenger ran out of fuel and had to land off the coast of Wales. A destroyer was despatched to tow the flying boat into port. While a patient in the Royal Naval Hospital in Swansea, Rolls received word he had been awarded a DFC.

After being declared fit again for active service, he was posted to the Publicity Branch of the Air Ministry. Here, he was involved in publicising the RAF's operations during a series of 'Wings for Victory' fundraising speeches. In September 1943, Rolls was sent to Manby, Lincolnshire, to undertake a six-month training course at the Air Armament School, after which he was posted to HQ, No 12 Group as a specialist armaments officer. In June 1944, Rolls was attached to the Bombing Analysis Unit and promptly posted to France.

Demobbed in January 1946, he secured employment in the public service with the Ministry of Works. In 1960, Rolls took a position at the Air Ministry as a senior information officer, overseeing the production of more than 150 training films for the RAF. Forced to retire in September 1975 due to failing health, Bill Rolls had a heart bypass operation in March 1981 and died following a heart attack in July 1988.

Spitfire VB BM309/MT-V of Plt Off Bill Rolls, No 122 Sqn, Hornchurch, Essex, June 1942

One of a number of Spitfire VBs to serve with the RAF that were paid for by the Bombay War Gifts Committee, BM309 was assigned to No 122 'Bombay' Sqn at Hornchurch on 10 April 1942 – at least seven Mk VBs marked with *BOMBAY CITY* titling were assigned to this unit in 1942. Plt Off Rolls flew the aircraft a number of times during the spring and early summer of 1942, but there is no way of confirming whether any of the four claims he made with No 122 Sqn came in BM309. The aircraft later served operationally with the 335th FS/4th FG and Nos 315, 303 and 313 Sqns, prior to being transferred to the Fleet Air Arm's 808 NAS in April 1944. Passed on to 759 NAS four months later, it was damaged beyond repair in a forced landing following partial engine failure in flight on 27 September 1944.

DES SHEEN

As the first Australian fighter pilot to fire his guns in anger during World War Two, Des Sheen would see considerable action in Spitfires during the early years of the conflict.

Desmond Frederick Burt Sheen was born in Sydney, New South Wales, on 2 October 1917. He had been interested in flying from the age of nine after he had witnessed an aerial display at the opening of Australia's Parliament House, in Canberra, in May 1927. Sheen subsequently joined the RAAF in January 1936 and undertook his flying training at Point Cook, Victoria. Transferring to the RAF 13 months later, he completed additional training in England and was then posted to recently reformed No 72 Sqn at Church Fenton, North Yorkshire, in June 1937. The unit had been the first in RAF Fighter Command to receive the Gladiator, and it retained the aircraft through to April 1939 when it transitioned to Spitfire Is supplied directly from Supermarine in Southampton.

The aircraft issued to No 72 Sqn were part of the first order for Spitfires placed by the Air Ministry, and a number of them would serve the unit until replaced by late-production Mk Is in August 1940. Sheen logged flying time in most of these early Spitfire Is, and he was allowed to adorn K9959 with his personal boomerang insignia. The Australian used this aircraft to down an He 115 floatplane that was attacking a North Sea convoy off Spurn Head, on the East Riding of Yorkshire coast, on 21 October 1939. Sheen engaged the Luftwaffe again on 7 December, north of Arbroath, Scotland, after seven He 111s from 1./KG 26 were detected heading for the Tay Estuary at midday. No 72 Sqn's alert section was scrambled from Drem, and six Spitfires took off. One of them was K9959, flown by Sheen:

When Plt Off Sheen joined newly reformed No 72 Sqn in June 1937, it had only recently become the first unit in RAF Fighter Command to receive the Gladiator I. Here, K6143 heads a line-up of nine biplane fighters at Gloster's Hucclecote factory in early 1937, just prior to their delivery to No 72 Sqn at Tangmere in March 1937. This aircraft, which remained with the unit until April 1939, was eventually written off in a landing accident at Khartoum, in Sudan, on 10 June 1941 while serving with No 117 Sqn.

We soon spotted the formation, which was carrying out an armed reconnaissance along the east coast. They must have thought that there would be no fighters this far north, so our presence no doubt came as a nasty shock to them. They had dropped down to low level in order to try and evade No 603 Sqn Spitfires [three of which had intercepted them and then been forced to break off their attacks due to dwindling fuel], so we, in turn, dived down to their altitude. I remember quite vividly zooming past Bell Rock lighthouse at eye-level in pursuit of a fleeing bomber.

As I commenced firing on my chosen target, a gunner in a second He 111 off to the left-hand side of 'my' bomber hit me with an accurate burst in the cockpit. I was struck in the ear with one round and hit in the backside with another, while a third ruptured my petrol tank [the latter was an incendiary round, which failed to ignite the fuel and was subsequently found in the tank by the groundcrew]. Petrol began to stream into the cockpit, and when I went in again to attack I began to feel dizzy with the fumes and decided to return home. Upon landing, I was soon bundled into an ambulance and

In April 1940, Flg Off Sheen 'volunteered' for service with the PDU after a signal was sent to No 72 Sqn asking for pilots to join the new unit. His CO, fellow Australian Sqn Ldr Ronald Lees, wrote the names of his pilots on to slips of paper and then placed them in a hat, and Sheen's was drawn out. He then spent the next four months flying photo-reconnaissance missions in specially converted, unarmed, Spitfire PR III Type Cs like this one (P9385, seen in May 1940 with Sheen at the controls) with No 212 Sqn from both Britain and France.

Thousands of miles from home, Flg Off Des Sheen left little doubt as to his country of origin by marking Spitfire I K9959/RN-J with a distinctive boomerang insignia beneath the cockpit. Frequently flown by the Australian in the first months of the war, Sheen and the fighter were photographed at Leconfield in October 1939. On the 21st of that month, he used it to down an He 115, followed by a third of a victory against an He 111 on 7 December – both Sheen and K9959 were hit in the latter engagement, which took place north of Arbroath. It would serve with No 72 Sqn until mid-August 1940, after which the Spitfire was converted into a photo-reconnaissance aircraft.

proceeded to spend Christmas convalescing in the hospital in Edinburgh Castle, which was most pleasant.

Sheen was posted to the Photographic Development Unit (PDU) in April 1940. Flying some of the RAF's first photo-reconnaissance Spitfires, he undertook missions over Italy from airfields in southern France. Awarded a DFC on 7 May, Sheen requested a posting back to No 72 Sqn and re-joined the unit at Acklington in July 1940. He would claim two victories on 15 August when *Luftflotte* 5 sent 72 He 111s from KG 26, with a 21-strong Bf 110 escort, to target RAF airfields in northeast England. Sheen's first success was against a Bf 110 fitted with a nose-mounted ventral tank, which he mistook for a bomb:

I latched on to a formation of seven Bf 110s [from I./ZG 76] that had begun attempting to turn in a circle, and I quickly singled out their leader. I initially misidentified the machine as a Ju 88 because I was mesmerised by what I thought was a bloody great bomb affixed to the aircraft's centreline. I took aim and fired at very close range, and the Messerschmitt simply blew up in front of me. That was very alarming, as I had to fly straight through the smoke and debris left behind by the now disintegrated fighter, but fortunately I emerged unscathed.

No 72 Sqn was sent south to Biggin Hill on 31 August, and the airfield was being bombed when the unit landed. With its new home temporarily rendered inoperable, the squadron transferred the next morning to nearby Croydon. Later that same day, Sheen was scrambled to intercept a large enemy force approaching London. Just as he was about to engage a Do 17, his fighter was hit by fire from a Bf 109 and Sheen was forced to bale out. On 2 September he was promoted to flight lieutenant, and three days later, while leading No 72 Sqn after its CO had been wounded, Sheen was shot down for a third time when his unit – forward deployed to Hawkinge – was bounced by Bf 109s while climbing through 25,000ft to intercept bombers heading for Thames Haven:

One of our 'weavers' shouted out a warning that he had sighted enemy fighters above us, but just as his voice crackled over the R/T, my aircraft shuddered as it was struck by cannon and machine gun rounds. I was hit in several places by shell splinters, and my oxygen bottle was punctured, which caused me to pass out. When I finally came to, my aircraft was in an uncontrollable vertical dive, so I forced the canopy back and released the harness pins in preparation for baling out. However, as soon as the straps came free I was sucked out of my seat, but then I was snagged by my feet on the windscreen, which laid me out in the slipstream of the aircraft along its spine. The Spitfire was rapidly nearing the ground, but fortunately I was thrown clear and immediately pulled the ripcord. My parachute opened at just 800ft, and my landing was broken by a copse of trees – so much so that my only real injuries were those sustained in the attack itself. The first person on

Twelve Spitfire Is from No 72 Sqn patrol the Northumberland coast in four loose vics of three in March 1941, the fighters flying from nearby Acklington. Flt Lt Sheen had claimed a rare night victory in one of these aircraft that month when he downed a Ju 88 heading for Glasgow.

the scene was a policeman on a bicycle who, while offering me a drink from his hip flask, asked, 'You left it a bit late didn't you?'

Sheen was taken to Queen Mary's Hospital in Sidcup, Kent, and following a spell of sick leave, he returned to No 72 Sqn in mid-October. He claimed his final victory in mid-March 1941, by which point his unit had been posted north to Acklington for a period of rest. The Luftwaffe's night-bombing campaign had by then been enlarged to include targets in No 13 Group's area of responsibility, forcing RAF Fighter Command to order day fighter units like No 72 Sqn to perform much-disliked night patrols in aircraft that were ill suited to such operations. Having spent many fruitless hours in the cockpit of a Spitfire at night during the winter of 1940–41, Sheen enjoyed a slice of luck on 13–14 March when he was vectored on to a Ju 88 during a period of moonlight, 'The bomber [which was targeting Glasgow] was exactly where the fighter controller indicated it would be, and I opened up with a long burst. This lit the enemy aircraft up like a Catherine wheel and started a fire in one of its engines. I pressed home my attack to the point where I almost rammed the bomber, my windscreen becoming smeared with oil from the stricken aircraft.'

Sheen was made CO of No 72 Sqn in April 1941, and he led the unit as part of the Biggin Hill Wing in sweeps over occupied Europe through to October of that year – he also

No 72 Sqn pilots stand in front of their Spitfire VBs at Biggin Hill in late July 1941 awaiting inspection by visiting dignitaries. Sqn Ldr Sheen is closest to the camera, wearing his distinctive navy blue RAAF uniform. He led the unit from April to October 1941, during which time it flew exclusively with the Biggin Hill Wing.

This studio photograph of Sqn Ldr Sheen was taken shortly after he had left No 72 Sqn, the Australian ace having received a Bar to his DFC at this time.

received a rare squadron-initiated Bar to his DFC that same month, with the citation for this award stating:

Since July 1941, Squadron Leader Sheen has led the squadron, and on occasions the wing, in 43 offensive operations over Northern France. He has carried out these missions with consistent skill and courage and, under his leadership, the squadron has attained a high standard of efficiency. On one occasion the squadron was menaced by a superior number of enemy fighters but, by his coolness and clever tactics, Squadron Leader Sheen saved his unit from suffering heavy casualties and succeeded in destroying at least three of the fighters. Squadron Leader Sheen has personally destroyed a number of enemy aircraft, including one at night.

After two years of frontline flying, Sheen subsequently held staff appointments and station commands in Britain (Manston, Skeabrae and Drem) and in the Middle East. Having attained the rank of wing commander, he was released from the RAF in 1947. Two years later, however, after dropping in rank to flight lieutenant, Sheen re-joined with a permanent commission. CO of the Royal Auxiliary Air Force's No 502 'Ulster' Sqn from 1950–52 (during which time the unit flew Spitfire F 22s and, later, Vampires) at RAF Aldergrove, Northern Ireland, he was then posted to the Central Flying Establishment's Air Fighting Development Squadron and, a year later, to RAF Leuchars, Scotland, as Wing Commander Flying. Subsequent appointments included the command of RAF Odiham (1962–64) and Group Captain Organisation at RAF Transport Command.

Following his retirement in 1971, Sheen found employment with BAC/British Aerospace as manager of the company's BAC One-Eleven and Concorde marketing teams. He retired from the aviation industry in 1982. Sheen passed away in Salisbury, Wiltshire, in April 2001.

Spitfire I X4034/RN-J of Flg Off Des Sheen, No 72 Sqn, Croydon, Surrey, September 1940

First flown on 30 July 1940, X4034 was issued to No 72 Sqn on 11 August and assigned to Flg Off Sheen. The first Australian fighter pilot to fire his guns in anger during World War Two, Sheen had enjoyed early success in K9959, which had also been marked with his boomerang insignia beneath the cockpit. It is possible that he flew X4034 in action against *Luftflotte* 5 when the North East was targeted in a two-pronged attack on 15 August, Sheen claiming two victories. He flew the fighter south to Biggin Hill on 31 August, and then moved to Croydon with the rest of No 72 Sqn the following day. Shot down on 1 September, Sheen was again forced to take to his parachute four days later when his formation of seven Spitfires was bounced while patrolling over Hawkinge at 25,000 ft. X4034 burst into flames after being hit by enemy fire, and Sheen baled out with shrapnel wounds.

JACKSON SHEPPARD

Jack Sheppard was just one of a number of Canadian pilots to achieve ace status flying Spitfires with the 2nd TAF in 1943–44 in the lead up to D-Day.

Jackson Eddis 'Jack' Sheppard was born in the North Vancouver suburb of Dollarton on 18 April 1920. Upon leaving school, he found employment with the Union Steamship Company working as a deckhand. Sheppard also joined the Canadian artillery militia at this time, prior to switching to the RCAF Marine Section in 1939. Initially assigned to the ground staff of Hudson-equipped No 120 (Bomber Reconnaissance) Sqn at Regina, Saskatchewan, from December 1939 to August 1940, he was eventually accepted for aircrew training and earned his wings flying Tiger Moths, Finches and Harvards with No 1 Initial Training School, No 10 EFTS and, finally, No 9 SFTS.

In August 1941, Sheppard arrived in Britain and was sent to No 53 OTU in Llandow, Wales, to convert on to the Hurricane. Three months later, the Canadian was posted to Hurricane II-equipped No 43 Sqn at Acklington. He remained with the unit for only a month, for in December Sheppard volunteered for service with the Merchant Ship Fighter Unit (MSFU), based at Speke, south Liverpool. Also equipped with Hurricanes, the MSFU

Plt Off Jack Sheppard briefly flew Hurricane IIs with No 43 Sqn from Acklington in late 1941 after completing his flying training, but he saw little in the way of action with the unit.

had been formed by the RAF to provide makeshift fighter cover for Atlantic convoys that were being targeted by German Fw 200 Condor long-range patrol aircraft.

On 10 February 1942, having mastered the art of flying rocket-launched Hurricanes from Catapult Aircraft Merchant ships, Sheppard suffered jammed controls in his fighter while circling the vessel he had just been catapulted from off the coast of Wales. Despite the aircraft crashing heavily when its port wing was ripped off after it hit the water at an angle, Sheppard survived the incident unhurt.

In February 1943, he returned to RAF Fighter Command when he was posted to Spitfire VB-equipped No 401 Sqn at Catterick. The Canadian-manned unit was transferred south to Redhill three months later, its arrival in No 11 Group coinciding with Sheppard being promoted to flight lieutenant and made a flight commander. Following two months of flying from the Advanced Landing Ground at Staplehurst, Kent, as preparation for operations in France in 1944, No 401 Sqn moved to Biggin Hill in mid-October, where it was equipped with Spitfire IXs. On 26 November, Sheppard claimed his first victory while participating in a high-cover escort for 72 Marauders bombing Cambrai-Epinoy airfield. The unit's operational diary noted, 'Flt Lt Sheppard got the first Hun since we've been on Spit IXs. Sheppard led his section down to the deck on a Jerry that had just taken off. After a five-minute chase, Sheppard destroyed the FW 190.'

Keen to engage the enemy, Plt Off Sheppard volunteered for service with the MSFU, based at Speke, in December 1941. Also equipped with Hurricanes, the MSFU had been specifically formed to provide fighter cover for Atlantic convoys that were being targeted by Fw 200 Condors. Here, Hurricane I Z4935 is being carefully lowered by crane on to a practice catapult shuttle at Speke in early 1942. The silver tubes in the foreground are propulsion rockets that will be loaded into the base of the shuttle once the Hurricane has been secured to it.

Clip-winged Spitfire VB EN921 was assigned to Flg Off Jack Sheppard of No 401 Sqn in June 1943, having previously seen service with Nos 309, 412, 421 and 416 Sqns. A well-used aircraft, it later spent time with No 504 Sqn, before being relegated to No 17 FTS in December 1944. By the time this photograph of EN921 was taken at Biggin Hill in early October 1943, Sheppard had been promoted to flight commander.

Sheppard's combat report for this action read as follows:

We were low Squadron of the Wing and flying approximately 1,000ft below and slightly in rear of the centre Squadron at 13,000–14,000ft. At 1215 hrs, I reported to Stylish leader (F/L MacDonald) that two FW 190s were taking off from the aerodrome (later proved to be Achiet) at six o'clock below heading northeast. The Wing Leader advised waiting and watching and the Squadron started a slow orbit to port. Decision to attack was withheld by the Wing Leader as a section of the close escort had detached as though to go down. It, however, reformed and order was given to attack when sighted again. Leading Yellow Section, I sighted one FW 190 three o'clock below, four miles northeast of Achiet aerodrome on the deck, and given permission, broke to attack.

We came down behind the enemy aircraft in line astern, closing fast at 450mph IAS [indicated airspeed]. Throttling down, I fired a short burst from dead line astern and overshot. Enemy aircraft, which had not seen us until I fired, then commenced violent evasive action. I pulled up to 200ft and dived down, firing a short burst and observing some strikes on wings and fuselage. The enemy aircraft was then using all available ground cover and jinking furiously. He led us over the aerodrome northeast to southwest, where I had to skid violently to avoid light flak bursting in front and underneath my aircraft.

Flg Off Sheppard's EN921 boasted one of the most risqué artworks ever to grace an RAF fighter, which proved particularly popular among the groundcrew at Biggin Hill.

By now a flight lieutenant, Jack Sheppard pauses briefly for the photographer prior to climbing into the cockpit of EN921 in early October 1943. This fighter was replaced by Spitfire IX MJ146 later that month, and Sheppard claimed his first victory with the aircraft on 26 November.

I chased the enemy aircraft down the railway towards Albert, giving him a short burst and observing strikes. Hopping over trees and hedges, the pilot was taking such violent evasive action that he hit the ground three times with his propeller, sending up dust. He then led us over Albert at roof height, turning to starboard. I gave him a long burst from 200 down to 75 yards, and observed strikes on the fuselage and wings. The cockpit cover came off in two jagged pieces. I swung into line astern, then over to the port side of the enemy aircraft, seeing flames surrounding the pilot's cockpit. A few seconds later he flew into the deck and blew up.

Sheppard's next success came on 7 March 1944 during a sweep over northern France, the Canadian engaging a lone Fw 190 encountered near the airfield at Beaumont-sur-Oise. The No 401 Sqn diarist recorded, 'Over France, Flt Lt Sheppard saw an Fw 190 on the deck just over the perimeter track and went down on it, with his section following. He engaged the Hun at treetop level and shot it down.' He was credited with his third Fw 190 destroyed eight days later near Cambrai-Epinoy airfield.

In April, newly promoted Sqn Ldr Sheppard took over command of Spitfire IX-equipped No 412 Sqn at Tangmere. His former squadronmate Bob Hayward described Sheppard as being a 'cool and calculating fighter pilot who did not agree with strafing the enemy on the ground'. His first victory with No 412 Sqn came on 10 May in a day of heavy action for the 2nd TAF – Sheppard's unit was part of No 126 Wing (which also included No 401 Sqn). Leading a sweep over Rheims, he and his squadron intercepted Fw 190s from I./JG 2, and although two were shot down, a pair of Spitfires from No 412 Sqn were lost in return.

The unit was posted to Bény-sur-Mer (B4) in France on 18 June, and Sheppard achieved ace status exactly two weeks later when he downed yet another Fw 190 southeast of Lisieux:

Flg Off H W 'Bud' Bowker checks the guns of his Spitfire IX at Bény-sur-Mer (B4) shortly after No 412 Sqn's arrival in Normandy on 18 June 1944. Note that a captured helmet is hanging off the starboard cannon muzzle and a newly acquired German motorcycle is leaning against the trolley accumulator. Bowker's CO at this time was Sqn Ldr Sheppard, who 'made ace' on 2 July in an engagement with Fw 190s south of Lisieux. Sadly, Bowker was killed in the same action, Sheppard noting in a letter he wrote to his widow, 'On the morning of the 2nd July, 1944, Bud took off with the Squadron to cover other aircraft that were dive-bombing targets behind the enemy lines. A number of enemy aircraft were encountered and the entire squadron engaged them. In the combat that followed, your husband was seen chasing an enemy aircraft which was diving toward cloud. I was unable to contact Bud by radio and, unfortunately, this was the last time anyone saw your husband. The squadron lost an excellent pilot and a very good friend when your husband did not return. Bud was very popular among his fellow pilots and admired for his keenness and ability as a fighter pilot.'

I was leading 412 Sqn covering [tactical reconnaissance] Mustangs when two Fw 190s were reported 2,000ft above and Blue Section climbed to engage. The whole squadron then climbed above the '190s when six more enemy aircraft were sighted climbing into the sun. There was five-tenths cloud in layers up to approximately 15,000ft. The '190s were using the cloud to evade interception, climbing and diving into it. At approximately 20,000ft, aircraft were sighted flying west – I called the squadron to reform as the other enemy aircraft had disappeared. I gave chase, and after three or four minutes Red and Blue sections closed and identified the aircraft as '190s and '109s flying in three sections. The squadron was closing from line astern out of the sun on 15 enemy aircraft when, at 3,000 yards, the enemy aircraft formation started a slow turn to port.

I engaged the port section of '190s which had started to break to port, closing on the last '190 of the section. At approximately 150 yards, and with 20 degrees of deflection, I fired a second-and-a-half burst of cannon and machine guns. I saw strikes on the wing roots, cockpit and engine. The enemy aircraft burst into flames and blew up. I had to pull up to starboard to avoid the enemy aircraft, which was now in pieces.

I called the squadron to reform after the short combat as we were all short of petrol, having been running on high revs and boost for some time.

Sheppard was shot down on 2 August when, during an armed reconnaissance, he became embroiled with Bf 109s near Argentan and fell victim to Unteroffizier Anton Schöppler of I./JG 5. Managing to evade capture, he returned to Allied lines 11 days later. Sheppard received a DFC on 22 August, the citation for which stated, 'he has taken part in many varied operational sorties including escorts to bombers, fighter sorties and defensive patrols. An excellent leader, he has set a splendid example by his fine fighting spirit.' Sent to a repatriation depot in early September, Sheppard returned to Canada the following month and was stationed in Vancouver until he joined Kittyhawk I-equipped No 133 Sqn at Patricia Bay, British Columbia, as CO in late January 1945. He attended the War Staff College in Toronto three months later, after which he was posted to HQ, Western Air Command in May. Eventually returning to Patricia Bay, Jack Sheppard was subsequently released from RCAF service in February 1946.

Spitfire VB EN921/YO-A of Flg Off Jack Sheppard, No 401 Sqn, Biggin Hill, Kent, October 1943

Adorned with art not routinely associated with RAF Spitfires, clipped wing Mk VB EN921 was the personal aircraft of future ace Flg Off Jack Sheppard during the summer and autumn of 1943. Delivered to the RAF in May 1942, the fighter had served with Nos 309, 412, 416 and 421 Sqns prior to it joining No 401 Sqn in June 1943. When 401 Sqn re-equipped with Spitfire IXs in October of that year, EN921 was passed on to No 504 'County of Nottingham' Sqn. It was eventually relegated to No 17 FTS and struck off charge in May 1946.

STANISŁAW SKALSKI

Stanisław Skalski was the ranking Polish fighter ace of World War Two, and he claimed nine of his victories in the Spitfire on the Channel Front and in North Africa.

Born in Kodyma, north of Odessa in Russia, on 25 November 1915, Stanisław Skalski moved with his mother to Poland in 1918. They would eventually be joined by his father in 1921 after he had escaped the Bolsheviks via Romania. Educated at Dubno College, Skalski joined the PAF in January 1936 and received flying tuition as a cadet at the Dęblin-based Officer Training Centre. He was commissioned as a lieutenant in August 1938 and posted to P.11c-equipped 142 *Eskadra* (squadron) of 4 *Pułku Lotniczego* (Air Regiment).

In the wake of Germany's invasion of Poland on 1 September 1939, Skalski made six victory claims to become the first Allied ace of World War Two, and the only PAF ace of the nation's ill-fated defence. Escaping to France via Romania and the Mediterranean, he volunteered for service with the RAF in January 1940. After being trained to fly Hurricanes, Skalski joined No 302 Sqn at Leconfield, East Riding of Yorkshire, on 3 August. As the unit was not yet operational, he requested a posting to a frontline outfit and was duly sent to No 501 Sqn at Gravesend on 27 August.

During his first nine days in action with RAF Fighter Command, the Polish ace claimed seven aircraft destroyed and two damaged prior to being shot down in flames by a Bf 109 near Dover on 5 September. Badly burned by the time he took to his parachute, Skalski spent six weeks in hospital recovering from his injuries. He eventually re-joined No 501 Sqn at Kenley on 16 October, and continued to serve with the unit until he was posted to Hurricane-equipped No 306 'City of Torun' Sqn at Northolt in late February 1941. It was issued with Spitfire IIBs four months later, followed by Mk VBs in September, and the unit was part of the Polish Wing at Northolt during the spring and summer of 1941. Skalski would claim five Bf 109s destroyed with the Spitfire between July and September of that year, and he received a DFC for his efforts.

In November he was posted as an instructor to No 58 OTU, before returning to operations with No 316 'City of Warsaw' Sqn at Northolt as B Flight commander in March 1942. Skalski became CO of No 317 'City of Wilno' Sqn, also at Northolt, two months later. Immediately prior to this, he made his final Channel Front claim in a Spitfire on 3 May:

I was leader of the Northolt Wing, which took part in a diversionary sweep in Circus 145. Biggin Hill and Kenley were the wings below us. Several times I was warned by Operations that small formations of enemy aircraft were in our vicinity. Between Audruicq and Guînes four FW 190s approached from the northeast at 27,000ft on our starboard side, making trails. My squadron was at this time flying at 25,000ft, and I warned all our pilots that the enemy was approaching to attack from the rear – I was flying in the sun about 2,000ft above and slightly behind one of the Biggin Hill squadrons. I asked Operations to warn Biggin Hill that enemy aircraft were behind them, but it was too late, as one of the FW 190s dived on them.

Seeing that the Biggin Hill Wing did not react in any way to this attack, I ordered my pilots to turn right while I attacked the diving FW 190 that was about 150–200 yards behind a Spitfire. I opened fire from about 500 yards, as I wanted to prevent the German pilot from getting in his fire. Making a three-quarter beam attack from above and closing to about 300 yards, I got in three bursts with cannon and machine guns. The FW 190 did not fire at the Spitfire, and after my third burst the enemy aircraft

Lt Skalski was photographed in the cockpit of his P.11c from 142 *Eskadra* in the summer of 1939. He emerged from the doomed defence of Poland as the PAF's only ace of the brief campaign, having made seven claims (six of them credited as victories) prior to escaping to France via Romania and the Mediterranean.

I should like to draw attention to the flying of the English squadrons. In line astern formation, they should keep a much better lookout behind them if heavy casualties are to be avoided, as I am certain that no pilot reacted to the attack described above. If I had not intervened at least two pilots would have failed to return.

I claim one FW 190 as probably destroyed, firing as I did from fairly long range, and the whole action only lasting a few seconds. Cine camera gun carried and exposed.

In November 1942, Skalski returned to No 58 OTU as its chief flying instructor, having also received a Bar to his DFC. His time out of the front line only lasted until early 1943, when he helped form the PFT (which was nicknamed 'Skalski's Circus') manned by volunteers.

A number of aces can be seen in this group photograph of No 501 Sqn at Kenley in late October 1940. Plt Off Skalski is sitting in the front row third from the right, and Sgt 'Ginger' Lacey is sitting at the extreme right. This unit was one of the highest scoring of the Battle of Britain, with Skalski contributing seven victories in just nine days prior to being badly burned when he was shot down by a Bf 109 on 5 September. He re-joined No 501 Sqn on 16 October and remained with the unit until late February 1941 when he was posted to No 306 Sqn.

went into a spin, evidently out of control. I was unable to follow it as 20–25 FW 190s were now positioning themselves to attack. I therefore ordered all our pilots to form a defensive circle flying to the right into the sun – about eight or nine FW 190s dived on 303 Sqn, flying just above us.

I observed one enemy aircraft attack a Spitfire from this squadron and I think his oxygen bottle must have been hit – shortly afterwards the pilot baled out southeast of Calais.

Immediately after the first attack a second one followed, but it did not develop as the enemy aircraft, at the last moment, broke away and climbed back into the sun. In the meantime, Operations ordered me to withdraw over the Channel owing to large numbers of enemy aircraft above us. Crossing the French coast near Calais, I flew as far as Dunkirk with the intention of covering the withdrawal of our forces. Near Gravelines I observed several aircraft flying below and to starboard on their way to the English coast. I then set course for Dover.

Sqn Ldr Stanisław Skalski briefs the pilots of his PFT 'Circus' in North Africa in the spring of 1943. Listening and watching are, from left to right, Flt Lts Karol Pniak and Eugeniusz Horbaczewski, WO Władysław Majchrzyk and Flg Off Ludwik Martel.

Its pilots were tasked with acquiring experience of operating as part of a tactical air force in preparation for the post-D-Day campaign in France. Flying Spitfire IXs on attachment to No 145 Sqn in North Africa, the PFT was credited with 26 victories in just eight weeks over Tunisia, with Skalski claiming three of them – the first of these, on 28 March, opened the PFT's score. The following combat report provides details of the engagement, which took place in the Tunis–Sfax area:

The flight was approaching Sfax at 8,000ft when Me 109s and Heinkels were reported below and seven Ju 88s were seen flying northwest at zero feet and Sqn Ldr Skalski [EN459/ZX-1] and Flt Lt Horbaczewski [EN267/ZX-5] went down to attack, the remaining Spitfires staying up as top cover.

Sqn Ldr Skalski saw two Ju 88s flying line astern and attacked the front one, leaving the second for his No 2. He fired two long bursts from 300 yards astern and above and

Spitfire F IX EN315/ZX-6, the top-scoring aeroplane of the PFT, was used by five different pilots to add to their scores, including three aces – Sqn Ldr Skalski, Flt Lt Horbaczewski and WO Mieczysław Popek. Photographed having its engine run up at Bou Grara alongside three other PFT Spitfire IXs in late April 1943, EN315 is marked with a PAF checkerboard insignia and five white swastikas. The latter denoted victories scored by various pilots in this particular aircraft, rather than the personal tally of one specific aviator.

saw pieces fly off the port wing. The enemy aircraft heeled over to the left as Sqn Ldr Skalski pulled up past it, crashing into a building in the northwest quarter of the town. An Me 109 was reported and then seen by Sqn Ldr Skalski making off to the northwest. Sqn Ldr Skalski then flew down one of the main streets of Sfax, strafing with cannon and machine guns. He set one truck on fire.

Following the PFT's dissolution with the capture of Tunisia, Skalski became the first Pole to lead a British fighter unit when he was given command of No 601 Sqn. Among the pilots he led during his time with this unit was Flg Off W G Matheson, who was fulsome in his praise of the Polish ace. 'Sqn Ldr Skalski was an outstanding fighter pilot and leader. He was always a very careful pilot and never did anything flash or reckless but was aggressive in action. He taught me how to see what was going on in the air. He seemed to know what was going on around us at all times, and must have had very good eyes.'

After further combat during the invasions of Sicily and Italy, Skalski returned to Britain in October 1943 and was awarded a second Bar to his DFC. Made wing leader of Spitfire IX-equipped No 131 'Polish' Wing at Northolt in December 1943, he then transferred to Mustang III-equipped No 133 'Polish' Wing in early April 1944. Skalski's final aerial victories came on 24 June when he forced two Bf 109s to collide and crash over Rouen without having fired a shot. These successes took his tally to 18 and two shared victories, two probables and four and one shared damaged.

While leading the PFT, Sqn Ldr Skalski routinely flew Spitfire IX EN459/ZX-1. However, on 6 April, it was being flown by fellow Polish ace Flt Lt Eugeniusz Horbaczewski when he shot down a Bf 109 for his sixth victory. Minutes later EN459 was hit in the engine by fire from another Bf 109, and Horbaczewski had to make a forced landing at Gabès, Tunisia, where it is seen being dismantled for repair.

Wg Cdr Skalski sits in the cockpit of his Mustang III FZ152/SS at Coolham ALG, in West Sussex, in April 1944. He had only recently become wing leader of No 133 'Polish' Wing, and he remained in command through to September. He was credited with his final aerial victories while flying a Mustang III on 24 June when he forced two Bf 109s to collide over Rouen without having fired a shot.

Awarded a DSO in August, Skalski was posted to the USA to attend a Command General Staff School the following month. Returning to Britain in February 1945, he became Wing Commander Operations with HQ, No 11 Group. Offered a permanent commission in the RAF following VE Day, he chose instead to return to Soviet-controlled Poland.

Initially serving in the PAF, Skalski was accused of spying for the 'American and British imperialists' (as were many other wartime PAF pilots who had returned from the West) in 1948 and brutally interrogated. Initially condemned to death, Skalski's sentence was subsequently changed to life imprisonment by the 'merciful' communists. Following Stalin's death in 1953, things slowly began to change in Poland, and Skalski was released three years later. Readmitted into the PAF, he rose to the rank of general and served until the early 1970s. He then headed up the Polish Aero Club until fully retiring. Stanisław Skalski passed away in Warsaw on 12 November 2004.

Spitfire IX EN315/ZX-6 of Sqn Ldr Stanisław Skalski, OC Polish Fighting Team (assigned to No 145 Sqn), La Fauconnerie, Tunisia, April 1943

First flown on 8 January 1943, EN315 was shipped to North Africa, via Gibraltar, in late February. Once in-theatre, it was issued to No 145 Sqn, which partially transitioned to Spitfire IXs in March 1943. It operated a mixed force of Mk VBs, IXs and, from June, Spitfire VIIIs. Assigned to the PFT, EN315 had an individual code number in place of a letter and a Polish checkerboard insignia forward of the cockpit. The PFT's most successful pilot was Flt Lt Eugeniusz Horbaczewski, who claimed three victories with the aircraft. Sqn Ldr Skalski was also credited with one of three PFT victories in EN315. The fighter moved to Malta with No 145 Sqn in mid-June, and it was destroyed there when its engine cut after the pilot overshot the runway at Luqa and hit rocks on 10 July 1943.

ROBERT TUCK

Bob Tuck was among the first Spitfire aces of World War Two, being in the vanguard of the action over the Dunkirk evacuation beaches and during the Battle of Britain.

Robert Roland Stanford Tuck was born in Catford, South London, on 1 July 1916. As with many high-scoring fighter aces, Bob Tuck was a talented marksman during his teenage years. Indeed, he was a member of the St Dunstan's College rifle team. After briefly serving as a sea cadet in the Merchant Navy from 1932, Tuck then worked in a window factory until he joined the RAF in September 1935. Upon the completion of his flying training, he was posted to Demon I-equipped No 65 Sqn at Hornchurch in May 1936. Two months later the unit switched to Gauntlet IIs, followed by Gladiator Is in May 1937. Tuck survived a mid-air collision with a wingman (who was killed) while performing aerobatics over Uckfield, East Sussex, in January 1938, the future ace taking to his parachute – he would bale out four times during his service with the RAF.

No 65 Sqn made the switch to Spitfires in March 1939, and Tuck subsequently took his experience of the type to recently re-equipped No 92 Sqn at Croydon in early May 1940. By then a flight commander, he engaged enemy aircraft on numerous occasions over Calais, Boulogne and Dunkirk from 23 May – Tuck was credited with five victories in 24 hours, followed by another two and one shared destroyed during Operation *Dynamo*. The last of his claims came on 2 June, when he intercepted both fighters and bombers in defence of the evacuation beaches:

When at 12,000 or 13,000ft over Dunkirk at 0800 hrs, I sighted three He 111s below and right, heading to, and almost at, Dunkirk. I led my section down out of the sun

Flg Off Tuck, in Spitfire I K9906/FZ-L, leads a flight of six fighters from No 65 Sqn on a training flight from Hornchurch in the early summer of 1939. Assigned to this unit in May 1936, he was a veteran fighter pilot by the time Spitfire Is reached No 65 Sqn as replacements for its Gladiator Is from March 1939. Following brief service with No 64 Sqn in April–May 1940, K9906 then spent time with an OTU prior to being converted into a Spitfire PR III Type C in February 1942.

and delivered two formation attacks and lots of oil was seen to come from one on the right. The formation was two vics of three. When breaking away after the second attack, six 109s came at me from above and out of the sun. The first one to attack me registered hits on my fuselage and tail unit. I turned quickly up towards it and he shot below me, and I was able to do a quick turn down on to him and waited until he pulled up out of his dive. I cut the dive and got very close on to his tail. I gave him a short burst of around 50 rounds per gun and he literally exploded in the air. I managed to evade the other five by diving into a layer of cloud.

After staying in the cloud for a few seconds I pulled up out of them, and right below – about 100ft – was an He 111. I gave him three short bursts of about three seconds each at about 150 yards from astern and on the quarter. One engine went up in flames and the machine spiralled down and crashed inland from Dunkirk. It exploded on landing and none of the crew used their parachutes.

On the way back, two more 109s attacked me. I expended the last of my ammunition on them and saw one spiral down into the cloud and bits flew off the other. Having no ammunition left, I returned to base.

Tuck was awarded a DFC on 11 June, with the citation for the decoration noting:

This officer led his flight in company with his squadron on two offensive patrols over Northern

Having dispensed with his battledress tunic on what was clearly a warm summer's day in Essex, Flg Off Tuck poses with his hands buried in his pockets in front of Spitfire I FZ-W.

France. As a result of one of these patrols in which the squadron engaged a formation of some 60 enemy aircraft, the Squadron Commander was later reported missing, and the flight commander wounded and in hospital. Flight Lieutenant Tuck assumed command, and on the following day led the squadron, consisting of only eight aircraft, on a further patrol engaging an enemy formation of 50 aircraft. During these engagements the squadron has shot down ten enemy aircraft and possibly another 24. Throughout the combats this officer has displayed great dash and gallantry.

Tuck continued to add to his tally of victories during July and August 1940, despite No 92 Sqn having been posted west to Pembrey, Wales, so that the unit could recover from its exertions during *Dynamo*. Tuck primarily engaged bombers in the early weeks of the Battle of Britain, including two Ju 88s on 14 August:

Ordered to patrol Barry with Blue Section at 16,000ft. On arrival approximately in patrol position above ten-tenths cloud, Blue 3 indicated three bogies behind and on my right. Did a quick turn towards them and identified them as Ju 88s flying in close formation at 16,000ft heading northwest. I broke up my section and we all carried out two or three beam quarter and astern attacks with little apparent effect. Enemy aircraft maintained formation and steady height and course. I then called up my section and instructed them both to carry out head-on attacks, but owing to heavy R/T interference they did not hear this order.

I proceeded well ahead and on the same level as enemy aircraft formation and then turned back head-on to them. I got in a dead steady burst of two seconds head-on to the enemy aircraft. When I had passed directly over him at about 50ft I pulled vertically upwards and looked backwards and downwards and saw that the No 3 enemy aircraft had broken away quickly from the formation and was losing height with a lot of heavy smoke pouring from both engines. He disappeared into the cloud, losing height, heading south or southwest.

The other two aircraft still maintained height and formation, so I carried out exactly the same head-on attack on the leading enemy aircraft. After pulling up vertically and looking back, I saw that precisely the same thing had happened to this enemy aircraft as to the No 3 enemy aircraft. I followed this aircraft down through cloud, heading south-southwest, but had great difficulty stopping behind it as apparently its engines were out of action. I lost this enemy aircraft in cloud and eventually came out below 15 miles south of Weston-super-Mare.

While I was looking for the enemy aircraft I had fired at, once I came down through cloud I saw a stick of five bombs land on the railway midway between Highbridge

Flg Off Tuck shows off his marksmanship during a clay pigeon shoot at Hornchurch in the spring of 1940. He would join No 92 Sqn as a flight commander at Croydon shortly after this photograph was taken.

and Glastonbury. I quickly looked round the sky and saw what appeared to be a Heinkel 111. As soon as I turned towards him he climbed into cloud and I lost him. I then returned to base to refuel and rearm.

Four days later, Tuck was shot down by return fire from a Ju 88, baling out over Horsmonden, Kent, after having claimed a Junkers bomber destroyed and one probable off Beachy Head, East Sussex, minutes earlier. On 25 August, Tuck's fighter was again hit while attacking a German bomber, this time a Do 17 intercepted off the Pembrokeshire coast. Despite being slightly wounded in the knee and leg, he managed to glide his Spitfire for 15 miles with a dead engine before crash-landing at Bosherston, Wales. When Tuck left No 92 Sqn at Biggin Hill for command of Hurricane-equipped No 257 Sqn at Debden on

Having claimed 13 victories in Spitfire Is with No 92 Sqn between 23 May and 25 August 1940, newly promoted Sqn Ldr Tuck was given command of Hurricane I-equipped No 257 Sqn at Debden on 11 September. He would lead the unit until July 1941, during which time he added seven more victories to his tally in the Hawker fighter.

11 September, his tally stood at 11 and two shared destroyed, one unconfirmed destroyed, one probable and three damaged in the Spitfire.

He had claimed a further seven victories in the Hurricane (and one in a Spitfire while visiting No 92 Sqn) by year-end. Awarded a Bar to his DFC on 25 October 1940, followed by a DSO on 7 January 1941, Tuck had been credited with five more victories by the time he was shot down into the Channel by Bf 109s on 21 June – he claimed two Messerschmitts immediately prior to being forced to take to his parachute. Rescued by a passing coal barge from Gravesend, Tuck returned to No 257 Sqn and was promoted to lead the Duxford Wing

Its propeller shattered and engine cowlings popped open from a heavy impact with the ground, Spitfire VB BL336/RS-T of Wg Cdr Tuck sits on its belly near a Boulogne-sur-Mer beach after its high-scoring pilot was forced to crash-land following multiple hits by 20mm flak at low-level on 28 January 1942. Tuck and his wingman, Flg Off A E Harley of No 401 Sqn, had had the misfortune of crossing the coast directly over a flak emplacement. The Spitfire's impressive victory tally attracted much interest from German troops in the immediate area.

During 1968, Bob Tuck was employed by Universal Artists to undertake the role of technical adviser for the *Battle of Britain* film – he was one of a handful of RAF aces to work on the motion picture. He is seen here with high-scoring Luftwaffe ace Adolf Galland at Tablada, in Spain, looking over ex-Spanish air force HA-1112 Buchóns that represented Bf 109Es in the film. Galland, who was also an advisor on *Battle of Britain*, had been a long-standing friend of Tuck. The latter was godfather to Galland's son.

the following month. He claimed two more Bf 109s in July and August, taking his final score to 27 and two shared destroyed, one and one shared unconfirmed destroyed, six probables and six and one shared damaged – a tally then only bettered in the RAF by Wg Cdr Adolf 'Sailor' Malan.

Following almost 18 months of constant combat, Tuck was replaced at Duxford in October and sent on a lecture and liaison trip to the USA with several other high-profile RAF Fighter Command veterans. Returning home in December, he was posted to Biggin Hill as wing leader. Tuck's time in the front line would prove to be short-lived, however, for on 28 January 1942, his Spitfire VB was hit by flak during a Rhubarb over northern France and he crash-landed near a beach. Immediately captured, he was hosted by fellow ace Oberst Adolf Galland at JG 26's HQ prior to being sent to a PoW camp. Escaping captivity on 1 February 1945, Tuck reached Soviet lines. He successfully used the Russian he had been taught by his nanny as a child to communicate with Red Army troops, and after remaining with them for two weeks as they advanced into Germany, he travelled east to Moscow and the British Embassy. Tuck was returned to Britain by ship shortly thereafter.

Participating in the September 1945 Battle of Britain flypast over London, he eventually left the RAF with the rank of wing commander in 1949. Tuck continued flying as a test pilot into the early 1950s, before becoming a mushroom farmer in Sandwich, Kent. Undertaking the role of technical advisor for the *Battle of Britain* film in 1968, Tuck had by then developed a close friendship with Adolf Galland, regularly visiting the German ace and enjoying hunting trips with him. He was also godfather to Galland's son. Bob Tuck passed away in Sandwich on 5 May 1987.

Spitfire VB BL336/RS-T of Wg Cdr Bob Tuck, OC Biggin Hill Wing, Biggin Hill, Kent, January 1942

BL336 was delivered new to No 124 Sqn at Biggin Hill on 28 November 1941, the aircraft being supplied to the unit when it replaced its Spitfire I/IIs upon arriving at the Kent fighter station from Castletown. The following month, the fighter was assigned to Wg Cdr Tuck after he became Biggin Hill wing leader, the aircraft wearing his RS-T code letters and victory tally. He had not had the chance to add to his score by the time he was brought down by multiple hits on BL336 from a flak battery as he and his wingman crossed the French coast near Boulogne on 28 January 1942.

GEORGE UNWIN

George Unwin was one of the most experienced Spitfire pilots in RAF Fighter Command at the start of World War Two, and he used this familiarity with the aircraft to claim 15 victories by the end of 1940.

The son of a miner, George Cecil Unwin was born in Bolton upon Dearne, near Barnsley, South Yorkshire, on 18 January 1913. Joining the RAF in 1929 as an apprentice clerk in Records, he was selected for pilot training in November 1935 and commenced his flying course at No 8 E&RFTS at Woodley. Three months later, Unwin moved to No 11 FTS at Wittering to complete his training, after which he was posted to Gauntlet I-equipped No 19 Sqn at Duxford. By the time his unit became the first squadron in the RAF to receive Spitfires, Unwin was a veteran aviator. He was chosen by his squadron commander to be one of the first non-commissioned officer (NCO) pilots to fly the fighter, on 16 August 1938, after which he undertook intensive flying trials with the aircraft in order to prove its suitability for frontline service.

The exhaustive trials programme completed by Unwin (and several other NCO pilots on No 19 Sqn) meant that he was as familiar with the Spitfire as any Supermarine test pilot by September 1939, having flown 15 different Mk Is in his year-long relationship with the fighter. Nevertheless, Unwin had yet to see combat by May 1940, and his first encounter with the enemy almost proved to be his last:

We had been keyed up and raring to go throughout the Phoney War, and with four years of experience already behind me, I felt confident in my ability to meet any challenge with the Spitfire as my mount. Despite feeling that my chances of success were good once combat was joined, I froze solid in the cockpit when the first Bf 109 attacked me [on 26 May 1940].

I could see this aircraft diving down in an arc towards me, with what looked like sparks lighting up his wings – I then realised he was shooting at me, and all I could do was sit there in the cockpit and watch him, I was so fascinated! I was shaken from this stupor when two shells hit my aircraft behind the cockpit, forcing me to take evasive action. Fortunately, I survived this brief moment of stage fright and never hesitated again – many pilots new to combat had similar experiences, but never lived to tell the tale.

My first victory was scored the following day, and it consisted of a cheeky Hs 126 spotter aircraft. The little bugger had used his superior manoeuvrability and slow speed

Spitfire I K9794 leads a six-strong formation of aircraft (one of which was flown by Sgt George Unwin) from No 19 Sqn on a flight from Duxford on 31 October 1938. The non-standard '19' on the fighters' fins were applied shortly before this press-generated sortie, and then swiftly removed once it had taken place.

Being the first operational unit to receive the Spitfire I, No 19 Sqn was routinely visited by the press in 1938–39. This neat line-up shot was taken at Duxford on 4 May 1939, by which time all the Spitfires assigned to the unit had WZ codes applied. The exhaustive flight trials programme undertaken by Sgt Unwin (and several other NCO pilots assigned to No 19 Sqn) meant that he had flown 15 different Mk Is by September 1939 – all of these aircraft featured in his logbook on more than one occasion.

to evade a series of attacks by Flt Lt 'Sandy' Lane and Flg Off Frank Brinsden over Dunkirk, during which time I held off and kept an eye out for enemy fighters. All the while he was rapidly retreating into occupied Belgium, and Lane finally gave up and ordered us to return to base. Just as they turned their backs on the Hs 126, its pilot straightened out to fly away. Feigning R/T failure, I dived on him out of the sun – he saw me too late, and despite an attempted stall and spiral dive, I pumped 240 rounds into the aircraft and it caught fire and crashed.

Unwin repeated this success three more times through to 4 June while flying patrols as part of Operation *Dynamo*. With France lost, he spent the rest of June learning the art of night fighting and getting to grips with the cannon-armed Spitfire IB. The latter proved to be less than successful, as Unwin explained many years later:

When we got hold of the first brand new cannon-Spitfires, we were more than a little perturbed by the fact that we had only six seconds' worth of ammunition to shoot. Little did we know that stoppages would restrict us from ever using all 60 rounds carried for each gun! To this day, no one has ever given me a suitable explanation as to how the 30 Mk IBs [supplied to RAF Fighter Command] ever passed pre-service gunnery tests.

With No 19 Sqn being assigned to No 12 Group, it had to wait until mid-August to see action in the Battle of Britain – often as part of Sqn Ldr Douglas Bader's controversial 'Big Wing'. Unwin had helped Bader convert on to the Spitfire upon his readmission into the RAF in late 1939, his future wing leader having initially served with No 19 Sqn. Between 16 August and 28 November 1940, Unwin claimed ten and two shared victories – all were Bf 109s and Bf 110s. The high point for him in terms of aerial successes came on 15 September. On a date now immortalised as Battle of Britain Day, Unwin flew two sorties as part of Bader's Big Wing and claimed the first of his three victories near Biggin Hill while participating in the morning patrol over South London. Unwin's combat report stated, 'I was Red 3 with Flt Lt Lawson. We sighted the enemy aircraft, who were in vics of three. The escorts dived singly on us, and I engaged one of them (Me 109) with a yellow nose. I gave one burst of six seconds and the enemy aircraft burst into flames. Pilot baled out. Enemy aircraft crashed approximately between Redhill and Westerham.'

After returning to Fowlmere, Cambridgeshire, and filling in his Form F combat report, Unwin had barely had time to catch his breath when word came through of eight to ten large enemy formations massing over the Channel. Scrambled late from their airfields in No 12 Group, the five-squadron strong Big Wing struggled to form up and gain altitude before tackling the enemy bombers, and their escorts, over London. Unwin subsequently recalled:

> I was lucky to survive that second sortie unscathed, as through my own stupidity I got separated from the rest of the wing. We were led through a gap in cloud over London by Sqn Ldr Bader of No 242 Sqn, and there in front of us

Flt Sgt Unwin and his Alsatian 'Flash' pose for the photographer on the wing of Spitfire I K9798 in June 1940 at Duxford following No 19 Sqn's combat debut over the evacuation beaches of Dunkirk just weeks earlier. During a handful of Operation *Dynamo* patrols flown from Hornchurch, Unwin had been credited with three victories. He had also claimed two enemy aircraft that remained unconfirmed.

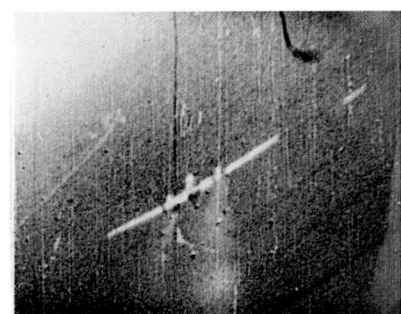
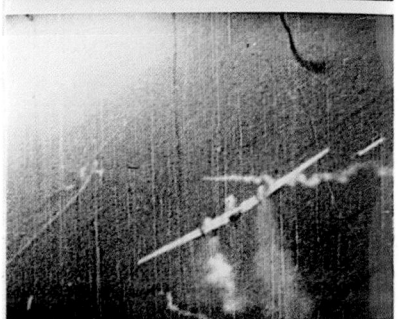
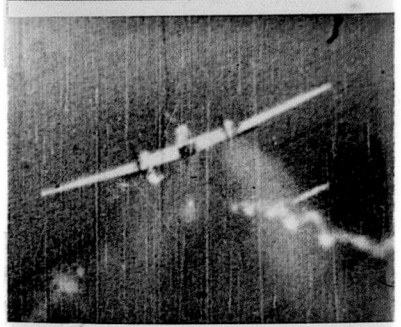
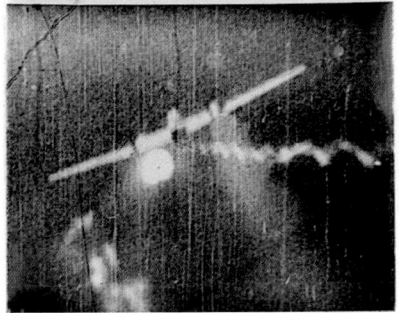

This sequence of frames was shot by Flt Sgt Unwin with a wing-mounted G.42B camera gun when he claimed a Bf 110 destroyed. The exact date of this engagement remains unknown, as he made seven claims against *Zerstörer* between 1 June and 15 November 1940. The fighter-destroyer's port engine has clearly been hit and is on fire. The corkscrewing smoke trails have been made by tracer rounds.

Spitfire IA X4179/QV-B is firmly chocked while Flt Lt Frank Brinsden runs the fighter's engine up at Fowlmere during the early evening of 26 September 1940. The aircraft's radiator flap is fully open – a necessity when the Merlin was running on the ground, as the engine had a propensity to overheat otherwise. The Spitfire had been delivered to No 19 Sqn from No 266 Sqn exactly two weeks earlier, and it was transferred to No 609 Sqn the day after this photograph was taken. The fighter had been used by Flt Sgt Unwin to claim three Bf 109s destroyed on 15 September, followed by a Bf 110 three days later. It was also flown eight times by 'Fanny' Brinsden between 20 and 25 September. X4179 subsequently served with Nos 66, 131 and 140 Sqns, before being relegated to an OTU in June 1942.

was what looked just like a pre-war Hendon Air Pageant flypast. We were at about 23,000ft and the bombers were below us at 20,000ft. I was transfixed by a squadron of Hurricanes struggling to engage these aircraft, and I had completely forgotten about the bombers' escort – I flew straight into the middle of them! The next thing I knew, literally hundreds of yellow-nosed Messerschmitts were whistling by all around me less than 100 yards away, so I pulled the bloody stick back and held it there! I gave the odd machine a quick burst as it flew past me and succeeded in forcing one to half-roll and dive into cloud below. I followed him down, but my windscreen froze at 6,000ft and he escaped.

I then climbed back up to 25,000ft in search of my wingman, but as was often the case with these aerial duels, the sky had gone from being heavy with aircraft to totally empty in a matter of seconds. After several minutes I spotted a pair of Bf 109s above me flying back in a loose *Rotte* formation towards the Channel, obviously intent on heading home. After a long chase, I finally caught them up as they crossed the Kent coast at Lydd, and after firing a long burst into the trailing fighter, it immediately burst into flames and crashed just offshore. Inexplicably, the leader failed to take any evasive action and he was shot down on fire into the sea seconds later.

These Spitfire pilots from Nos 19 and 616 Sqns were photographed between operations at Fowlmere in October 1940. Flt Sgt Unwin is flanked by 'Flash' and 'Rangy', while sitting on his right is Spitfire ace, and No 19 Sqn CO, Sqn Ldr Brian Lane. His counterpart at No 616 Sqn, future ace Sqn Ldr Howard Burton, is standing second from the right.

I had survived the mission simply because the Spitfire could sustain a continuous rate of turn inside the Bf 109E without stalling – the latter was known for flicking into a vicious stall spin without prior warning if pulled around too tightly. The Spitfire would give a shudder to signal it was close to the edge, so as soon as you felt the shake you eased off the stick pressure.

Unwin received a DFM on 1 October 1940, the citation for the decoration stating, 'This airman has displayed great courage in his attacks against the enemy and he has destroyed ten of their aircraft. On a recent occasion, when returning from an engagement alone, he intercepted a formation of enemy bombers escorted by about 30 fighters and destroyed two of the fighters. He has displayed skill and courage of the highest order.'

A Bar followed on 6 December, Unwin having recently been promoted to warrant officer. In February 1941 he was sent to No 16 EFTS in Derby as an instructor. He fulfilled this role – latterly with No 2 Flying Instructors School at Montrose – until October 1943, when he undertook a conversion course on to the Mosquito. From April 1944, Unwin spent six months on operations with No 613 Sqn as part of the 2nd TAF, before seeing out the war as an instructor with the CGS at Catfoss.

Remaining in the RAF post-war, he fulfilled a series of staff jobs until he was posted to Habbaniya, Iraq, in late 1949, to take command of Brigand-equipped No 84 Sqn. Unwin led the unit to Tengah, Singapore, in April 1950, and subsequently flew combat missions from there over Malaya until August 1951, when he broke his leg playing football and was posted back to Britain. Having been awarded a DSO in March 1952 for his service in Malaya, Unwin undertook further staff roles until his retirement with the rank of wing commander in January 1961. Settling in Dorset, George Unwin passed away on 28 June 2006.

Spitfire IA X4425/QV-H of Flt Sgt George Unwin, No 19 Sqn, Fowlmere, Cambridgeshire, September 1940

X4425 first flew on 13 September 1940, and it was assigned to No 19 Sqn five days later when Mk IAs replaced Spitfire IBs due to the unreliability of the latter type's 20mm cannon armament. It was frequently flown by Flt Sgt Unwin, the 15-victory ace claiming a Bf 109 destroyed while at the controls of X4425 during a patrol over the Thames Estuary on 27 September. He had the fighter adorned with the Popeye art seen here beneath the cockpit on the port side. After being transferred to No 92 Sqn at year-end, X4425 was passed on to No 57 OTU in March 1941. Damaged in an accident in July, the aircraft was repaired and issued to No 61 OTU four months later. X4425 was written off while still serving with this unit on 4 April 1943 when it crash-landed on a beach at Llanddulas, Wales, after the fighter had been flown into a sandbank.

LANCE WADE

Lance 'Wildcat' Wade was credited with more victories than any other American pilot to serve exclusively with the RAF in World War Two.

Born in Broaddus, San Augustine County, Texas, on 18 November 1916, Wade was christened L C by his parents. He subsequently adopted the forenames Lance Cleo to satisfy RAF regulations in 1940. Kept busy on the family farm while still at school, Wade moved to Tucson, Arizona, in 1934 to take advantage of the US government's New Deal programme in the wake of the Great Depression by enrolling in the Civilian Conservation Corps. While driving teams of mules, building roads and planting trees as part of his employment, Wade also earned his private pilot's licence after he and some friends purchased a light aeroplane. He then tried to join the US Army Aviation Cadet Program but was rejected due to his lack of higher education.

Undeterred, Wade travelled to Canada in December 1940 and joined the RAF instead. With 54 flying hours in his logbook, he was sent to the Spartan School of Aeronautics in Tulsa, Oklahoma, where an RAF Refresher School had just been established. Wade had completed his training by April 1941, after which he was shipped to Britain and posted to No 52 OTU at Debden to undertake his conversion on to the Hurricane. Subsequently posted to the Middle East, Plt Off Wade flew a Hurricane to Malta from the carrier HMS *Ark Royal* on 13 September 1941 as part of a 46-fighter reinforcement brought in aboard this vessel and *Furious*. With Malta experiencing a rare lull in the Axis campaign to subjugate the island, 23 of the Hurricanes were sent on to Egypt the following day – one of these aircraft was flown by Wade, who was assigned to No 33 Sqn once in the Middle East.

Flying missions over Libya, the American had 'made ace' by the year's end, with seven aerial and six strafing claims in successful clashes with both German and Italian aircraft during the short-lived advance on El Agheila (codenamed Operation *Crusader*) and the retreat to Gazala that followed. No 33 Sqn replaced its combat-weary Hurricane Is with Mk IIBs in February 1942, and Wade was awarded a DFC three months later. Promoted to flight lieutenant and made a flight commander in late June, he continued to inflict losses on Axis fighters and dive-bombers during the Allied retreat to the Alamein area of Egypt as the Afrika Korps advanced steadily eastward. On 16 September, during Wade's last flight of his first tour, his Hurricane IIC was hit twice in a dogfight with an Italian C.202 Folgore – the first time his aircraft had been damaged by an enemy machine, prompting the American to record in his logbook 'He was good.'

Flg Off Lance Wade was photographed at Gambut, in Libya, shortly after receiving his DFC in May 1942 for shooting down six Axis aircraft and damaging a further seven on the ground. He achieved his success while flying Hurricane Is with No 33 Sqn, and he would go on to make a further 11 claims (eight of which were credited as victories) in-theatre with the unit in Hurricane IIB/Cs through to 11 September – his tour ended five days later.

Spitfire VB BR390/ZX-N was serving with No 145 Sqn at Hamraiet, on the Libyan coast, when Flt Lt Wade joined the unit as a flight commander in January 1943. Fellow American Flt Sgt MacArthur Powers had enjoyed success with this aircraft when he damaged a Bf 109 on 2 November 1942. Powers, who made five claims in Spitfires, became an ace flying P-40 Warhawks with the USAAF over Tunisia in April 1943.

A Bar to Wade's DFC was announced in October, the citation to the decoration stating:

Since being awarded the Distinguished Flying Cross this officer has destroyed seven enemy aircraft, thus bringing his total victories to 15. In September 1942, during a reconnaissance patrol, his aircraft was attacked by some eight Italian fighters. Flight Lieutenant Wade, however, fought them off. By his skill and determination he contributed materially to the success of the reconnaissance and much valuable information was obtained. Flight Lieutenant Wade's courage and devotion to duty has been an inspiration to all.

Sqn Ldr Wade ruefully examines the damage to the wing tip of his Spitfire IX at Goubrine North after aerial combat with Axis fighters over the Gulf of Tunis on 6 May 1943.

With his tally standing at 12 and two destroyed in the air and one on the ground, Wade was sent home for a period of rest. Flown to the USA aboard a Pan American DC-3, he joined an RAF delegation in Washington, D.C., before heading to New York to participate in a press conference at the Rockefeller Center. Coverage of Wade's exploits duly appeared in the 14 October 1942 edition of *The New York Times*. Briefly loaned to the USAAF, he toured training establishments before ending up at Wright Field, Ohio, where he test-flew the P-39 Airacobra, P-47 Thunderbolt and P-51A Mustang. Wade was also approached to join the USAAF during this period, being offered a higher rank and increased pay to tempt him to make the switch. 'Thanks, that's mighty fine,' he replied, 'but I'd rather keep stringing along with the guys I have been with for so long now.'

Returning to operational flying in North Africa in January 1943, Wade was posted to Spitfire VB-equipped No 145 Sqn as a flight commander. Made CO by the month's end, he added to his tally in a series of fierce engagements fought with Bf 109s during the Battle of the Mareth Line in Tunisia in March. Wade received a second Bar to his DFC at the end of the month, the citation accompanying the award stating that the American ace was 'the leader of a squadron which has achieved much success in recent operations. During March 1943, the squadron destroyed 21 enemy aircraft, four of which were shot down by Sqn Ldr Wade. By his great skill and daring, this officer has contributed materially to the high standard of operational efficiency of the squadron he commands. Sqn Ldr Wade has destroyed 19 enemy aircraft.'

By early April, No 145 Sqn had partially re-equipped with Spitfire IXs, and Wade used one to claim three more victories as Axis resistance in North Africa crumbled. Flying from Malta, the unit supported the invasion of Sicily in July, before moving to the newly captured island shortly thereafter. By then, No 145 Sqn was also flying Spitfire VIIIs, as well as Mk VBs and IXs, and Wade led the unit to southern Italy in September. He claimed his final victories on

Commanders of the units forming Spitfire-equipped No 244 Wing in Italy in the autumn of 1943. They are, from left to right, Sqn Ldr Stan Turner (OC No 417 Sqn), Sqn Ldr 'Hunk' Humpherson (OC No 92 Sqn), Wg Cdr Wilfred Duncan Smith (wing leader), Gp Capt Brian Kingcome (wing CO), Sqn Ldr Lance Wade (OC of No 145 Sqn) and Maj 'Bennie' Osler (OC of No 601 Sqn). Of these pilots, only Humpherson failed to 'make ace'.

2 October while heading up a patrol of eight Spitfire VIIIs. Spotting a formation of Fw 190 *Jabo* at 12,000ft off Penne, on the Italian coast, Wade led his formation in a climb to engage the enemy, positioning his charges to approach from behind and below. He subsequently wrote in his combat report, 'After gaining this position, and approaching unseen to within 200 yards, I destroyed the rearmost Fw 190 with a burst of cannon fire. I then moved behind the next fighter, and with another burst sent the enemy plunging earthward.'

When he ended his second tour on 16 November, Wade's score stood at 22 and two shared destroyed, one probable, 13 damaged, and one destroyed and five damaged on the ground.

No 145 Sqn CO Sqn Ldr Wade shares a joke with his adjutant, Flt Lt Norman Brown, at Triolo, in Italy, in the autumn of 1943. Behind them is a Spitfire VIII marked with a No 145 Sqn insignia. From June to September 1943, the unit had flown four different Spitfire variants (Mks VB, VC, VIII and IX), before finally settling on the Mk VIII. Wade would make his final five claims (two of which were victories) in the Spitfire VIII in October–November 1943.

This photograph of Sqn Ldr Wade was taken at Triolo on 12 November 1943 – nine days after he had claimed his 24th, and last, aerial victory, and just four days prior to him ending his second frontline tour. Promoted to wing commander and posted to Air Vice-Marshal Harry Broadhurst's staff at HQ, DAF, he would perish in a flying accident on 12 January 1944.

Promoted to wing commander and joining the staff of the DAF, he was killed in a flying accident at Amendola, Italy, early in the new year. The demise of the leading American Spitfire ace was witnessed by Capt Paul Carll of the 57th FG's 64th FS:

It occurred on Wednesday, 12 January 1944, at about 1500 hrs. Lance was flying a Spitfire V, and in his role as CO of the RAF's No 239 Wing, he had come over to visit our CO, Lt Col Archie Knight. He arrived at about 1400 hrs. They had their meeting, which lasted for about an hour, and Lance prepared to leave. Our strip lay east to west. The wind was from the east, and Lance took off from west to east. The west end of the runway was directly south of our tent.

I watched him take off, and as soon as he got off the ground and picked up his wheels, he did a slow roll. He remained low and did a 180-degree left hand turn. He came back parallel to the runway, between our tent and the runway, and started another slow roll. He fell out of this one right before my eyes. His left wing hit the ground and the aeroplane crashed and burned furiously. Lance had no chance. The Spitfire V he was flying was used as a utility aircraft by the Headquarters flight of No 239 Wing, while its frontline units were primarily operational with newer model Spitfires. Speculation was that Lance had not made allowance for the underpowered Mk V. There was no room for error when performing a manoeuvre like that.

The award of a DSO to Wade was gazetted less than two weeks later.

Originally buried with full military honours in a British cemetery in Italy, Wade's body was subsequently repatriated to Texas and re-interred in the McKnight Cemetery in Cushing, Nacogdoches County.

Spitfire VB ES252/ZX-E of Sqn Ldr Lance Wade, OC No 145 Sqn, Bou Grara, Tunisia, March 1943

ES252 was delivered to the RAF in November 1942 and shipped to North Africa on board SS *Empire Clive* the following month. Once in-theatre, it was issued to No 145 Sqn just as Flt Lt Wade joined the unit as a flight commander. Made CO of the squadron in late January 1943, he used ES252 to make three claims against Bf 109s between 8 and 22 March. The fighter remained with No 145 Sqn until August, after which it was assigned to the Northwest African Air Force. ES252 was struck off charge in April 1945.

BIBLIOGRAPHY

Books

Boot, Henry and Ray Sturtivant, *Gifts of War – Spitfires* (Air-Britain, 2005)
Bowyer, Michael J F, *Aircraft for the Few – The RAF's fighters and bombers in 1940* (PSL, 1991)
Bracken, Robert, *Spitfire – The Canadians* (Boston Mills Press, 1995)
Brew, Steve with Mike Bradbury, *A Ruddy Awful Waste – Eric Lock DSO, DFC & Bar* (Fighting High, 2016)
Cameron, Dugald, *Glasgow's Own – 602 (City of Glasgow) Squadron* (Squadron Prints, 1987)
Caygill, Peter, *Spitfire Mark V In Action* (Airlife, 2001)
Caygill, Peter, *The Biggin Hill Wing 1941 – From Defence to Attack* (Pen & Sword, 2008)
Cooper, Anthony, *'Paddy' Finucane and the legend of the Kenley Wing* (Fonthill, 2016)
Cull, Brian and Bruce Lander and Heinrich Weiss, *Twelve Days in May* (Grub Street, 1995)
Franks, Norman, *Fighter Leader* (William Kimber, 1978)
Franks, Norman, *Buck McNair – Canadian Spitfire Ace* (Grub Street, 2001)
Franks, Norman, *Fighter Command's Air War 1941* (Pen & Sword, 2016)
Gray, Group Captain Colin, *Spitfire Patrol* (Hutchinson, 1990)
Jefford, C G, *RAF Squadrons* (Airlife, 2001)
Matusiak, Wojteck and Robert Grudzień, *Osprey Aircraft of the Aces 127 – Polish Spitfire Aces* (Osprey Publishing, 2015)
McRoberts, Douglas, *Lions Rampant – The story of 602 Squadron* (William Kimber, 1985)
Morgan, Eric B and Edward Shacklady, *Spitfire – The History* (Key Publishing, 1993)
Nichols, Steve, *Osprey Aircraft of the Aces 83 – Malta Spitfire Aces* (Osprey Publishing, 2008)
Nijboer, Donald, *Osprey Aviation Elite Units 35 – No 126 Wing RCAF* (Osprey Publishing, 2010)
Olynyk, Frank, *Stars & Bars – A tribute to the American fighter ace 1920–1973* (Grub St, 1995)
Parry, Simon W and Mark Postlethwaite, *Dunkirk Air Combat Archive* (Red Kite, 2017)
Parry, Simon, *Battle of Britain Archive Vols 1 to 12* (Red Kite, 2015–22)
Postlethwaite, Mark, *Wing Leader Photo Archive No 1 – Supermarine Spitfire Mk I in RAF Service – 1936 to the Battle of Britain* (Wing Leader, 2020)
Price, Dr Alfred, *Osprey Aircraft of the Aces 5 – Late Mark Spitfire Aces 1942–45* (Osprey Publishing, 1995)
Price, Dr Alfred, *Osprey Aircraft of the Aces 12 – Spitfire Mark I/II Aces 1939–41* (Osprey Publishing, 1996)
Price, Dr Alfred, *Osprey Aircraft of the Aces 16 – Spitfire Mark V Aces 1941–45* (Osprey Publishing, 1997)
Robinson, Neil and Mark Postlethwaite, *Wing Leader Photo Archive No 6 – Supermarine Spitfire Mk V in Europe and North Africa* (Wing Leader, 2021)
Rolls, Flt Lt W T, *Spitfire Attack* (William Kimber, 1987)
Ross, David, with Bruce Blanche and William Simpson, *The Greatest Squadron of Them All, Volume 1* (Grub Street, 2003)
Shores, Christopher and Clive Williams, *Aces High* (Grub Street, 1994)
Shores, Christopher, *Aces High Vol 2* (Grub Street, 1999)
Shores, Christopher, *Those Other Eagles* (Grub Street, 2004)
Shores, Christopher, Brian Cull and Nicola Malizia, *Malta: The Spitfire Year – 1942* (Grub Street, 2001)
Shores, Christopher, and Giovanni Massimello with Russell Guest, Frank Olynyk and Winfred Bock, *A History of the Mediterranean Air War 1940–1945 Vol 3* (Grub Street, 2016)
Shores, Christopher, and Giovanni Massimello with Russell Guest, Frank Olynyk, Winfred Bock and Wg Cdr Andy Thomas, *A History of the Mediterranean Air War 1940–1945 Vol 4* (Grub Street, 2018)
Tan, Jon E C, *Aces, Airmen and the Biggin Hill Wing – A Collective Memoir 1941–1942* (Pen & Sword, 2016)
Terbeck, Helmut, Harry van der Meer and Ray Sturtivant, *Spitfire International* (Air-Britain, 2002)
Thomas, Andrew, *Osprey Aircraft of the Aces 80 – American Spitfire Aces of World War Two* (Osprey Publishing, 2007)
Thomas, Andrew, *Osprey Aircraft of the Aces 81 – Griffon Spitfire Aces* (Osprey Publishing, 2008)
Thomas, Andrew, *Osprey Aircraft of the Aces 87 – Spitfire Aces of Burma and the Pacific* (Osprey Publishing, 2009)
Thomas, Andrew, *Osprey Aircraft of the Aces 98 – Spitfire Aces of North Africa and Italy* (Osprey Publishing, 2011)
Thomas, Andrew, *Osprey Aircraft of the Aces 122 – Spitfire Aces of Northwest Europe 1944–45* (Osprey Publishing, 2014)
Thomas, Andrew, *Osprey Aircraft of the Aces 131 – Spitfire Aces of the Channel Front 1941–43* (Osprey, 2016)
Thomas, Nick, *Hurricane Squadron Ace* (Pen & Sword, 2014)
White, Andrew, *Flyer* (Fighting High, 2022)

Websites

Spitfire Performance Testing – www.spitfireperformance.com/spittest.html
The National Archives – www.nationalarchives.gov.uk
Aces of WW2 – acesofww2.com
Royal Air Force Commands – www.rafcommands.com